C000216480

In the presence of White Feather

Conversations with a Spirit Teacher

Received through the mediumship of
Robert Goodwin

Compiled and edited by
Robert and Amanda Goodwin

In the presence of White Feather

Conversations with a Spirit Teacher

Copyright 2005 Robert and Amanda Goodwin

All rights reserved. No part of this publication may be reproduced or transmitted in any form or by any means, electronic or mechanical, including photo-copying, recording or any information storage or retrieval system, without either prior permission in writing from the publisher or a licence permitting restricted copying.

ISBN 0 9535210 2 8

Other White Feather publications

Truth from the White Brotherhood

First published 1998

Available from Psychic Press, The Coach House

Stansted Hall, Essex CM24 8UD

The Golden Thread

First published 1999

Available from R.A. Associates, Suite 62 Beacon Buildings

Leighswood Road, Aldridge, Walsall WS9 8AA

Answers for an Enquiring Mind

First published 2002

Available from R.A. Associates, Suite 62 Beacon Buildings

Leighswood Road, Aldridge, Walsall WS9 8AA

Visit the White Feather Website:

http://web.ukonline.co.uk/mandrob

Email: mandrob@ukonline.co.uk

whitefeather@bluecom.net

Cover design: Dolphin Associates

Printed in the UK

Published by R.A. Associates

This book is dedicated to thinkers everywhere.
With grateful thanks to all who have contributed to our understanding,
from this and all other dimensions of existence.

To our children and families,
we have always tried to do our best for you,
and always will.

Readers should be aware that White Feather's teachings are exclusively oral and the contents of this book have been transcribed from recordings of his communications between 2002 - 2005. Wherever possible the text remains true to the spoken word despite some inevitable repetition and only punctuation has been added in the interests of continuity.

We would like to thank all who have given their time and energy to attend either private or public trance sittings with us and for their enthusiasm, kindness and patience. We hope that our editing of the original transcipts meets with your approval. We have attempted to retain the respect that you deserve at all times throughout this publication and any authors comments which have been added are again only for the purposes of continuity or to further enhance readers' understanding. Some names have been changed to protect privacy and any which bear a resemblence to persons living in this or the next world are purely coincidental.

We would like to thank everyone connected with this work, particularly those who have recorded public demonstrations on our behalf and of course those unseen souls in the spirit realms whose love, guidance and protection is palpable.

Without you, this book would not have been written.

Contents

In the presence of White Feather

Foreword - By James McQuitty

During the past twenty-five years I have read the teachings of practically every spirit sage in print. These have included Red Cloud, Ramadahn, Chan, White Eagle and Silver Birch. When I first read the teachings of White Feather, to my delight, I knew that I had found a teacher of equal distinction. One who was in touch with the modern world and issues pertinent today, and willing to impart his personal understanding and insight on a wide range of subjects.

On a few occasions I have personally been privileged to witness demonstrations of his communications through the trance mediumship of Robert Goodwin, on such occasions the differences between the personalities of Robert and White Feather are clear for all to see. In these few words I cannot prove authenticity of any White Feather communication. The 'proof' is in the ring of truth that, as read, will resonate within the heart and the soul of all open-minded seekers, At least this is how I have found it to be, I hope it will likewise be the same for you.

Like all renowned spirit teachers that have imparted wisdom to those of us upon this earth plane, his answers and teachings are presented in a simple and easy to understand way. At the same time they so often take that step further, to stretch and illuminate the mind.

This may read like a reference, and why not? For I have found that all White Feather books uplift, inspire and spiritually educate in a way that only genuine spirit communications can. For this reason I truly and wholeheartedly recommend their reading.

James McQuitty
Spiritual Author, Healer and Lifelong Seeker

In the presence of White Feather

Preface

To the reader of this book, whoever, wherever and whenever you are, you can be assured that you are living in troubled times. That you have sought out these teachings is perhaps indicative of your search for a deeper meaning to life that goes far beyond mere curiosity. For in all probability you feel an inner disquiet resulting from your daily interactions with the world around you. A world in which reliance upon materialism, combined with a basic denial of spiritual values and teachings leaves you with a void that can only be filled when those higher aspects are properly addressed and can play their parts in everyday existence.

Thus it is that either consciously or unconsciously you are engaged upon a search – a search for contentment, for happiness and for spiritual fulfilment. That quest will have lead you along many pathways. For some it will have meant searching endlessly and perhaps fruitlessly for books of real teaching amongst the many that now line the shelves of the 'Mind, Body & Spirit' or 'New Age' sections of bookstores. For others it will have been to embrace one of the many new age therapies, either as a practitioner or a recipient. For yet others, it will have involved journeys to spiritual retreats in an attempt to connect with the inner self and find peace away from the stresses of modern life. Perhaps some will have embraced a meditative approach whilst others will simply have tried their best to live life in accordance with their spiritual beliefs and values, whatever they might be.

All of these pathways and any others that enable the disciple of spirituality to embrace the pathway of the soul, are worthy of note. For each must find their own way, in their own way.

What is important is that this innermost desire to strive for the highest within and the need to live a more spiritually centred life should not become overshadowed or negated by worldly events to which so much importance is attached but which, when seen from their true perspective are of little consequence in the grand scheme of existence.

Never forget what you are and the truly awesome potential that each of you has for greatness. In this earthly lifetime you are but dreamers, within a dream. When you awaken to the real nature of your existence you will recognise that all of the experiences that have gone before within the framework of time and space have only served to bring you to a realisation of your true nature, which is beyond time and space. Above all, strive to see through the mists of illusion and the web of deceit which will be thrown over and around you in an attempt to cloak down your true nature. Never lose sight of your higher directive and always seek to be true to the voice that speaks without words and the truth that has no label, for these are from your higher soul. If you are told what to think and do by others and are 'educated' into ways which do not encompass respect, kindness, tolerance, truthfulness and love for every living form, then you can know that your pathway lies elsewhere. Reliance upon materialistic values will only lead you into a blind alley. The one who desires true spirituality always seeks the broad highway of non-conformance and individual expression and only sheep allow themselves to be lead where others determine they should go. The eagle however, that most majestic of creatures, soars high above the landscape, a captive unto no one and a silent witness unto much.

In these troubled times in which you live, look always through the eagle eyes of the spirit and strive to soar above the mundane, the mediocre and the irrelevant. You are your own pupil and your own master. All questions and all answers lie within and all happiness is to be found in the discovery of the bliss that lies at the heart of the innermost self.

Introduction

This is the fourth in the series of White Feather books. The previous titles have been a compilation of questions and answers put to the Spirit Guide and transcripts of recordings from such encounters on the public platform. In creating this new volume we wondered how we might expand somewhat, give a little more time to explore more deeply certain subjects, how we might reach those souls who would not wish to go to a meeting but none the less have their own questions to ask and at the same time further document some of the wonderful question and answer sessions we have had in the public arena with those who have attended there.

The aim of this book is to reach out to as many as different people as possible. There are many who would not choose to go to a 'trance evening' in a Spiritualist church. We firmly believe that spiritual philosophy should be accessible to everyone - the teachings affect us all. Spirituality is not owned by churches, the learned or a 'gifted few'. It is a blueprint for living that encompasses all of those people and institutions but is not theirs exclusively.

Sometimes the environment in which we work can be off-putting to some so it is for this reason that we wanted to open our home to anyone who wished to ask their questions in a more relaxed atmosphere and to allow those who came a longer time to enjoy a 'One to One' session with White Feather. We have had tears of joy, tears of sadness, laughter and happiness but the overwhelming feeling from our sittings has been one of love both from the spirit world and the reciprocal emotion from our sitters who without exception have said they found the experience poignant, thought provoking and ultimately of great benefit.

There is no mystery in spirit communication. It is natural. An awareness of and interaction with the vibrations of energy that exist at various frequencies all around us means that we can tune in to a source of information that is universal, available to everyone - an information super highway. Science is now confirming what we have known instinctively for aeons of time. Energy cannot be destroyed. All things are connected and it is in that connectedness that we can access the wealth of knowledge and wisdom that is ours for the taking if we are open to receive it.

In the world of quantum physics observation of something can alter it. Whether it be local or remote the change still occurs. The energy being directed can have a profound effect on the recipient and if the sender's intent is positive amazing things can happen. Would this not explain how absent healing might work or how telepathy can occur?

We do not however need to be physicists to enjoy the benefits of such knowledge. Communication of any kind is dependant upon the meaning of a message being conveyed effectively. We hope that this book will answer some of your questions in a way that is meaningful to you.

We ask you to be open to its teachings and inquisitive about finding additional answers for yourself but above all enjoy your own personal journey of enlightenment through its pages.

'Sunflower'

November 2004

"At times man thinks that he is at the summit, the pinnacle of power and achievement in your world. But these things are transient and in reality he stands, but a little way from the foot of the valley."

The New Physics 1

Our world view of what is considered to constitute 'reality' is constantly shifting as new theories and discoveries reveal to us more and more of the possible nature of existence. Spirit guides have of course, traditionally informed us that we are much more than just flesh and bone and that the physical universe, as vast and unfathomable as it may appear, is only a fraction of the totality that is life.

Space and time, those two essential postulates at the heart of modern physics have been recognised as being parts of one another and more recently the term 'spacetime' has been employed to describe the apparent relationship that each has with the other. Indeed, to speak of space without time, or time without space would be unthinkable in the modern era. Not only that, but new discoveries at the 'quantum' levels have further revealed that mind and matter are also linked in a similar way, as is so called 'matter' and 'non-matter'. In fact, the whole world of sub-atomic existence is proving to be far stranger than we could ever have imagined.

Spirit guides, to their credit have always spoken to us of the oneness of all life. Down the ages they have revealed to us that we are indeed all parts of each other and that matter is but the husk and 'spirit' the reality.

White Feather has himself, on many occasions spoken in this vein, but as knowledge has increased upon the earth, so those in the spirit realms have been able to impart information which, even fifty years ago, would have been incomprehensible to mankind.

Today, despite the many difficulties which face humanity worldwide, and flying in the very face of the increasing reliance upon a material lifestyle which seems to be engulfing mans collective psyche, the new discoveries of science are proving what many materialists, atheists and ignorant minds have long thought either highly improbable or downright impossible - that we are at the very heart of creation. We are God, and God is us, each and every one. Here in typical fashion, the spirit sage begins his oratory on the subject with his by

now, customary style of greeting. His words, both encouraging and profound reveal a deeper insight into the knowledge and information now being afforded to those prepared to suspend their conditioned beliefs and who are ready to move on to a new stage of enlightenment:

White Feather: "As we link with you tonight we seek as always to impart something of worth and of value. To offer a measure of certainty where there is doubt, understanding where there is confusion and enlightenment where there is ignorance, and to this end I thought it would be helpful to say a few words concerning what I refer to as 'the new physics'. For there are many changes taking place, as there always have been and always will be, upon and around your earth. None more so than in the fields of endeavour that link with scientific study and research. There are those free thinkers and modern day explorers who are prepared to push beyond the boundaries and the decreed barriers that represent and enclose man's current understanding. The tragedy for the most part is that these individuals are scorned. They are ridiculed and denied the necessary help to support, to continue to pursue their explorations. But of course this is nothing new. Throughout man's history individuals who have been at the cutting edge of discovery have never been afforded an easy journey and have seldom been recognised by their own people in their own time. Indeed, history will inform you that many of these deeper thinkers were, in their own time regarded as heretics. Some were even put to death, in the physical sense, and it was not until many centuries later that their discoveries and the truths that they sought to expound at the time were recognised as being correct.

Today, upon your world the story is much the same. For even though man has advanced in some areas of his intellect and mental prowess and at times excels, nevertheless there are still a great many closed minds who are not prepared to venture beyond the accepted norm and what has become entrenched through many years of indoctrination.

Science is a wonderful tool for discovery and correctly applied enables the mind to push forward unto greater and greater discovery and deeper and deeper understanding, and yet, used incorrectly it can easily form a barrier to further progress as is so often the case. Much of current thinking over the last few centuries has been based around the teachings of Newtonian physics which in their time were ahead of their time and did a great deal to further man's knowledge and understanding of how the universe, the physical domain, operates. There were of course other great minds who added to this knowledge, there have been many since. Most recently Einstein, who even as I speak continues his work in my world as do many of the great thinkers who once walked upon the earth. Einstein at least, had begun to gain a grasp of the complexities and intricacies of the sub-atomic world and the implications that has for the relationships between all facets of life. Perhaps it can be stated that generally, the old world view of the structure of form and its relationship with itself at many levels was one of separation, where objects such as planets, galaxies and stars and even individuals such as you and I, although existing within the same dimension nonetheless did not have any connection as such, between one another. Of course, seemingly outside forces such as gravity acted upon these bodies and that in a sense, assumed a link between them. But modern thinking and recent discoveries into the world of the quantum mechanical level has revealed what we as teachers of spiritual truths have always sought to impart; there are no divisions between the various facets of life at whatever level they exist and that all, in reality is connected.

Recently it has been discovered that man himself is a partaker in the creation of what is loosely termed 'reality'. The very fact that his mind and his being is able to observe matter, influences the way that, that matter operates and determines to an extent the way that path unfolds. If we take an example; light. It has been discovered that light has many properties and that it can appear as both a wave and a particle at the same time - a kind of duality. This in itself has proven to be an extraordinary discovery for humanity and perhaps even more so is that when that light is observed in certain conditions its form 'collapses' into one or the other - either a wave form or a particle form. The very act of observation seems to determine the way that these sub-atomic particles or 'quanta' of light behave. Through observation it seems to be that matter falls either side of the line, as it were, creating the 'reality'. But it has also been noted that even if light, in its observation becomes a particle then its opposite, the wave, also seems to exist at some other level or dimension. Transversely, when the wave is observed then the particle exists somewhere else in another dimension. This is a very complex and deep teaching in the sense that those who have little understanding of the study of quantum mechanics and sub-atomic particles may find this a little difficult to comprehend, but in reality what scientists have and are discovering is what we have been speaking of in many ways for a long time. Trying to communicate this understanding to mankind - that the physical level is only one facet of a much greater whole and that 'death' is not the end of life but merely a progression from one state to another.

What happens you see, when man observes his world and his consciousness impinges itself upon it is that not only does he bring into being the very reality of which he is a part but he also creates an imprint upon his higher self. A record, if you like of all that occurs in his life. All that he has been, all that he is, all that he will be. And when the light form collapses into the wave or the particle, whilst the one aspect settles into what is regarded as the physical reality in which you live, its opposing aspect or other half creates the etheric reality which is also as comprehensive and complete as your physical dimension. So every act, every thought, has this duality in that it has a physical aspect but also an etheric, spiritual aspect. This is why everything that you do, think, say, is recorded upon the etheric, upon the etheric body and when death occurs those energies, those memories if you like, are taken up into the higher spirit body and travel with you. This is why you actually create the spirit body that you have. You are doing it now. We have always stated that you create that body, by your thoughts, by your words, by your actions, by your deeds. But the new physics is offering to humanity, through the scientific body that explores it and delves within it, tangible evidence and proof that this exists.

Another discovery that science has made is that when one observes a particle - let us say an atom or a facet of it, and that instance of observation changes its behaviour, then a subsequent change may also occur in a particle some distance away which is linked to the very particle which is being observed. Distance is no object in this law of observation and explains to an extent why there is no separation between anything. Scientists are baffled how a particle in one place can affect a particle in another place when seemingly, there is no connection between the two. Of course there is a connection! It is a minute sub-atomic connection, but it exists nonetheless, although science has yet to 'see' it. Have we not always stated to you that when you send forth a thought, it reaches another, either in my world or in your world and I am sure that many of you have evidence of this. That which you may refer to as telepathy, clairvoyance, clairaudience of clairsentience. These are only labels. The fact is, a thought is a powerful medium and travels through the ether, through time and space and connects one to another. Indeed, the very principles that we employ when communicating with your earth are founded upon the basis of thought transference. For when we link with you through this instrument we do so through the power of thought. From spirit, through spirit, to spirit. From mind, through mind, to mind. We do not have to make 'physical' contact as it were. We can do so through the power of thought directly, when applied with the knowledge that we have in the right way.

So there has to be a connection between all things. Not only animate but also inanimate. For make no mistake, all are parts of the same whole. When you look around you, you see divisions. You see space between objects. When you look into the night sky and see the stars, see the sun and the moon, you perhaps believe that you have no part of them and they no part of you. And yet perhaps another part of you senses a connection between you. In truth, you are connected to the farthest star in the most distant galaxy and to the highest of the high in my world and the lowest of the low in yours. The fact that you cannot always register these extremes of the spectrum does not mean that you are not connected to them. For you operate within a 'bandwidth' that is largely of your own making. Because the frequency at which you operate and vibrate is in accordance with what you are and have become through your past actions, your past lives and also of course in a physical sense, with the vehicle through which you have to operate, which itself is limited to a small range of frequency and vibrations in the physical universe. But of course you are receiving information upon many other levels of which you are not always consciously aware. Nevertheless you are giving forth and receiving information at all times as you sail upon the ocean of being.

If science is to become anything other than a tool for industry, for those who seek to earn wealth from it by prostituting it for their own ends, then it must break free from the restraints which are imposed upon it by certain individuals and corporations whose material desires outweigh their spiritual endeavour. Science is not the be-all-and-end-all. But it is a wonderous mechanism for discovery and when it is allowed to operate with the divine principles upon which all true discovery is founded - that is the inner desire to know and to understand, to embrace, then it will reveal to humanity much about itself and its place in the universe. It is a wonderful truth to know that you are one with all things. Very humbling I would say, for it brings home the reality that you are not greater or lesser than anyone or anything. Man has no privileged position to have dominion over other creatures and life forms anywhere. He is himself a creature of evolution through which the mind of the spirit has found a greater opportunity for expression. But he must endeavour to achieve humility through the recognition of that through which he has come."

The teacher went on to emphasise that man still has a long way to go in evolutionary terms and needs to encourage the 'New Physics' to grow so that scientific discovery and spiritual understanding can harmonise and develop with each other:

White Feather: "At times man thinks that he is at the summit, the pinnacle of power and achievement in your world. But these things are transient and in reality he stands, but a little way from the foot of the valley. He has to earn the right, by harmonising all aspects of his being into a state of balance and equilibrium that encompasses the physical, emotional, mental and spiritual aspects and that recognises in the very heart of its being that it is of the spirit and that its relationship with all of creation is essential.

When man forgets that from which he has emerged, he loses sight of what he is and what he may become. The greater soul is the humbler soul. The most enriched soul is the one which has the utmost compassion, empathy and understanding for those who have yet to reach the self same awareness and spiritual growth.

The new physics, if it is allowed to flourish, to become mainstream, will naturally succeed the previous world view and take man into a new age of discovery. These are exciting times. There is much to be positive about. Man is a multi-dimensional being, existing in a multi-dimensional matrix. He exists and has his being upon many levels simultaneously. The discovery and comprehension of this alone, has many implications for humanity. Not least, the challenges to organised and orthodox religion, which has clung for many centuries to outmoded views. To dogma, creed and to ignorance. There are many who stand to lose a great deal in your world. But in losing, there must be a recognition that they have so much to gain. Whether or not they can rise to the challenge and have the courage to let go of that to which they have stubbornly clung for so long, is the burning question. I have said before and I will say again; that those who have decried what we have said, the spiritual knowledge and truth, the evidence which we have always sought to impart, may yet be the very ones who embrace it. Because the truth you know, has a strange way of imposing itself. You can deny it and deny it and deny it, and yet it persists. It is only when you come face to face with it, perhaps for the umpteenth time that you cannot any longer reconcile its reality within the limited map of the world and you gently melt into the understanding of what is. Man can shut his ears, close his eyes, lock and bolt the door to his mind and its thoughts but the truth will not go away. Just as the sun rises each morning, so the truth will seek ever to rise in his heart. When he accepts what is and yields to its wonderous certainty then he will indeed take great steps forward."

The understanding that there are no clear distinctions or boundaries between the various facets of creation, physical and non-physical and that what appears to be solid and substantial in physical terms, may really be nothing of the kind - the atom for example, is said to consist largely of emptiness - leads to all kinds of questions concerning the location and nature of various aspects of our being. Where is our soul? What is the mind? Here, on another occasion whilst addressing a live audience in Birmingham, England the guide was asked about the location of memory:

White Feather: "That is a good question. The memory is not held just in the physical body and when you 'lose' a memory, it is not lost, it is only lost in the physical sense. What you must comprehend if you can is that the mind and the brain are not the same. The brain is not the mind, the mind uses the brain just as the spirit uses the physical body.

Scientists would have you believe perhaps that the brain is the mind and that the thoughts are contained within the brain, but they are not. Consciousness and mind exist throughout the body. Within every cell and within every atom of the body. In fact the whole body thinks and yet it is the mind and the spirit that uses the physical organism.

You must understand that when at death, the spirit withdraws from the physical body, all of the memories including those that you think are lost, things which you have forgotten, they are all there because they are preserved in the spirit body. Do you understand that? Does that help you?.........good!"

The fact that the guide commented on consciousness and mind existing throughout the body is congruent with modern day discoveries about the nature of the mind and its operation through the body. Scientists have discovered that every organ of the body and indeed every cell 'thinks' and cellular memory is a very real phenomenon. Mediumship too, has demonstrated down the ages that mind is not located exclusively in the brain. The ability to 'read' a manuscript through the fingertips or even the toes is not unheard of and the numerous cases of 'remote viewing' and OBE's (out of the body experiences) are relatively common and well documented. Other phenomena such as psychometry (the gathering of information from inanimate objects) and reading the auric field are also indicative of a mind that exists both beyond the physical body and also leaves its residual energies

within a similar 'field' encompassing an object which has been associated with a particular individual.

The phenomena of 'spacetime' which has already been touched upon is another aspect upon which consciousness impinges itself. How often have we experienced dreams or insights in which a past or future event seems to be reaching out to us? Can memory be both past and future tense, and if so can we actually have memories of events which have yet to occur in our current existence? If Einstein is to be believed, then time itself is relative, and both past present and future may coexist together. *(See also page 135).* **Here is what White Feather had to say on two separate occasions:**

White Feather: "Well, you know, you are spirit, you are mind and when at times you are able to raise above the level of the physical, the body, then you are able if you have earned the right to gain glimpses into what you would call the future.

Now the future is something that exists at this level and at other levels of perception. There are levels in my world in which past, present and future are one. They are not the same as in your world because you live and exist within what I call linear time, but when you are able to raise the consciousness, perhaps in the sleep state or in meditation or in moments of attunement, you are able to glimpse into the past and future. It is rather like opening the windows of the mind and looking outside at that which was closed to you. Do you understand that? If that happens then it is because you have earned the right to know it. What you have to do is learn to have the responsibility that insight and that knowledge brings, because it is a gift, you have earned it. It is a gift but it brings responsibility, you have to use it wisely."

Questioner: "But how will I know if what I am seeing is correct?"

White Feather: "You will find that if your motive is right you will reach that level in your perception where you will see truthfully. You WILL see truthfully and anything that you see will be there to be seen because you are meant to see it. It is there as a help, sometimes it may appear as a warning or a sense that you have to avoid a situation or even take a particular course of action, but it is there to help you, not to hinder you.

Where there are those who say they have insights into the future and they see the death of another, the passing of another, again you know you must question what they are seeing, why they are seeing it, who they are........because not all such insights are as they appear to be. There are those who touch a lower psychic level and believe me there are many mischievous minds on the lower planes of my world that take great delight in putting fear into the hearts of some misguided people in your world. But I do not think that is the case in question."

Questioner: "The problem I have is that I had a vision of someone heading into serious trouble and I didn't know whether or not to warn them......."

White Feather: "Well, it is not for me to judge you on that and question you. If you saw it and you felt strongly enough, if you have registered it to such a point that you felt a strong sense of right and you felt you had to impart that knowledge and warn them, or help them in that situation, then that would have been perhaps the right thing to do. But ultimately, it would have been their responsibility, not yours. If you didn't do that it is no reflection upon you because it is quite a responsibility that is carried and one does not always have the sense of purpose in that what one has seen is the truth. You doubt yourself don't you? You doubt it and you think 'well, have I really seen that?' and you are fearful of whether or not to pass this message on. It is no reflection upon you, but you will find that like all gifts of the spirit, if you cultivate them, if you develop them they will get stronger and there will be no doubt and you will have to act if you are true to yourself upon the true message that you see and that you are given. So I would cultivate it."

On the second occasion the guide had been asked whether it was right and proper to be able to glimpse events before they 'happen':

White Feather: "What do you want to know? As with the previous questioner you have earned the right. What you must understand is that time in my world is not the same as it is in your world. In your world you are experiencing things through a linear time. In my world time is not the same.
You know, Einstein I believe it was, who said that time is relative. It is relative to where you are and the speed at which you move. In my world we are able to see time a little more differently than you in your world. We can see further ahead, into the future and what happens is that when you are receiving these premonitions, it is either you, yourself who is temporarily able to escape this linear time upon the earth and glimpse into the time frame of my world and 'see into the future', or else it is someone in my world who is giving you that information that they have acquired so that you may be forewarned, or forearmed as it is said, of some event that is yet to 'happen'. That is not given to frighten you. It is given to help you. But it can only be given because you have earned the right to receive it. Does that help? Does it answer your question?"

Questioner: "Not really."

White Feather: "Did it help you at all?"

Questioner: "Well, the thing is that when I gave the person the message that I had been given, they didn't believe me and I question myself."

White Feather: "Well, that is a matter for them. You know, I speak about a lot of things and no one believes me! But I do not concern myself about whether or not they believe me. All I know is that the truth is the truth is the truth and I speak it as I know it. If they choose to believe it then I am pleased. If they do not then that is a matter for them.

The truth was given to you, you accepted what you were given and you gave it to others. They were at liberty to accept it or reject it so do not reproach yourself for that. You did what you had to do. Let me say to you that it won't be the last time."

As understanding and yet as uncompromising as ever White Feather always makes his point in a way that seeks to demonstrate his unswerving loyalty to that which he professes to know as truth whilst never setting out to offend one who holds a different viewpoint. He simply attempts to impart the facts as HE understands them and leaves his enquirers to decide for themselves the validity of his philosophy.

One thing however is certain, the desire for greater knowledge, whether through mainstream science, mediumship or other esoteric disciplines will persist for as long as man exists. For the quest to understand the universe in which he temporarily resides, his own nature and his ultimate destiny beyond the physical domain is one which is intrinsic within him and which drives him on upon the endless journey which is his destiny.

The 'New Physics' is replacing the 'Old Physics' as the views of Galileo, Newton, Einstein and other prominent scientists and philosophers are being gradually modified to accommodate the latest theories and findings. In time these too will give way to even deeper insights as new discoveries reveal yet more of the true nature of being. Whether or not the 'ultimate equation' that encompasses a theory of everything will be attained is a matter for conjecture. The very nature of the spirit in all its forms is one of progression and White Feather, along with many other spirit guides has pointed out that perfection is virtually unattainable. And yet, we cannot but continue to pursue our instinctive drives to learn and evolve. Like dogs chasing their tails we spin around and around in ever spiralling circles of change. In days gone by, a major new discovery or breakthrough occurred perhaps once in a millennium. Then it became once in a generation. Then once in a decade. Now it is perhaps, one major discovery every week. Soon it may be every day that a major breakthrough is made and a new dimension is added to the understanding of the collective consciousness of mankind.

Somewhere an old saying emerges out of the ether: 'May you always live in exciting times'. This we do. For we are men. We are God. We are eternal.

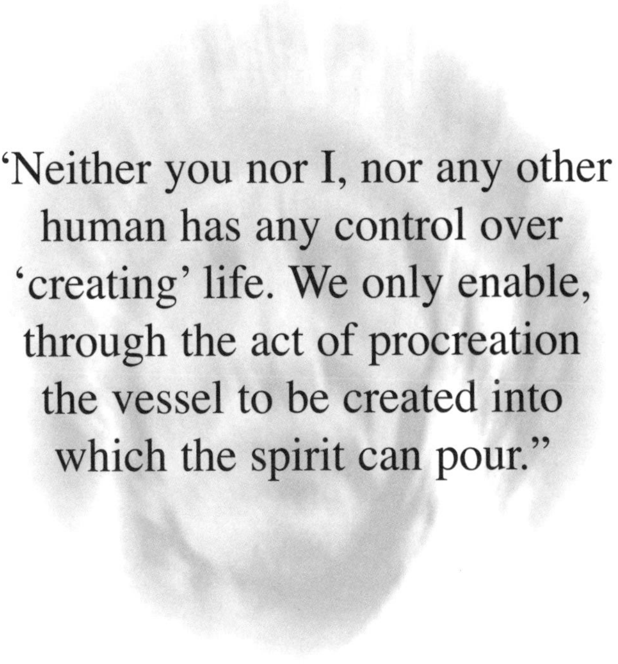

"Neither you nor I, nor any other human has any control over 'creating' life. We only enable, through the act of procreation the vessel to be created into which the spirit can pour."

one2one

Seeking a Child 2

When we decided to give selected individuals the opportunity to enjoy a 'one to one' discussion with White Feather, a personal friend who was aware of our work with the spirit guide offered to become the first to speak with him in a specially arranged private sitting. Pam, as it transpired, was in search of answers regarding her quest to start a family. A successful businesswoman in her mid thirties, she instinctively felt that the time was ripe for her and her husband to have their first child. They had been trying in vain for many months to conceive and Pam felt that, having 'affirmed' for the pregnancy, things should have been starting to happen. White Feather however, whilst affording his usual respect and kindness was keen to point out that in spiritual terms at least, things do not always unfold in the timescale that we would wish them to:

White Feather: "May I impart my usual greeting to you all tonight.....and I use the term ALL deliberately for even though your temple is compact, we are not confined to its boundaries and there are many souls who gather with us and who wish to share in this joyous communion of worlds and of minds. As it is, I welcome again the opportunity to fill the cup of your understanding, that it may overflow with the truth of the spirit. How I hope and pray that you may drink deeply of it, for its waters not only purify the soul but also enable the spirit, through coming into understanding and awareness of its divinity, to free itself from the self imposed prison in which it has temporarily placed a facet of itself, albeit to learn through life's many vicissitudes. Because as I have said so frequently of late, truth it is, which is the liberator of souls. When there is ignorance, there breeds fear, superstition, anxiety, trepidation and all of the other negative aspects to which the human condition seems to be so prone. But where there is truth, there cometh light that banishes darkness, that removes ignorance and sets the soul upon a wonderous journey that takes it from its prison to a state of liberation. And there is no greater freedom than that of a liberated soul.

I sense a little apprehension in the atmosphere tonight but that is a good thing because as always we work upon the vibration of spontaneity. I am not concerned or perplexed at whatever questions you may have for me, for I trust in the divine law which operates with a mathematical precision to enable the answers to be forthcoming, if not from my own wealth of understanding then from those who stand at my side.

Let me, for the uninitiated amongst you just reiterate that we, like you have a long way to go upon the journey of unfoldment. We are not all knowing and all wise. We have much to learn but remain humble as we set forth on our task because as you may perhaps learn from us, we also learn from you. It is a two-way thing and that is as it should be because there is no teacher who is not also a pupil and no pupil who is not also a teacher.

Let us then share in this joyous time of communion and reveal to each other what truths and what secrets and what inner knowledge and understanding we may have.

Are you happy?"

Pam & Amanda: "Yes."

White Feather: "Good. Then let us hope that in this joyous time ahead, happiness will overflow and we can add to it and polish the facet of the diamond of the spirit which awaits our words. Sunflower (Amanda), you know the procedure that we always follow, so I will invite the opportunity to ask any questions which are appertaining to tonight's proceedings."

Pam: "I have a number of specific questions but I'd like to start with a general one. The general one is just asking if there is something ......I know on my journey there will be a lot that I need to discover for myself.....but there maybe something that you feel that I would be grateful for some help with.........whether there is something that you feel that I need to know now?"

White Feather: "There are many things which each of us have to unfold and discover. You know, part of the wonder of life's journey is not always knowing what awaits us around the corner, but the joy in discovering through the adventure of life the lessons that we need to understand and help us in our unfoldment and the recognition of the divinity that lies within us. Perhaps the greatest lesson for each of us is in service.....serving the Great Spirit. Because in serving the Great Spirit so we too are served. In giving forth so we too are given unto. Because service is the coin of the spirit. Service is the passport of the soul and in serving others selflessly, so we too are served by the same laws that we invoke when we give forth from ourselves.

On a personal level, perhaps one of the greatest lessons that you have to undertake and to encounter is to learn the art of patience, because you have many virtues.

Looking into your heart I can see that, and I speak not with the voice of criticism, but with the voice of love when I say that patience is not your greatest virtue. When you learn patience then you will invoke laws that will operate, that will draw energies to you and conditions to you that otherwise may have been denied you, through your impatience. It almost a paradox, but it is a great truth when I say to you.....and perhaps I can invoke words that so often are spoken in your world, that 'less is often more'. If you wish to move forward then learn stillness. If you wish to have answers then learn to close your ears to the material world, in which there is so much chatter and listen to the still voice of the spirit that speaks to you. In patience there is great strength. In patience, there is great movement forward. When man is restless and impatient he is an enemy unto himself. He blocks the very forces of the universe which would if they were given free reign unfold him in their gentle love and lift him to the heights of joy and freedom which he seeks. But in his impatience, and I speak now not just of those here, but of mankind generally.....man wants everything handed to him on a plate. He wants answers now. He wants deliverance now. He must learn patience. In calmness, in fortitude he invokes the law of cause and effect which will bring to him that which is his soul's desire and if you can culpably cultivate this, through repose, through gentleness, through calmness you will find that many things will be brought to you."

Pam: "That's a perfect answer. Sometimes we hear things which our soul knows and to be told it again is perfect, so thank you for that. As you may know, one of the things that I desire, and I believe for all the right reasons......I desire with my partner to make a baby and we have felt the 'soul' of the baby very strongly......once a couple of years ago and once last year and then a little bit this year, and yet the soul hasn't found...hasn't come.....in the physical form. On the one hand that saddens me greatly but on the other hand I also realise that until now it may well have been the wrong time, but every time that I seem to turn a corner in a new thing or a new realisation, I then believe that then, is the right time. But this comes back to your last point of 'patience'. I wonder if there's anything there that I need to know because the baby is welcome to come now....?"

White Feather: "Let me speak....because I know that in answering your question, which I will do, that many others will at some point come into awareness of these words which I am about to offer, and I have to say first of all that we have to clarify for many reasons, certain points to which you refer. Let me state first of all that spirit is master, matter is servant. You speak of 'creating' a baby and I understand the terms that you employ when you say that.....the language used....but no one 'creates' a baby. No one 'creates' life, do you understand that? What happens is that a vessel is created through the sexual act that permits the spirit, or a facet of it to incarnate into the body of matter if the conditions are right and if it chooses to do so. Neither you nor I, nor any other human has any control over 'creating' life. We only enable, through the act of procreation the vessel to be created into which the spirit can pour. Into which the spirit can enter. That is the first point. Secondly, you say you have sensed the soul of the 'baby'.....which you may well have done, but you must recognise also that there is no 'child' awaiting to enter into your body....there is a soul awaiting. The soul that comes to many upon your earth may be an older soul than the one through which they incarnate. The fact that one senses it as a child does not necessarily mean that it is younger soul that is about to enter into the body. That has to be recognised, do you understand that?"

Pam: "Yes."

White Feather: "I have to clarify those points for others who may read these words or listen to these words, that you must recognise. As to the point of entry, when, through the act of procreation a vessel is formed, at that moment there is life created and spirit, if it chooses to, will enter into that vehicle. There is no life without spirit, there is no spirit without life. But spirit is the master. Man cannot create life, you cannot create life. You can only provide the means for life to enter. To that point, there is a time and a place for everything. There is an old saying you know, that 'for everything under the sun there is a time and a place.' That time, for the entry into your world will only happen when it has been reached, and not before. Nothing that you or I or anyone may do can interfere with that process. As I have said on many occasions; when the fruit is ripe it falls from the tree. If you try to force it, if you try to pick it before it is ready then it is a bitter fruit and I will say to you that there is a time and a place and when that point is reached then there will be no effort required on your behalf other than the normal act that you will undertake. Because the spirit will enter when it has chosen to do so, when the point has been reached for that to happen. Do you understand?"

Pam: "I understand it and thank you for that. My question therefore leads to the fact that because I am now reaching on in years......I am thirty five, soon to be thirty six.......in modern times one thinks that is getting a bit late. We have been trying, we have been aiming for a baby for twelve months.......there are some tests that can be done by modern science and I am not sure whether to go down that route or to go down that route without yearning, with total understanding that it is when the baby, when the soul is ready, but making sure that the vessel is able......."

White Feather: "It will do no harm to proceed with the tests but let me reverse this somewhat and say that sometimes precautions are taken in your world to prevent life from entering......what you refer to as sterilisation and yet still happens. Why is that? If man has such mastery over life that he can prevent it, why does it still occur? Even perhaps many months or years after that operation to prevent fertilisation from occurring, yet life still occurs. That is because man and matter have no mastery over the spirit and whatever the outcome of your tests, whatever the prognosis, it does not matter to the point that, if it is meant to be, it will be and the spirit will come when it is ready, that you must understand. Man has great technological knowledge in many fields including medicine and science but he has yet a great deal to learn and understand about the workings of the spirit and the way that natural law operates and let me say to you this; if it is that a spirit is to enter into your world there is nothing that man can do to prevent it because it will do so, despite what you may think."

It was obvious at this juncture that the guide was giving answers which were beginning to inspire still deeper questions from his guest, something which often occurs when White Feather engages in a dialogue with those seeking knowledge:

Pam: " Two questions follow on from that. The first one is that although I am happy to do the tests I feel awkward about asking my partner to take them. If we take them.......and we know that the soul is meant to be, then perhaps I don't need to ask him to take them, although for my peace of mind it would be quite nice to do the tests......"

White Feather: "I think peace of mind is an important piece of the jigsaw in this equation because the mental aspect and to an extent the emotional aspect have their effects upon the physical. Mind is very powerful. It works upon many levels in many subtle ways to influence and affect the physical body, the endocrine system, the hormonal system and many other facets that contribute to the overall health of the being and the fertility of the physical form. When you address the emotional and mental aspects then you are also, in effect addressing the physical. You cannot separate and divorce one from the other at this level and where you refer to 'peace of mind', that is a wonderous statement in itself. 'Peace' of mind. Because the mind, when it is at peace, reflects those energies throughout the body and throughout all systems and so where there is peace of mind there is harmony, there is wholeness, there is health and there is a greater aspect of fertility. So you have to encompass the whole in this."

At this point the guide, through his medium, leaned forward and looked into Pam's eyes, something which he does when he wishes to 'see' more deeply into the psyche and also to establish a more intimate connection with the sitter:

White Feather: "Let me ask you a question......and I already know the answer......is there great love between you and your partner?"

Pam: "Yes."

White Feather: "Where there is love there should be no fear, no apprehension, no wavering, no doubt. There should be oneness, there should be support, there should be harmony. Put fear and doubt, trepidation and worry and anxiety out of your heart. They play no part in an awakened and enlightened soul. Go forward in love. Where there is love between two souls there is a great bonding. There is a power, a great energy and force at work. I think it would be a good thing to undertake the tests because then you will have more peace of mind, more direction and there you will be calmer within yourself and can reflect not only inwardly and within you both but also throughout the rivers and currents of energy that flow between you and embrace you."

Pam: "Thank you. Another point leading on from the idea of helping the soul to realise how welcome it is but also understanding the concept of patience and allowing it to come in its own time............is there anything that as a couple or individually we can or should do to let the old or new soul come in from the baby to my life?"

White Feather: "Let me say this to you; when the soul is about to enter into the physical form, to reincarnate, or even to enter into that for the first time, there are many aspects of which you are unaware, which have to be considered. In the case of a soul who is an 'older soul' shall we say, who has lived many times upon the earth, but a facet of which has chosen again to reintroduce itself into the body of matter, it has earned the right more often than not to choose its parents.
Do you think that any soul linking with you would simply do so by chance, who happened to be passing by and saw the opportunity to 'dive in'? I think not! I think it would have considered its options very carefully and would have been drawn to you because it recognised that within you and your beloved it had something with which it found affinity. In fact it would be that very self same thing that it recognised within itself that would draw it because like always attracts like.
So you do not have to welcome this spirit that is as yet unknown to you, as you would welcome a stranger knocking upon your door because it is no stranger. One whom you have yet to discover may know the actions of you, so allow that guest to invite itself, to make itself known in as natural way as possible, because recognise this; that where there is a choice of parentage and of vessel into which to incarnate, a wise soul will deliberate and weigh up, ponder and consider very carefully its options before making that choice.
Why does it do that? Firstly because as I have already said it recognises that it has an affinity with its parents but more importantly it chooses to come in to the body of matter to learn particular lessons and to outwork perhaps, some Karmic aspect which has yet to be unfolded. So it is important that it makes the right choice.
In my world we don't make mistakes. We *don't* make mistakes, understand that."

Pam: "Thank you for that. In our modern society we have computers and lap-tops and I spend.......have been spending up to twelve, seventeen hours........."

White Feather: (interrupting) "Too much time!"

Pam: ".....my question is, even without considering the baby, how much time is healthy to be in front of a computer, my lap-top.....but then the next question is that in front of the laptop with a baby in my stomach....."

White Feather: "You must recognise that the energies, the vibration, the frequency given out by your computer screen and your television and your other electrical phenomena and gadgetry do not help, do not assist in any way.......in fact they can hinder the progress of the spirit through the physical form, so I would heartily recommend that you reduce this and consider very carefully your options because energies, even though you cannot see them and the vibrations that emit from these electrical sources are very powerful and they can indeed interfere upon many levels....with your own physical body, certainly they would do with that of a child that you may carry within you."

The spirit teacher seemed to be pointing out that the relatively new problem of electromagnetic pollution, which has recently been highlighted by those investigating the use of mobile phones, microwave ovens, computers and other equipment which generate electrical fields, could have a direct bearing on health, a thought which had already arisen in Pam's mind and which was obviously giving rise to concern:

Pam: "I was thinking that it could be realistic to reduce my computer hours to three hours a day, would that still be too much?"

White Feather: "Whatever hours you spend, divide it by four and then divide it once more. So you have to cut it back. You have to do this. Certainly the amount of time that you spend - and to a lesser degree you too Sunflower (Amanda) and the one through whom I speak also (Robert). It's not healthy. One can become a little blasé about these things. It is the old story you know, again if I can paraphrase one of your sayings 'What the eye doesn't see, the heart doesn't grieve about'. But ignorance is not always bliss and just because something is unseen it does not mean that it does not exist, that it does not carry any potency. Man is surrounding himself by electromagnetic energies, electric currents, and this is creating many stresses, not only within the home but within his physical and to a lesser extent his etheric body which a resulting in disease and suffering. Some of the forms of cancer which are emerging in your world are due to the electric currents which are also present in your modern day lives. And until man addresses this problem and sacrifices his materialistic desire for monetary gain and replaces it with a recognition of his spiritual dimension and its requirements then I'm afraid his suffering will continue to increase."

Pam: "So if I reduce........I recognise this need which is why I have asked the question........if I reduce my twelve hour working day or more down to a one hour day......."

White Feather: "....a sensible level! Excuse me, I'm sorry to interrupt but you know, you have many answers to the questions and you even tell yourself the answer. You even listen to what your higher self is telling you, but you then don't act upon it. That is your downfall. That is, if I can refer back to your earlier question 'what do I need to do in my life now?', allied to patience it is to listen to what your soul is telling you and then act upon it. It is one thing to have knowledge, it is another to act upon it and to live it. That is perhaps a great lesson for yourself and for for the many in your world, to learn to act upon."

Having taken White Feather's point, Pam turned her attention to a different aspect of her life, asking the guide if he could advise her with a business venture that had its own spiritual implications. The sage responded firstly in a humourous fashion before imparting his guidance.

Pam:"I usually push it down, I understand it. The next area of questioning if I may be so bold is that we have stumbled upon ......yes, we'll call it a business opportunity, whether it is giving in the way that you mentioned before, we have made a highly significant impact on the health of so many people which warms my soul and gives me great purpose for making a difference and makes me very happy......it also gives me a significant fun challenge for something I believe in strongly. I am keen to know, and I'm sure you know what the venture is......I'm keen to know your thoughts on this and potentially ideas for direction."

White Feather: "Would you want me to be your marketing manager!?"

Pam: "No! I think again it goes back to listening to my inner soul and I will have the answers. But then I could do this with all of these questions and I think you're a lovely man and I would like your answer!"

White Feather: "Well it's a relief that I don't have to be your marketing manager! But let me say in all seriousness that anything which allies that which is beneficial to man's constitution whether physically, emotionally, mentally and most importantly spiritually, then it has to be applauded and I think that what I have been able to even ascertain through various sources is that the individuals and the collective minds who are directing and driving this particular venture of which you have become a part are doing so out of the right motive which is essentially a spiritual one but which obviously does derive material benefits along the way. And that is perfectly acceptable. Why should one be enlightened and yet poor? It is not written into the laws of the universe that knowledge and wisdom have to go hand

in hand with disparity and poverty. Where you have a truly enlightened soul, there you will find that the bounty of the universe comes to that soul effortlessly. It does not have to go and strive and labour hour upon hour to obtain the coin of your world or to feed itself, or to have a roof over its head. These things come to it.
If I can use the words again that are so often spoken by the one who is referred to as the Nazarene, 'If you follow me and love me and my Father, all other things shall be added unto you.' That may be an old fashioned saying but it is as true today as it ever was because truth is timeless.
All you have to do to be successful is to recognise and hold fast to your principles and your motives. Motives are everything, and if you do that you will find that the other things of a material nature, which may at first have drawn you and compelled you and pulled you in, will be added unto you. As I said earlier; less is more. If you stop striving, if you stop trying so hard then you will find that with ease these things will come to you. It is almost, on the surface of it, a contradiction in terms, yet this is the true way in which the universe works. The law of least resistance, the law of least effort. I have heard it referred to as 'the lazy mans law'. That is a nonsense. We are not talking about being lazy or lacking effort or desire. We are talking about serving humanity and the Great Spirit that YOU may be served. Where the motive is selfless, where it is altruistic......and I'm not speaking of that 'face' which some may present, their 'public image'.......... what I am talking about is what lies in here (White Feather pointing to his chest). You may know that, but then you will find that these things which are necessary in your world and which we understand that you have to have to survive will be added unto you with ease, without effort.........fact."

Pam: "Thank you. May I ask you another one. Moving subject now to.......I want to ask you something which is ......difficult to ask. In our society there are many images of a sexual nature and of what is expected and this puts thoughts and concepts into the mind of anyone watching media, reading books etc. Now, my question is that in nature, you do not see sheep or any of the birds having sex every day or every few hours. In our society I think because of the media and the expectations we are therefore given, it leads to a lot of disillusionment, disappointment etc. The reason why I ask this is because some men feel they must have sex all the time, by the media, because that is what everyone else is doing. For some females, we feel that we don't want it everyday, but that it is put upon us by our partners and for others we feel that because the concept is that everybody else is having sex everyday because that's what we see in the media, that because we may not be having it everyday, something is wrong ......that our partner does not love us as much.....however if we look at nature, and we are part of nature, they do not have the same expectations or the same actions and my question is that in going back to a less, quote "civilised" world, what would be the norm, understanding that everyone is different? Understanding that every couple and every relationship is different? Can you give us some indication because I think the media has given us such expectation......it is so destructive to relationships, whether there's too much sex or too little sex......"

White Feather: "Yes, I understand the thrust of your question. I understand the difficulties that obtain and you put your point very well, very articulately. There is indeed great pressure brought to bear by those in your world who have a vested interest in selling the concept of sexual activity and also other areas, non sexual, due to other agendas of which you are not always aware. Some of which are monetary, others which are of a more insidious nature and have brought about over a succession of generations, in the first instance a lowering of the age of sexual consent in your world, but also a general loosening of attitudes and a degrading of morality, shall we say. All of these are many aspects of the same overriding concern which we have, in which sex is sold to you as a commodity or an act which should be undertaken because it is expected, in the same way that you are expected to fit a particular 'model' in physical form or in behaviour, in the clothes that you wear or your speech, in the activities that you undertake because it is considered to be 'normal', whatever that is. What has been lost is the essence of the spirit which is its uniqueness, which is its individuality. Because every facet of the spirit is individual. You are not the same as anyone or anything that has ever been or ever will be. You are totally unique. Yet man, in his regimented world of dogma and creed, ceremony, ritual and labelling, seeks to fit everything into a particular format or pigeonhole where it must conform and sexual activity is high on the agenda because it is such an emotive issue. Because it encompasses not only the physical act but also the mental and emotional aspects of humanity also. This in turn, has an effect on man's spirit and his spiritual development. Man is the only creature upon your earth that undertakes the sexual act simply for pleasure, without the need to procreate. If you look at the animal kingdom you will see that the sexual act, which is performed in the open, without any modesty, quite unashamedly by the creatures of the field is undertaken because of the act of procreation. Of course there is a sexual desire and an attraction between the male and the female of the species and that part of the act itself and humanity, let me say, before man reached a level of intellectual development which he now enjoys......I am talking now of a time going back to the cavemen and beyond that, also was part of this level of expression where the sexual act was a matter of procreation. Now that desire and impulse has been overtaken by the desire for sex for sex sake only. For titillation, for the desire of the ego mind and the ego self. For self gratification and self satisfaction. And this is a great pity for it denies the true expression of the spiritual aspect which should be inherent within everything that is undertaken upon your world.

As to what is normal or what is expected, as you say so rightly, every 'individual' is that. There is no norm. The sexual act should be performed not only through and for the physical gratification, that is a small facet of it, but because it is a part of love. Love is the greatest force in your universe and the physical act of sexual activity should be a part of love and a loving relationship. There is nothing greater than that expression, do you understand that? Am I making sense?"

Pam: "Yes."

White Feather: "....so what you have to try to do, if there is understanding between you and your beloved......and I think there is because you are very close and at similar levels of understanding and spiritual development.....there should be a recognition that there should be no expectation, no pressure, no conforming to what is expected of you. That when you perform the sexual act it should be a joyous union of two souls who recognise their deep love for each other and that they are truly parts of one another. That is the greatest expression of the sexual act that man can attain."

Pam: "You've answered my questions so fantastically and I am very, very grateful. I have one last area that I would like to touch upon if I may and that is with regard to 'soul mates'. I think I understand what soul mates are and I think that I am with my soul mate. We almost met ten times over ten years and when it was the right time for us we actually met. My perception on many different levels is that he is my soul mate but I would quite like to hear your view or what your definition, for want of a better word is, of a soul mate?"

White Feather: "There are what I call 'facets' of the same individuality and there are also what I refer to as 'affinities'. Where you have a true 'soul mate' as it is referred to then it is a facet of one's self, of one's higher self. An aspect, if you like of the same diamond of the soul. And it is somewhat rare that these two facets should meet upon your world although it does occur. What is more often the case is that one encounters an 'affinity'. By an affinity I mean one with whom one has shared many lifetimes, many incarnations into the world of matter. One with whom one has linked through many expressions, many experiences both light and dark, high and low, negative and positive, good and bad. And through this, over successive lifetimes has become truly an affinity, a similar vibration, a similar level of unfoldment, a kindred spirit. Very often affinities choose to enter into the world of matter at the same time. To reincarnate, to undertake particular tasks, to outwork Karma and very often to meet up and to work together and help one another with their individual lessons and where these two affinities meet there is an instant recognition. Not neccesarily on a conscious level, but on a deeper level there is a recognition that they have lived before in the physical sense and that they have loved before and are parts of each other. Where those facets meet there is a true coming together of affinities and there can be no separation, do you understand that?"

Pam: "Yes.......and can you have more than one soul mate?"

White Feather: "You can have more than one affinity because you must recognise that over successive lifetimes you interact and work with many souls and so you form many affinities. But there is only one true 'soul mate' in my understanding."

The topic of 'soul mates' and 'affinities' is one which White Feather has touched upon before, but he was relishing the opportunity to expand further upon this subject and was clearly enjoying his discussion and the further question that followed during which he made a veiled reference to the house cat which had begun howling to be let in on the proceedings.

Pam: "Something that happened to me a few years ago was that I perceived on a model, social criteria standard that the relationship that I had with my soul mate wasn't going where social pressure would demand that we should make it go, so I made the decision to leave my partner but my soul screamed internally and externally for two days to the point where it was definitely not ME crying because I had made the decision, but my soul absolutely howled and my partner's soul came to me that weekend when I had made the decision to leave. So my question there is I suppose it's a recognition that there is something quite strong because even if on a physical, mental, social pressure level I had decided that it was time to move on, my soul would not under any circumstances let me do that......"

White Feather: "I understand that. I think there is another soul that is howling as well! But in answer to your question, or your statement, sometimes you know, the heart's wish is not the soul's desire. Very often you know, you act from a particular level.....and I broaden this out now......you can act from many levels within your being. From the lower ego state, from an emotional level, from a mental level, neither of which may be truly from a soul level and the soul will let you know instinctively through that aspect of your mind which is sometimes referred to as the conscience, but which I call the 'compass of the soul' because it always points to the truth. You don't always want to listen to it, you shut it out even though it screams at you. You shut it out and you act through your own will and desire to partake of whatever pathway you think is right for you. But the soul cannot be denied and its voice, even though it may be a whisper, is the loudest voice you will ever hear. The great thing is when you acknowledge it and you listen to it and then act upon it. Because then, truly are you acting from the soul and not from the lower."

Pam: "Thank you for that. You mentioned about another soul howling. Are you able to clarify that?"

White Feather: " I was referring to your own statement, that your soul 'howls'. That is what I meant. Very often the soul will speak to you in whatever means it can find to communicate. Sometimes it does so through bodily pain because that is the only way that it can speak to you. Sometimes it will speak through the dream state. Other times through a moments inspiration it will burst forth like a seed into your mind. Sometimes it will just be a 'nagging feeling' through the conscience that what you are doing is not as it should be. Equally, when something feels right it is probably because your soul is in accord with it and you sense that in your whole being. The problem that man has is that he does not listen, not to himself. He does not listen and then he goes against his own wishes, the wishes of his soul. If only man were in more attunement with himself then you would find that many answers would come to him. When the storms blow you know, the tree bends. The blades of grass bend with the wind and the breeze. That which defies it, and is rigid, breaks. Man has to learn to bend to the wishes of his spirit. If he did this he would be guided so often, correctly to the truth."

Pam: "And to tune in more, to become more at one, one goes back to the very first thing that you mentioned which was to learn patience. Are there other pointers that you can suggest......others, being with the nature of taking time out......feeling and seeing through the wonderment of life, meditation.......are there some other aspects that you have found and perceived to be of particular good use?"

White Feather: "There are so many, because there are many ways to reach a central point. Sunflower will know that I often say 'many paths lead to one place'.....that's right isn't it? But you know, all of the things which you have mentioned are helpful. Overall I would say, learn to love, even your enemies, even those whom you may despise initially or who may despise you, because they are parts of you. Recognise that you are a part of everything that is. From the lowest of the low to the highest of the high. There is nothing from which you are separated, segregated or divorced in any shape, manner or form. Learn simplicity. Man over complicates the simple and in doing so his loses sight of the very essence of his being, which is to BE. Give service wherever you can, not that you may receive but knowing that as you do, you *will* receive. Seek always to temper your acts with kindness, with gentleness, with love, with sincerity, with altruism and with a desire that you can fulfil your own purpose and also serve that of your brother, which is a part of yourself. These things are all truths. They are all encompassing and all enduring. They have not changed since time immemorial. Nor will they ever change. Life, in essence is simple. It is to BE. It is to SERVE. It is to LOVE and it is to recognise your true oneness with the spirit. When you do that the fear of death, the fear of suffering, the fear of this or that or the other, the constant struggle and striving to exist......all of these things fall away from you and the universe of which you are often speaking, will respond to you. This is what you have to understand. It is one thing to 'affirm' something, but it is another to understand how it operates and to live it, quite simply. Simplicity is the great teacher that man has overlooked and forgotten. When man gets back to simplicity he will reach a level of profound wisdom that even I cannot express."

Pam: " I would hug you if I could. Thank for answering all of my questions."

White Feather: "I hope that I have been able to, in some way afford you the answers that you have sought. I feel so often inadequate because I cannot express the totality of the spirit through the clumsiness of your earthly language. But if I have in any small measure been able to express the rich bounty of the spirit and it has helped you in any way, then I am grateful."

Recognising that Amanda may have been feeling left out of the proceedings but sensing that she may have a question of her own the spirit messenger gently enquired of her whereabouts:

White Feather : "Sunflower......are you still there? You have a question......"

Amanda: "Intuitively and instinctively as a mother, I feel that my children aren't where they should be at times. How much do I involve myself with that, when it is very painful to watch things happening and I have to stand back......instinctively I want to take them away from it but I don't know spiritually if I should?"

White Feather: "You know, you have already answered your question yourself. But a few hours ago you said, correct me if I am wrong 'you are where you are meant to be and everything is as it should be." Try to understand that the universe is governed by laws and not any one of us, neither you nor I, your children, your pets.....anyone or anything can be other than where it is meant to be at that moment in time.

The natural instincts of a loving parent are to be protective. To throw one's arms around one's offspring, to protect them from all harm and difficulty. But sometimes the greater lesson is in the experiences which they undergo, which neither you nor I can always register and see, unless we are able to look deeply in to their hearts and souls with the eyes of the spirit.

But I want to say something to you. You have experienced difficulties, not only within your own relationships with your parentage but also with those in your immediate circle, including your offspring. There will be times in the future where there will be continued difficulties, but I must say this to you now, and I want you always to remember this: They will always be on your pathway. They will ALWAYS be on your pathway."

Amanda: "Whether or not they live here ......"

White Feather: ".....they will ALWAYS be on your pathway. A kite may go soaring off into the heavens but it's thread is tied to your hand. No one else's. And a gentle tug will soon bring it scurrying back to you.......there."

With the evening drawing to its close and many questions having been answered it seemed that an enjoyable time had been had by all, except perhaps by the feline who could not be allowed to participate in the proceedings.

Amanda: " Thank you for your time. Thank you very much and on behalf of us all please take our love with you. I am sure we take yours with us. Thank you and God bless you."

White Feather: "The love which has greeted me here tonight is overwhelming and I want to thank not only you but also the many others who stand at my side to listen, to work, to serve. Together we have achieved much this night and I know that the words which have been faithfully recorded by your machine will reach ears other than ours and souls which are as yet, unknown to us. And that is the greater love, that is the greater destiny, that is the greater service and for that I am grateful. Thank you all, thank you both and may the love of the Great Spirit play its music ever upon the strings of your heart."

Postcript: After the sitting with White Feather had ended, we were able to impart information to Pam from a relative in the spirit world who had lived in her birth-place of Malta. Details of his house and surroundings, the name of town in which he had dwelt along with other relevant facts and descriptions were given and subsequently confirmed when Pam made a telephone call to her father.

"One can look at nature and see many examples of synchronised expression. One only has to witness a flock of birds or a school of fish that turn with one graceful movement as if one entity."

Synchronicity 3

We have all experienced events in our lives from time to time that have appeared as either random 'coincidences' or to which we have attributed as being part of our own personal fortune, either positively or negatively. Things which were unpleasant at the time we may have referred to as being 'bad', whilst other events which had a positive effect in our lives may have been regarded as 'good'. Seldom do we ever stop to consider that these happenings could be the result of subtle, yet powerful connections, outworking themselves at the unseen levels of existence to play a distinctive role in our lives.

White Feather often speaks in what he terms a 'scientific' way when talking of things which fall beyond the normal scope of our five senses, employing terminology frequently used by the scientific community such as 'quantum physics' and 'non-locality'. Yet he manages to use this language in the simplest ways possible so as to appeal to the understanding of those less familiar with these terms.

Here, he tackles the subject with his usual panache, weaving a web of spiritual understanding and deeper philosophy with the latest discoveries of cutting edge science to provide the reader with a more concise version of what in truth, is a complex phenomenon:

White Feather: "May I greet you once more with the undying love and radiant warmth of the infinite mind. It is a delight to have this opportunity to communicate with you once more and to endeavour to impart a teaching of value and worth. Whenever we link with your world a great deal of care and attention is paid beforehand to ensure that all criteria are met. For ours is an ordered world and as such each communication, whilst containing a great deal of pure spontenaity, still requires some planning and careful thought. For we know we will encounter certain aspects with which we will have to contend to ensure there is a smooth transference of the subtle thought energies that we employ when operating through mediumship.

We have to contend of course with the various idiosyncrasies of the human condition in its individualised state and the numerous vagaries of mediumship itself which can often, to use your terminology 'throw a spanner in the works'. But where true attunement can take place, there the great power of the spirit can flow in harmony and accord and much in the way of spiritual teaching and all that accompanies it can be conveyed.

I have said many times before that the law governs each and every aspect of life and even though man has freewill to choose, to decide to an extent his pathway, those choices and those decisions must still fall within the operation of natural law which cannot be abrogated. On the surface it would seem to many observers that life is a series of events which are unrelated and which at times appear separate and fragmented. Many of life's experiences are put down to chance or fate, or luck and randomness. And yet in a universe that is controlled and regulated by the application of natural law, these things do not exist. In reality they are but an illusion and can often trick the mind of the uninitiated or the ignorant. But the more evolved soul will recognise and understand that the application of thought, word and deed through one's freewill instigates the operation of natural law and its outworking and thus it is that those things which are regarded by some as being accidental or the result of chance outworkings can be recognised and seen for what they are - the true outworking of the law.

This is why I thought it would be helpful to say a little on this occasion about what is sometimes referred to as synchronicity. What is synchronicity? Again, it is often referred to or thought to be mere coincidence and yet coincidence per se does not exist, but is of itself part of a greater expression of natural law and of which synchronicity is an integral part. One can look at nature and see many examples of synchronised expression. One only has to witness a flock of birds or a school of fish that turn with one graceful movement as if one entity. In truth they are part of a group soul with group mind which operates in a synchronised manner to coordinate thought and movement. This happens almost instantaneously. It is not as if each individual creature has to make a conscious effort to think which way to turn or to manouver. Just as you do not have to think when you raise your arm or take a step. It just happens, because there is a part of you that coordinates those bodily movements without conscious effort.

But what of synchronicity when applied to the human condition? You have all, I am sure, experienced events in your life where what is termed as chance or fate seems to have given you a helping hand. Where events have conspired to bring about for example, a meeting. Someone whom you needed to meet at that time, who later went on to play an important part in your life, perhaps even changed the course of your earthly existence. And looking back you say 'were I not to have met this soul my life would have been different, how lucky I was!' And yet, could it not be that the events which brought that about were not random but actually orchestrated at a deeper level of being without you consciously having to do anything?"

The guide went on to explain in more detail how we all make 'connections' with other aspects of creation which in turn orchestrate events that later become manifest at the physical level of creation:

White Feather: "Those of you who are of a scientific mind may understand the nature of quantum physics and the concept of non-locality as it is termed by your scientists. Where any aspect of life is not localised in one place or point, but is everywhere, within all space and time. Thus it is that when you think and your thoughts have an energy, you are making a connection with other aspects of life upon other dimensions, unbeknown to yourself. Your thoughts are imbibed with the very essence of your being and when those thoughts are filled with intent and deep desire then they set into motion laws that operate at a quantum level, that link those thoughts with other thoughts and other beings and individuals with minds of a similar nature. The consequences of these connections are not always instantly recognised or evident but can come about in a seemingly random way, even though they are not, at some later point.
Let me give you an example of how synchronicty operates; let us suppose that you have taken an interest in a particular subject. Let us say 'sunflowers'. Because of your interest you think a great deal about sunflowers. You may even paint pictures of them or plant them in your garden. You may wear clothing adorned with the pattern of the sunflower or engage in other activity relating to your interest. When one day you walk into a bookshop there happens to be a book that falls of the shelf and lands at your feet. You look down and there upon its cover is a sunflower! Amazed, you pick the book up trying to work out how it is that this coincidence has happened. Now the sceptic will say that was all that it was, a mere coincidence. It was the mere operation of chance, a throw of the dice. And I have heard it said that 'eventually it was bound to happen and one does not choose to recall all of times that it did not'. That does not explain why it happened and furthermore it may not explain how, when you return to your home carrying the book a friend whom you have not heard from, perhaps for many years, contacts you and begins talking about sunflowers! Another coincidence perhaps? Or could it be that the energies of your thoughts and your intentions have made unseen connections in the quantum world that have brought the results that on the surface, seem random and yet which are the result of synchronicity in operation."

This knowledge seems to explain not only how coincidence takes place but has many deeper implications for other seemingly non-localised events that occur such as absent healing, remote viewing, clairvoyance, clairaudience, clairsentience and telepathy.
White Feather continued his explanation by revealing how we are all engaged in a constant process of communication with the subtle energy fields which both interpenetrate and encompass all aspects of creation:

"You must understand that you are all transmitting and receiving stations. You give out and you take in energies upon many, many levels of your being. Not only physically but also mentally, emotionally and spiritually. Thus it is that you are constantly weaving this web of links along which travel these microscopic, minute energies. You live and move and have your being within this ocean of energies and you are forever establishing pathways both internally and externally that link and bind you to others, often without your conscious awareness.
So when you have an event or an experience in your life that seems random or coincidental recognise that it is far from being such but is the result of a synchronised sequence operating within natural law and outworking itself at the physical level of being."

Intriguingly the spirit sage went on to reveal how man once had the ability to manipulate physical matter and could actually learn to do so again by understanding how the power of his will and his mind affect the atoms of which it is composed:

"Now the more inquisitive amongst you may wonder whether it is possible to consciously manipulate and orchestrate events in this fashion. It is possible as long as one understands the way in which the law operates and the intent and the motive is a good one. Man, if he but realised it, has control over matter. Man can create, mould, shape and form matter by the power of his will and his intent through the application of his mind. And yet this ability has become lost to a great extent because of his descent into materialism. If he but realised it, he would remember what he has forgotten and recognise that his spirit and his mind can operate in such a way as to make matter subservient to the will. At the moment the reverse is the case. Man has to labour with his hands, with his physical energy to construct, to manipulate, to mould and to build with matter. There have been races upon the earth who did not have to manipulate matter in this way, who understood the techniques of the mind and the spirit, who recognised that matter was not master over spirit but that spirit was master over matter. When man recognises that he is first and foremost a spiritual being then he will understand that he has control over many of the lower aspects of order. That will not come about however until such time as he also recognises the responsibility that it brings. Whilst he continues to live in the illusionary world that he inhabits he will remain a slave unto the lower order, encased within the physical body. Only glimpsing momentarily the divine that lies beyond the earthly prison. Those who through their meditation and aspiration glimpse a higher environment of light and spiritual unfoldment will understand that of which I speak. So recognise the power of the mind, the power of the will, but most importantly the power of the spirit. Understand that synchronicity is a very vital part of life itself and that everything and everyone is connected. There is no separation. There is no isolation. All is one."

At the time of compiling this book it has become evident that more and more literature is appearing on this, and related subjects. It is as if humanity is on the one hand being shown the deeper implications of its actions whilst on the other is becoming aware that it stands upon the shores of a greater knowledge and understanding than ever before. A revelation which could lead to numerous radical changes in the way we live whilst upon the earth. If we can actively bring about synchronous events through the power of our intent then the world is our oyster. Realisation of the relationship between mind and matter coupled with the knowledge that they are both aspects of the same 'energy' that is life itself, imparts an understanding that is far reaching in its consequences for the future of all life on this planet. As learned teachers down the ages have informed us, we are not flotsam drifting upon the ocean of randomness, prey to every passing wave or current. We are the ocean and everything within it.

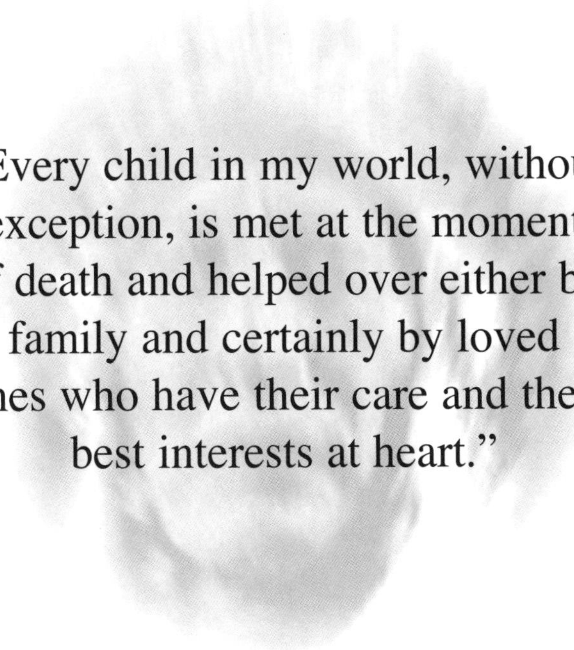

"Every child in my world, without exception, is met at the moment of death and helped over either by family and certainly by loved ones who have their care and their best interests at heart."

one2one

Loss of a Son 4

Gee came to us with some trepidation but with an open mind. Still harbouring grief from the death of a child soon after birth, she came seeking both comfort and evidence that her son was both alive and happy in the next life. Although naturally nervous to begin with, Gee warmed to the kind words and comforting sentiments of the guide and became reassured that her 'lost' child was still very much in evidence around her. As always White Feather was able to expand on the topics covered and touch upon sensitive but important issues that affect so many individuals. In this highly charged sitting the guide begins with a talk upon the subject of 'Belief' before inviting questions of his guest.

White Feather: "May I greet you with the supreme love of the Great Spirit and welcome again this opportunity that has presented itself and that allows me to speak with you, who are seekers of answers. How often we have trod this path. How frequent have been our visits. How many times we have trodden in these footsteps, and yet we do not get weary. We are not tired and always we are refreshed by the scenery that we find and the peoples that we encounter, by the enquiring minds who so often ask questions that deserve answers. It is always a pleasure to speak with those who are prepared to listen because so often we find in your world that those who have listening ears and enquiring minds are at a premium. So often, we find individuals are engaged in trivial activities which do nothing to enhance the beauty and the richness of the spirit. But where we find those individuals or groups who are prepared to invest their time and their energy, to discipline their thinking, to reach out and touch the spirit, there we find the spirit power can enter into their awareness and reach deep into their consciousness and touch the heart of their being, to lift them, to inspire them, to guide them, to enrich them and as I've said so often, this work is immeasurable. By what yardstick do you measure spiritual progress? Upon what scales can it be balanced? What criteria can be used to calculate its effectiveness?

What is ripe for one individual, is not for another. For spiritual progress is measured not by earthly measurements, but by the spiritual changes that take place within each and every soul in an individual way. Just as one cannot and view the hands of the clock, waiting for them to move, so one cannot always stand and witness the spiritual growth within an individual. Yet in both cases there is movement and growth is always from the lower to the higher. From the gross to the refined. From darkness to light, from ignorance to truth, from captivity to freedom. This is a glorious thing because it means that everyone who is upon this pathway is reaching forward, not only towards the Great Spirit but towards a recognition of their own state of being. To know themselves and become one with their individuality. And where one finds, residing at the heart of one's being, the very power that created the universe and all that resides within it, that is a glorious recognition. For then one truly becomes empowered. One recognises that within the self, is the greatest power of all. The power to conquer all fear, all doubt, all ignorance, all superstition. This power, as wonderous as it is, encompasses the greatness of love, altrusim, kindness, gentleness and light. For where there is truth, where there is understanding, there darkness resides no more.

You know, beliefs are very powerful things. Before I invite questions tonight I want to say just a few words concerning this aspect of man's thinking. Because you will find within so many individuals that there is a belief system to which they adhere. So often when one comes into a belief, it is the result of past experiences, actions and events that have shaped and moulded the way in which the mind thinks and behaves. And out of this series of experiences come behaviours and out of behaviours grow beliefs. Now there is nothing wrong with having a belief, indeed one has to believe in one thing or another because without beliefs one is like a ship without a rudder, drifting aimlessly upon the ocean. But the difficulty arises when the belief is so strong that it directs the vessel of the self into waters that are very confining and limiting, where the winds of spiritual truth can no longer dictate as they should, the journey of the soul.

You know, it is one thing to believe, it is another to know. One can believe in something but it does not necessarily follow that it is correct, that it is truth. But to know something, is quite different. For when you know, then to that knowledge you can add belief. It is better to have knowledge and fact and add belief and even faith unto it than to have belief and faith without knowledge. You see the difference?

So how do you know that which you believe is correct? I have said so often in the past that when one comes into an understanding it goes beyond belief, because one knows with evey pore of one's being, with every cell, with every facet, with every fragment, that it is correct. Nothing can dissuade you otherwise. This is not arrogance. This is not placing oneself above others it is simply a recognition of that which is, because it lies within the heart of the being. For that is ultimately where truth resides. You may find it outside of the self but ultimately it forms a harmony with that which resides within. Where you have this harmonisation, where you have synchronicity, there it is that the recognition, the fact that what you are sensing, what you are thinking, what you are experiencing is truth and goes beyond words, beyond books, beyond dogma, creed, ceremony and ritual. Truth does not reside in any religion yet it may be found in one. Truth does not reside in any group or society or creed and yet it may be found there. Truth does not reside exclusively in any individual and yet it may be found there. Because truth is within.

What I am stating to you is not a paradox, it is a fact. But you have to come into a recognition of it. Let me give you an example; have you ever in your lives encountered something that you did not like? Let us say that as a child you did not like apples or pears, whilst others around you enjoyed the bounty of these fruits and then you reached a certain age and your tastes changed. Suddenly that which you found distasteful had a glorious sweetness to it and was in accordance with your pallate. What a change opening up to you in your life. Because of this change you had come into harmony with something which you once found abhorrent and which you disliked and it is the same rule with life and its experiences. There are things with which you do not concur because you do not understand them, they are foreign to you, because they are outside of your belief system. But when through experience you search more deeply, your vibrations change. Your perception alters and you come into an awareness of that which before, was denied to you. It was outside of that which you would have recognised. Now a wonderous vista has opened up to you and truth, like a great ocean pouring through a tiny crack in a wall opens it up and pours into the heart of your being and fills it with light. This is how when you go beyond belief into the realm of that which truly is, always has been and always will be, it comes about.

So be prepared in your lives to have beliefs, not beliefs which are set in stone, that are rigid, that are unbending, unswerving, but beliefs which can be tailored, which can be altered, which can be remodelled, remoulded, transformed. A mind which is rigid, which is hardened by life's experiences can often become bitter and set in its ways. Then the subtle energy of the spiritual truth that we speak of finds it difficult to find a lodgement. But where there is suppleness, where there is pliability, there you will find that truth can enter and bring with it all the richness and bounty of the spirit."

Sensing that Gee may have been feeling a little nervous the gentle spirit ambassador enquired if everyone was happy. Amanda replied that she was but upon hearing no response from the invited guest, the guide turned to her and asked the same question once more:

White Feather: "Are YOU happy?"

Gee: "Reasonably....."

White Feather: "Well let us hope that by the end of the evening we can ensure that your happiness has increased. For that is our purpose. To bring happiness, to bring light, to bring information. I know that there are a few questions that you have for me and that is something which I always delight in, as do those who stand at my side. So Sunflower, perhaps you will start the proceedings in your customary fashion."

Amanda (Sunflower): "Gee, do you have a question you would like to ask?"

Gee: "I would like to know if he is alright?"

White Feather: "You are referring to the one to whom you are closely attached?"

Gee: "Yes."

White Feather: " You mean the one in my world?"

Gee: "Yes."

White Feather: "The one in my world is in the brightest of health and radiance. There is no sickness, there is no disease, there is no suffering, there is no regret. All is well and let me say that the one to whom you refer, who WAS and IS and EVER SHALL BE a part of you is happy and content and making progress in the realms of light as it was intended that he should. The sadness remains in your heart, but in his heart there is no sadness. The only sadness is that you are sad. When you place flowers on the spot and when you speak to the grave you are speaking to an empty place, for he is not there. He is with those in my world, with whom he shares an affinity and he is within you, in your heart and around you. This you must understand. Sadness is so often prevelant where there is a passing, where there is distress but we must not hold that sadness forever. There is a time to be sad, there is a time to cry. There is a time also to rejoice that the soul no longer has to encounter the harshness of the material world and the physical 'reality' but is set free in the realms of its true nature which is its home. As I have said so often; where there is love, there is no separation. To you at times, there is a vast chasm between you and yet it is but a hair's breadth."

Gee: "Do you know who he is with?"

White Feather: "There are many with whom he has an affinity. Members of family but also those with whom there is a friendship link. You must recognise that we have in my world what I refer to as 'realms of the children' where children play with children. Where young souls are with young souls. Where there is much laughter, gaiety, happiness and rejoicing. Not for them the tears of sadness. Not for them the thoughts of dispair and pain, but for them the joy of being with other souls, other children. Of being cared for, loved, looked after, educated - not in the ways of the earth with its trappings of ignorance, spite, hatred and darkness, but in a ways of the spirit. Oh, what joy it is to be a child growing up in the spirit world. For here one is not fed the doctrines of religion. One is not accustomed, as is the case in your world everyday of the taunting of other children, the spitefulness, the vindictiveness and the materialistic aspects and concepts of your world. Here the soul is unfettered and can experience truth and joy. This you must understand. Do not despair, do not cry for me, for I do not cry for you."

At this point Gee was a little overcome with emotion and was unable to ask further questions of the guide. Acknowledging this, the guide suggested that Amanda continue:

White Feather: "Sunflower, let us come back to this point later. Perhaps you have questions of your own. We can come back to this aspect when the time is ready."

Amanda: "Ok. I don't know what to ask after what we have just experienced....?"

White Feather: "Well let me continue then for a while because I think it might be helpful to those present here in your world but also to those in my world to say a little bit about the children's realms in my world. First of all I want to point out that there are many souls gathered here in my world listening to this conversation and my love and my thoughts reach out to them as it does to you. To visit the realm of the children is a wonderous experience in itself. Children you know, are such bright souls and sparks of light. They are great teachers. They provide great inspiration. One can learn a great deal from a child. I personally have learned as much from a child as I have from a great teacher, a great soul and who is to say that a child is not also a great teacher and a great soul? The realm of the children is filled with laughter and joy. They spend their activity or time in a mixture of learning and playfulness, often a combinaton of the two. They attend what you would come to regard as a 'school' because their mind, their soul, still has to learn as it would have done upon the earth because that particular facet that is expressing itself through that form still has many things to understand, to grasp. But you must recognise that the mind, in my world, can grasp things much more quickly than it can when having to operate through the physical brain of matter. This is why children in my world pick up things and grow intellectually as well as spiritually far more rapidly than is often the case in your world. We have great teachers who help them and who love and care for each and every one of them. Each child is afforded the same time and effort, love and attention as the next. We do not have favourites. One is not neglected to the exclusion of another. One is not placed upon a higher pedestal and serviced more than another. Each is afforded their own time because it is recognised that each is a special soul in its own right. So there is opportunity to explore the realms of music and linking with animals. It is not uncommon in my world to see a child riding upon the back of a tiger or standing upon a lion or sitting upon the back of a giraffe! In your world these things would be impossible, in my world animals and children play together as great playmates as if they were brothers and sisters. There is the opportunity to study the various sciences, to look at the history of life as it truly is, not as it is portrayed through your history books, which are a sham. There is the opportunity to view the stars and the galaxies and so often you will find that the true gifts of these children, which they have earned through past lives and which are spiritual gifts, come to the fore. And it is not an uncommon sight to see children in my world who, were they upon your world would appear around the age of, shall we say six or seven, playing together in a great orchestra, playing songs and symphonies of the masters. You look at this and you think 'how can these young children have grasped this complicated music and these instruments.....they are so young? And yet you see that the spirit yearns and grasps these things so easily and swiftly in my world than it does in yours and so these things come more easily to the growing mind, the growing soul."

White Feather went on to tackle the question of grief, a problem for those left behind on earth when a loved one passes on:

"Now, what about the ones who have been 'left behind' in your world? What about the parents who so often are filled with despair, grief and in some cases guilt? There need be no guilt. There need be no grief beyond the initial shock that transpires. You must remember that every passing occurs because it is meant to be. Because of the laws governing that. There is no chance, fate or accident. Whenever anyone passes into my world it is because laws are called into operation that necessitate that passing at that time. When a child passes it is because in reality its time has come to do that. From the childs point of view the initial shock is brief, it passes swiftly and there soon comes a recognition of what has transpired. Very quickly a child is able to be reunited from my side of life with its parent even though they cannot sense it so often. They are not aware that the child is there with them, but from the child's point of view, they *are* there with them. They can see you, they can hear you, they can be in your midst, in your house, in their own room and their own space and that is perfectly natural. They are helped to understand what has happened, they are taught and they are helped to recognise that the ones left on the earth plane cannot always see them or hear them as they themselves can do and they are educated into the whys and wherefores of the spirit transition, the spirit world and all that is encompassed. Very quickly they are moved on to the realms of joy and happiness and there is no suffering. This you must understand.

So often, when you see a child passing into my world the last picture that you are left with is one of the child suffering. But that is only momentary. It is only a short time span and it is only in the physical world. Very often the physical body can suffer but the soul, the spirit, does not feel it. There is no pain in death, no suffering in death, only happiness. That you must recognise. Every child in my world, without exception, is met at the moment of death and helped over either by family and certainly by loved ones who have their care and their best interests at heart. What is buried in the grave or cremated is only the remnant, only the shell. It is not the real self. It is not the individual. The individuality of each child is retained as is every soul who passes into my world and that continues in an unbroken sequence at the moment of death."

Amanda: "If the soul that passes is only upon the earth a very short time, from a soul perspective would it have a memory or an understanding that it was to pass quickly?"

White Feather: "The soul would know before it came. The soul would know before it came upon the earth that its earthly sojourn was to be short. But during that time it may have learned the lesson that it came to learn when it came to the earth."

Amanda: "Would it be HIS lesson....because it obviously leaves its mark upon the parents for such a long time afterwards.......such a hard thing?"

White Feather: "What lesson......what lesson is learned by an individual that does not also have its impact upon those who surround that individual? Who is to say that the lesson that is learned by the individual is not also a lesson for those around it? What passing of a child does not affect the parent? Whose is the greater lesson, the child's or the parent's? Whose is the greater experience and who is to say that the child did not incarnate for that very reason, to help its parent to learn that very lesson?"

Amanda: "And would the parent know what that lesson would be or is that something which she would come into an awareness of as time goes by?"

White Feather: "As times goes on one always comes into an awareness of a particular lesson, particularly if it is a Karmic lesson which carries greater import for the progress of the soul. At the moment that the event occurs and for a little while after one does not always recognise the lesson that is being learned through the experience that has been undertaken because the pain is great, the tears flow, the heart bleeds, the soul cries out 'why has this happened, why me?' The mind is in turmoil. So often you find, although not always the case, that individuals question themselves. Could they have done more? What did they do that they shouldn't? What did they fail to do? Where does God come into the equation? It is only with the passage of time that one can reflect in a way that is........what shall I say....... less involved, where one can take a step back and one can analyse. Then perhaps one can recognise that within that experience was a great, great lesson. It could not be seen at the time but nevertheless was a lesson which both the child and the parent agreed beforehand to undergo, to help each other. That is the great truth.

If one can go beyond despair, beyond bitterness, beyond grief one can see that within each experience there is a lesson to be learned that will equip the soul of every individual, as a means to quicken its vibration and enable it to move forward into a realm of light. You know, what is often a defeat for you is a victory for the spirit. What is despair for you is rejoicing for the soul. I have stood at your gravesides, I have stood and watched your bodies being lowered into the ground in a coffin. I have stood at your burial chambers, I have seen the tears flow and the bitterness from your hearts but if you could look from my side you would see the rejoicing when we are welcoming a soul back from the darkness of the earth to the light of the spirit realms. It is a great, great ocassion for us. What is heartbreak for you is rejoicing for the spirit for we are welcoming home one of our own.
You have to look if you can, not with the eyes of matter but with eyes of the spirit and you will see that these are not the acts of a vengeful God who seeks to punish you, or hurt you, but a God who is all knowing and all loving and who has, ultimately, your best interests at heart."

The question of whether a parent will be able to locate and recognise their child in the spirit world when they themselves pass over is one which often gives rise for concern. Amanda picked up on this very point and asked the guide what would happen in this event:

Amanda: "If the child goes into the spirit world, when the parents pass over, is the 'baby' still a 'baby'? Obviously there is recognition from a soul level but would that child appear as the baby it was when it passed so that the mother and father would understand?"

White Feather: "Absolutely. The 'child' would always appear in such a form as to be recognised by its parents. If that child passed as an infant then it would appear as an infant. It will be there waiting for you in your 'home' or whatever place of residence you take up when you come to my world. You will find that child will be waiting for you. It may be that in a very short time it could reappear as it has 'grown' to become if that is appropriate and that, ultimately of course could be a great shock to the soul of the parent to find one that had grown to adulthood and with whom it did not share that transition, so always you will find that the appearance of the individual is tempered to the needs of the parent and it is quite appropriate that the soul should appear as it had passed for a little while or as long as is necessary for both parties."

Amanda: "Obviously there are a lot of emotions around at the time, but is it possible for a child to die because of something that somebody else didn't do correctly? If that is the case how does that affect........"

White Feather (interuptting): "This is a particular bone of contention is it not?"

Amanda and Gee: "Yes."

White Feather: "Try to understand that individuals do of course make mistakes. You will understand that they have to make decisions and no one is perfect. Not you, not they, not I. Sometimes people do things out of malice, other times because they are tired, or because they are incompetent or simply because they err for whatever reason. Try to understand that would not influence the knowledge of the soul of the child who came into the body because the soul would know beforehand that was to transpire. You must recognise that all things in your world are known. It does not mean to say that freewill is excluded and that life is like a play in a theatre, which you are acting out and that all things are predetermined, because that is not the case. The soul knows the landmarks of it's journey upon the earth. It knows about certain events that are meant to transpire. That does not exclude freewill, but it knows what is to transpire and it would know that its time upon the earth would be short. Nevertheless that would not deter it from entering into the body to give that body the opportunity to learn the lesson, to quicken its own progress, not to mention its effects with the other members of the family in a Karmic sense as we have already mentioned. Do you understand that?"

Amanda: "Yes. It is very difficult in a situation like this though where the question of negligence is on the minds of those involved.......would you be able to tell us at all whether..........because it is very difficult to let go of those feelings of bitterness.......are you able to say that this baby would not have survived in spite of any medical intervention if it was meant to come and go as quickly as it did? Is that what you are saying?"

White Feather: " If the spirit decides upon a course of action that is necessary for it there is nothing and no one in your world that can prevent that from happening. Whatever measures are taken, whatever directives are employed, you cannot hold the spirit when its time is ready to be released from the body of matter. I know you would perhaps argue and say that well, we have 'life support machines' that we can use to keep the physical body alive but I can only emphasise that spirit is master, matter is servant and when the time has been reached for the spirit to withdraw there is no machine, no doctor, no drug that can be applied that can prevent the passing. Now, I understand of course the implication that one can shorten one's life through inadequate procedures, though tampering or through incompetence and of course these things upon a vunerable child's body can have an impact. Of course, if the body is injured then the spirit can no longer operate through it and will withdraw, resulting in what you call 'death', but I can only emphasise again that the soul knows before it comes. At the soul level there is an awareness of that journey which it is undertaking and if it chooses to touch your world for a few moments then perhaps it is learning a greater lesson and performing a greater service than if it were to reside there for eighty or ninety years.Who are you to say how to look from the soul perspective?"

Amanda: "If that's the case then, as difficult as it may be, is it appropriate to forgive those people who were around and involved at the time?"

White Feather: "Let me say something to you which you want to have an answer to. In the case in question there was no malice, no vindictiveness, no deliberate incompetence. Measures could have been taken that would have changed to a certain degree events that transpired but it is not right to hold those responsible for the passing of the child because there was no action or attempt or incompetence that was born out of malice that resulted in that conclusion. I can only look with the eyes of the spirit and say that there is a greater lesson to be learned and that *is* being learned from the events that transpired and continue to this day to unfold. The spiritual lesson encompasses a great deal more than the physical events. Let me say this to you; you have undergone a great deal of suffering in one form or another but if you look back sister, through your life, you will see that there is a common thread that keeps re-occurring, rather like the thread that resurfaces in a tapestry, rather like a current that keeps coming to the surface of a river in flow. There is a thread that keeps re-occurring and the individuals that are drawn to you and that will keep re-occurring in your life, are of a certain type of character and spirituality. Everything that comes to you, every experience, carries with it the opportunity to learn, to digest that spiritual lesson. This is not a criticism it is merely an observation. You have chosen this particular life and all that you encounter within it to quicken your soul. Without any doubt this is why at times you find individuals who present to you, difficulties, where you have to assess, weigh up, consider, and discern. Through this your soul is being equipped and you are growing spiritually at a rate that you cannot yet assess. It is the same with the passing of your beloved child which even as I speak stands upon your shoulder. He came to help you with the same lessons which you are now learning. You have to learn to use your spiritual gifts. Let go of bitterness, let go of guilt. Let go of all these things and use the wonderous shower of light which even now burns brightly within you. You are a soul which has the capacity and the ability to give light out to many who are in darkness. But how can you do that? How can you be a beacon unless you yourself have been in darkness? How can you be a healer unless you yourself have known pain? How can you help the suffering unless you have suffered? It may seem that this is a bitter pill to swallow but it is a medicine of the spirit that will equip you with all the necessary components to be a great soul.

You will help many souls in this lifetime. You will touch many souls, you will help many souls. You will even help souls who are passing into my world. You will be there when they pass. You will help their soul on its way. You will help the souls who are in grief. You will touch those mothers who have lost children. You will touch those whose tears run down their faces because they are so beset with grief and are beside themselves. You will help them because you gave gone through that.

Now let me tell you one further thing that no one upon this earth can know; your beloved child is guiding you. He is working through you. His voice speaks through your voice, his hands rest upon your hands, his heart beats with your heart. You are working together. You are never apart. Never, ever apart."

Amanda (still asking on behalf of an emotional Gee): "How.....when someone desperately wants to help someone else and you've got that within your heart......and you sometimes have to say to somebody 'no that's it, draw a line under it, they have to go'.....for your own self preservation how do you spiritually come to terms with that because everything within you wants to help the person to the enth degree, yet it's physically, emotionally and spiritually sometimes just not possible.......you can't give anymore. How do you reconcile that?"

White Feather: "Because the motive is a good one. The motive is to help and to serve and if it is filled with love and respect then it is that which counts. Sometimes you know......let me borrow a term from your world...... 'you have to be cruel to be kind'. I'm not advocating cruelty but what I'm saying is that sometimes you have to make provision to shut one door that another may open. You must recognise that spiritual development brings with it, responsibility. Sometimes you have to say things and do things which are not in agreement with others of a lesser understanding than you. Truth is like a knife. It can cut. Sometimes it wounds, but it can also heal. What is important is that you give the truth as you understand it. If that sometimes offends others reasoning minds then that is their responsibility, not yours. You have only given it as it is. The thing is, that you do that with love and kindness, never with malice. Never with wrong intent. Always with the desire and motive to help. Sometimes you know, if you have to take a bottle of poison from a man's hand to stop him from poisoning himself even though he thinks that he needs that poison to live, then it is better to do it. I know always that you strive to operate from the motive of the spirit, of the highest that is within you. You do not have an ounce of malice within your heart. I recognise that. We all have faults because we are all imperfect. Perhaps your greatest fault is that you trust too much. Perhaps it is better that through this you grow spiritually and if that means that you do not trust quite so easily it is not a bad thing.
You know, there are many kinds of trust. You can have a blind trust, just as one can have a blind faith and that is not a good thing. It is better to have a trust based upon experience and faith based upon fact and knowledge. It is not spiritual to have a blind trust, but if you can have a trust that is based upon a knowingness, upon a discernment, upon a spiritual understanding of people, places and events, borne out of personal experience, isn't that a better kind of trust? For then you will know whether to go forward or to stay back. Whether to speak or to be silent. Whether to imbibe or whether to withold. Then you will truly be growing spiritually."

Amanda [to Gee]: "Anything else you want to ask?"

Gee: [Emotionally]"I don't think so....."

White Feather: "I hope I haven't upset you too much!" That is never my intent. You know, tears are wonderful things. We can cry for many reasons. But you know, perhaps the greatest tears are tears of joy, tears of recognition, tears that come from deep within the self because we recognise that we have been touched deep within our heart. Let me say that you are never alone, never forgotten, overlooked or neglected and your most beloved of beloved is closer to you than you can ever realise. You only have to reach out your hand."

It had been an evening charged with emotion, but one in which the guide had reached out in love and compassion, not only to those present but to many whose hearts have been wounded by the pain of loss. There can perhaps be no greater pain than that incurred through the loss of a child and it is hoped that the words of the wise sage can bring comfort and hope to all who find themselves in the midst of grief. As the spirit messenger says; you are never alone.

Postscript: *After the sitting we sensed the presence of Gee's spirit son in the room and were able to give evidence that he is indeed close to her and aware of events in her life. One of the messages he imparted demonstrated something of which we could not have known beforehand. He said to us "What is this about the lipsticks? I know what you have been doing with them!' This meant nothing to us, but when we mentioned it to Gee she smiled, opened her handbag and took out a range of half used lipsticks whose tips had been worn away into various unusual shapes. Apparently, that very day she had been laughing with others with whom she worked about how the lipstick ends resembled various objects. We also later discovered that upon her return home, Gee was greeted by a white feather which was lying on the floor as she opened her front door. Evidence indeed that we are never forgotten and that our loved ones are never very far from our side.*

Gee later sent us a copy of a photograph of the lipsticks which had been taken weeks prior to the sitting. (See Fig.1)

Fig 1.

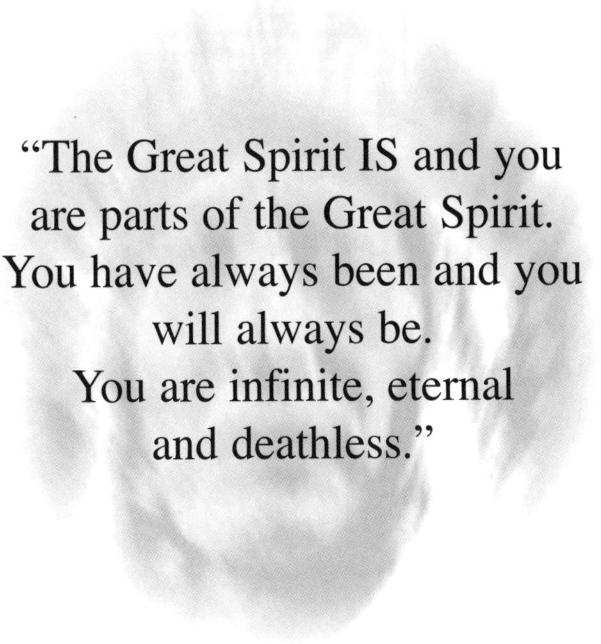

"The Great Spirit IS and you
are parts of the Great Spirit.
You have always been and you
will always be.
You are infinite, eternal
and deathless."

Many Minds 5

"It is as always a great honour and privilege for me to speak through this instrument to you who are seekers of truth for it enables me once more to take up the pallete of knowledge and wisdom that I may add a little more colour to the canvas of your understanding. For as I have said so frequently, it is truth which ultimately is the liberator of souls. It is truth which sets the individual and the collective, which is humanity, free from its self imposed prison and enables it to soar like a bird into the infinite planes of truth and understanding.
Some of you I know, I have spoken to before, many of you I have not, but my message is the same to you all for the Great Spirit does not recognise many of the boundaries and barriers that are imposed upon the material form. The Great Spirit pays homage and adherence to no creed, no dogma or religion. The Great Spirit is not black or white or red or yellow. The Great Spirit IS and you are parts of the Great Spirit. You have always been and you will always be. You are infinite, eternal and deathless."

White Feather opened with those words one evening, addressing an audience who had come to witness his communication at a specially arranged trance evening in a small village centre. After greeting those present the guide went on to impart his teaching, touching firstly upon the subject of spiritual attributes before later inviting questions of those seeking knowledge:

"Like you I am part of that same Great Spirit. I am not a deity, I am human as you are. But I always reiterate this point for those who may be in awe. You have nothing to be in awe of because I am like you, human in every regard. I have a body just as you do. The only difference is that it vibrates on a finer link, on a finer energy than does your physical body of matter. In that respect I function on a higher plane. That does not mean that I am better than you, that I am greater than you in any way. It only means that I have been able to slough off the physical body and retain the etheric, astral and spirit bodies which enable me to function at this level. It is not my intention to lecture you tonight because I seek not to preach any dogma. I seek only to impart a few simple truths that may appeal to your reasoning capacity and anything I say which offends that, you are at liberty to reject. For I seek to win you over not by brute force or by stating that something is a fact which must be accepted without question, I seek to enable your reasoning minds to intervene and to operate for you, that you may come into your own understanding.

I want to say just a few words briefly, before I invite any questions, about what I refer to as 'gifts'. I don't mean the kind of gifts that you impart to another at anniversaries and birthdays and suchlike, I am referring to the gifts of the spirit which each of you have in degree. Because you are all gifted. You all have gifts of the spirit whether or not you employ them. Whether you utilise them in your day to day lives is another matter, but you have them nevertheless. But why is it that you have gifts? Why is it that some seem to have more gifts than others? That some seem endowed with greater gifts than others, supposedly? To understand this, on the face of it, simple question, perhaps requires that you undertake a study and become aware of the principles of life itself. Because let me say to you........and I have never shyed away from the difficult topic of reincarnation, that you aquire gifts over a period of time which involves more often than not, many lifetimes of living upon the physical world of matter. And through these experiences, through learning the lessons of life which you encounter, the soul is quickened, the spirit enriched and you earn by right the aquisition of certain gifts.

Now, you may say that 'this is all very well but White Feather, have you not stated before that it is never the totality of the self that comes into the body of matter when it reincarnates? That there are many facets, like there are many sides to a diamond, and it is only one facet that reintroduces itself into a new body?' That is a fact, but what you must understand is that even though you cannot recall in this conscious state, your past lives, even though you cannot remember them and there are very good reasons why that applies, nevertheless the gifts that you have earned and have accumulated through your past lives, you carry with you into your future experiences. It would not be right would it for you to have earned something only for it to be taken away from you or to be stored on a shelf for use at some later date? You must understand that whatever you aquire, it adds to the lustre of the diamond and when a facet comes into the physical world as it invariably does, to reintroduce itself into the body of matter that it may outwork a Karmic debt or render a particuar service to humanity it brings with it those gifts that it has earned.

How often have you seen what is referred to perhaps as a 'child prodigy'? One who is young of age in your world and yet is an old soul. One who has perhaps, wonderous gifts? Perhaps one who can play a piano or an instrument, or who has the gift of healing? One who can speak, who has acquired a great knowledge at an early age and you say 'yes, they are a genius'. But could it be that they are bringing those gifts with them because they have earned them in their past experiences, their past lives? This is what you must recognise.

You have earthly gifts, you have material gifts and you have spiritual gifts which endure from life to life. They endure beyond time because YOU are beyond time in the physical sense and when you have earned them no one can take them away from you. In fact no one can take anything away from you once you have earned it, whatever it is. Whether it be 'bad' or 'good' it is there, indelibly written upon the index of your soul and I say to you this; that if you are able to look at an evolved soul in my world and look at the index of that soul, you will see that written there for all time are the good and bad, the light and the dark, the negative and the positive aspects of everything that soul has undertaken. Because what you are, as you have created yourselves, is there. You cannot hide it. You can wear a persona in your world, you can put a mask on, you can clothe your body, you can wear make-up, you can do all manner of things to disguise what is beneath, but in the eyes of the spirit you are naked. You are as you have created yourselves and that you must understand. That is why it is so important that if you have gifts, even if they are gifts which you think of as being insignificant, you utilise them.
Service you know, comes in many forms. People think that to give service of the spirit you must be a great healer or a great clairvoyant or a great orator, you must stand upon the platform or have books published or articles written about you. The great soul can work in the field, upon the street, within the quiet sanctuary, unnoticed, unheard, unseen by many eyes and yet that soul touches other souls. It reaches minds, it touches hearts and that is the greatest gift of service. It is service that is the passport of the spirit. It is service that is the coin of the soul with which you tarry. It is service that equips you with the means to move onward and to reach out into the great spiritual realms wherein lie all the gifts that the spirit has to offer. There is much more that I could say to you but I don't want to take up your valuable time and I want to try to get through to as many individuals as I can tonight. Let me just say before I commence that there are many souls in this of your temple tonight. Many souls. Not just you who sit upon these seats, but many in my world who are gathered here. Who number over a thousand and who come to join with you to listen, to enjoy and to understand the wonderous power of the spirit as it seeks to flow into your world, bringing all the richness and beneficence that it has to offer."

Peparing to invite questions, White Feather demonstrated his sense of humour, something he often does as a way of lightening the proceedings, by commenting upon the chair in which the medium was sitting:

"Can I just say Sunflower before we invite questions, this is the first time I have ever sat on a deckchair! I hope that it doesn't take anything away from the importance of the occasion!"

Amanda: "I hope you don't fly backwards because you really don't need to be lying flat out."

White Feather: "Everything is under control."

Amanda: "Ok......who would like to start us off with a question?"

At times an audience can be slow to commence asking questions of the spirit guide, not through lack of interest but simply because no one likes to be the first to raise their hand and speak out. On this occasion though, White Feather's humourous comment seemed to have had a relaxing effect on those present and the first of many questions came very swiftly, with a gentleman who ahad a query about the controversial subject of reincarnation, a topic close to the spirit sage's heart:

Questioner: "Do we have to reincarnate or do we get to choose?"

White Feather: "There is of course an element of choice if you have earned the right to choose. No one compels you to reincarnate. No one stands over you with a stick! The Great Spirit does not command it of you, but there comes a time when there is a realisation within you that unless you reintroduce a facet of yourself back into the body of matter to outwork whatever Karmic aspects need to be addressed, perhaps to put right an imbalance, then you cannot move on in my world. You will remain at that particular level, do you understand that? So you are not compelled in that sense. It is a choice that comes from your own mind and your own soul, but it is an informed choice that recognises that in order to move on into the higher realms of spirit you have to put right the loose ends that you may have left here upon the physical earth. Do you understand that? Does that help you?"

Questioner: "Yes thank you."

Amanda: "The next question please........."

Questioner: "Is it true White Feather that there are a lot of people queuing up to come down here?"

White Feather: "That's quite a quaint phrase to use 'queuing up'......let me say that there are many souls who wish to return to the earth and there are sufficient vehicles for them to do so. The difficulty that sometimes presents itself to the more evolved soul is finding the right vehicle that will equip it to learn the lessons it knows and desires to learn, has earned the right to learn and to enable it to render perhaps, a particular kind of service that it chooses to do. That can take a little time. For example; I had to choose the instrument through whom I speak at this moment. I did that very carefully. Even though we were aware of each other before his entry into the physical world I still had to make sure that everything was correct, that I had the necessary affinity and that conditions were right to enable me to undertake the work that I now do. Were conditions not right then I would have had to have operated through another. So there are many things that come into the equation and the more knowledge that you have, the more refined that you are, the more difficult it can be at times to choose the right vehicle into which to be reincarnated. Does that make sense to you?"

Questioner: "Yes, thank you."

Questioner: "May I ask you White Feather, when we reincarnate do we come back into the same family group?"

White Feather: "Very often that does happen. It is not written in stone, there is no law that demands it but very often of course, where there have been past experiences that have born out certain relationships that may have incurred again Karmic debt, then it makes sense that individuals reincarnate together again when the time is right to outwork their joint Karma and in some cases group Karma. It does not always follow of course that you will have the same relationships. For example, your father in this life may be your daughter in the next and so on and so forth. That isn't of great importance. What matters is the spiritual relationship, the spiritual lessons to be learned and the laws which have to be outworked."

Questioner: "White Feather, to work through your instrument do you have to be in good health......physical health?"

White Feather: "If you are talking to me, I have perfect health. If you are referring to the instrument through whom I operate.......if you are referring to Robert then there has to be a certain level of health obtained to enable me to operate effectively. If that health becomes compromised then it makes it more difficult for me to operate in the way that I would like to and that has to be taken into consideration. Whenever we speak in this manner, at this level, there are many imponderables you know, that we have to accomodate. The health of the medium, his temper, his wellbeing generally, the congregation or the audience, the people who come and bring their own energies, sometimes their own difficulties, the weather, the building..........all kinds of things that perhaps you wouldn't think of immediately that we have to contend with and certain precautions have to be made beforehand to ensure that we can obtain the level, the depth of control that we desire to work in this way. Does that answer your question?"

Questioner: "Yes thank you. What I was also wondering as well.......if the instrument was to incur physical bad health and he was working through a form of trance, would the communicator step back to leave him to nurse his physical condition?"

White Feather: "Naturally we try to help. We advise where we can and we try to work with those in your world and in my world who can bring healing, who can restore harmony and balance to the physical body. But if the point is reached where to link through that medium whose health was not as it should be, would endanger the medium or would compromise the communication to the point of where it lost its effectiveness, then we would have to withdraw. We would do so reluctantly but we have to weigh up and consider all factors to operate in this way."

The agenda swung back once more to the theme of reincarnation with the next question concerning the rememberence of past lives:

Questioner: "Why is it that some people can remember their past lives, particularly children and yet seem to forget later in life?"

White Feather: "Well the simple fact is that when they come into your world, they are closer to my world. As life progresses, in a sense.......although in the truest sense not.......but in one sense, they become more distant because they lose their innocence. It is rather like, you know, a river. The closer you get to its source, the purer it is but when it flows towards the ocean it widens and many other tributaries flow into it and colour it so that by the time it reaches the ocean it is a little more muddied than when it commenced its journey. Do you understand that?"

Questioner: "Yes.....and could I ask as well, is it usually children that have died violently in a previous life, whether they be children or adults, that have more of a memory of that previous life?"

White Feather: "Not necessarily. It can happen........if it was a very traumatic passing in the past life that made such an impact upon the individual, certain aspects of that can be carried forward into a new experience and I have seen and witnessed that happen and sometimes those difficulties can manifest in a mental disquiet, certain physical phenomena and 'blockages' which have to be cleared so that harmony can be restored. This is why sometimes......although I do not advocate the use of hypnosis 'willy nilly' shall I say, this can be an effective tool in clearing those blockages, as can other forms of healing and therapy. You must also understand that where there is a particular traumatic passing, when that individual finds themselves in my world they are helped, they are healed and I have said this before; there are occassions where they can pass into what I call 'The Halls of Forgetfulness' where that vivid memory and shock to the spirit, even though it cannot be taken away from the index of their soul, can be removed to the point where they cannot remember it, so that it does not disturb their future development. But their soul may still choose to come back upon the earth to outwork a particular aspect. Do you understand that? Its rather a complex issue in fact. Hope I haven't complicated it further for you!"

Questioner: "No, I just wondered why some children can be quite happy knowing that they've lived previously."

White Feather: "Hmmmm. Let me give you an example; Sometimes you know.....this is a simple explanation for a more complex law......... but sometimes you know, you find an individual who is born with a particular 'birth mark' on their skin and you say 'why has that occurred?' Is it just purely something that happened in the womb? Is it a physical aspect that has caused it? Or perhaps it is a mental aspect that has brought that about and has resulted in that effect being made apparent on the physical body? Certain aspects of what you call stigmata, where you have marks appearing on the physical body, even now can be brought about by the mind, by past memories and other aspects which can come into play. Because the mind is very, very powerful and it carries with it these energies and this is why some in your world at sometimes in their lives have deeper seated psychological problems that require expert help and healing to redress the balance."

Questioner: "Thank you."

Amanda: "The gentleman at the back please."

Questioner: "At the moment it's becoming more and more materialistic, how does White Feather see us moving towards a more spiritual world?"

White Feather: " It is difficult. You know, so often son I am asked this question and I would like to give the answer that one day your world will be a wonderous place where all will live in harmony and all will be happy and joyous in the knowledge of the spirit. But it is a difficult journey that lies ahead of humanity because man's intellectual capacity and his spiritual understanding do not keep pace with one another. He is intellectually advanced, he has aquired great technological knowledge, but spiritually he's puny. He is like a little child in infancy and unless you can balance and harmonise these two aspects of his higher and lower being then you will not have the 'Garden of Eden' that many would like in your world. The other thing to consider as well of course, is that the physical universe, the material universe is not perfect. Matter cannot be perfect by its nature and the soul or the spirit comes here upon the earth like a stone sent skimming across the waters of life, to touch upon the experiences that it offers. Some which you consider to be good, others bad, some which you know as light, others as dark, some positive, some negative and you know it is through this polarity that the material universe and your earth offers, that the soul equips itself for its ongoing journey. It quickens because of this. So in actual fact this polarity serves a great purpose for the soul.

If you had not experienced captivity, how could you know freedom? If you had not been through darkness, what would you know of light? If you had not seen black, how would you know white? You have to come through this spectrum, through this rainbow of experiences - the light and the dark, the high and the low, the male and the female and so forth, so that you may learn and in that sense your earth serves a great purpose to the spirit. Does that help you?"

Questioner: "Yes, very good."

Lifting the proceedings once more the guide enquired if everyone was happy and received a positive repsonse before the evening continued with a question which perhaps mirrored the concern of many of those present:

Questioner: "Could you tell me about the state of the world we live in?......it's difficult to understand.......the destruction of the rain forests......it's worrying just why we keep getting told different things, different aspects......you don't know what to believe in the end."

White Feather: "Who is telling you different aspects?"

Questioner: "Well.......I mean, some people say it's going to be really cold and some people say it's going to be hot and the seas are going to rise......"

White Feather: "Ah, you mean 'The Scientists'?" [Laughter from the audience]

Questioner: "Hmmm"

White Feather: "Those of you who know me will know that I have little regard for the scientists even though they are sometimes revered as the 'Gods' of the modern age. They have a great deal yet to learn because they work within their limited framework.

There's an old saying you know, that 'Man takes what meanings please him' and one source will say one thing and tomorrow they will say something different. What you have to learn is to sift through all of this chaff to find the gold, the golden thread, the golden ore that runs through life and then you will find the real truth and you know, ultimately, where does truth lie? It doesn't lie 'out there', it doesn't lie in that book over there, it doesn't lie in the words of that scientist or even that great teacher. It lies in here [the guide pointing to his chest]. It lies in your heart. That is where you will find truth.

If you want to see, then open your eyes and look. If you want to hear, then shut your ears to the babblings of humanity and listen with the ears of the spirit. There you will find the truth comes to you. It won't come in a blaze of glory, in flashing lights. It will come in a whisper, but it will be the loudest voice that you will ever hear. It is the voice of the spirit speaking through your heart. That is where you will find truth. But, referring to the previous question, your world will never be perfect.

It is only a learning ground. It is a learning field. Sometimes it is a battlefield for the spirit but it is a place where the spirit can be quickened, because remember that you are not first and foremost bodies with spirits. You are spirits with bodies. It is the spirit that is the real, eternal you."

Questioner: "Could it be that scientists and technologists are also inspired spiritually as well? Surely not all of their life, all of their inspiration comes simply from logic?"

White Feather: "That is of course, very true and I would never say otherwise. The problem arises where the ego-mind and the logical mind - of which scientists tend to be rather left brained, logical people by the very nature of their being - overtakes or discards the right brained spiritual aspect which seeks to work through that. But of course there are exceptions, there always have been and there always will be. For example, I know of many brilliant medical people, surgeons, those who perform the most complex and intricate operations on those who are in need of them in your world, who are guided by unseen hands from my world. They don't even know they are being guided. They don't even know that the spirit operates through them. They have no idea and yet it does. What matters is the result. What matters is what happens to the one who is in need.

What I am speaking of is in general terms where we must seek to have a marriage of the scientific and technological with the spiritual and esoteric because if you bring that together, if you can marry those aspects together, there, in potential, you have greatness and man and humanity as a race, will be propelled forward far more swiftly than if either one is utilised to the exclusion of the other."

Questioner: "Well I was going to say, as technology and knowledge improves, obviously there are deep and concerning questions about the element of freewill and the extent to which man engages in the creative process, particularly in human creation."

White Feather: "Again son, I have encountered this question - and it's a very viable one to ask.......let me state once more quite categorically that man cannot create life. Man can create the vehicle into which life comes, but he cannot create life. Even though he thinks he does, he does not. Through genetic experiments, through cloning, through employing the technological advances in understanding the genetic coding of DNA and so forth, man is changing the face of humanity. He is changing his own destiny. But as I have said so often, even if you clone a form, you cannot clone the spirit. You can have identical twins, similar in every aspect and yet they are different because they have different souls within them. You can look at a forest of trees and they all look the same, yet they are all different and man has to understand that despite his technological prowess, he has to except and understand that he cannot divorce the spiritual aspect from it. He does so at his peril.

That is a warning, not from me, but from an understanding of the way that the law operates and if he continues towards imbalance then he will do harm to his physical progress.
You know son, if you take a shoe off your left foot and walk with one shoe on your right foot the chances are you will go in a circle. You know that Sunflower, you've heard that, *[the guide turned towards Amanda]* and that is a very apt way to describe the path which humanity is taking because this reliance upon science to the exclusion of the spiritual aspect of his own being is bringing about a chasm is terms of progress between his lower state and his higher mind and that is what I am referring to. That is what has to be addressed. Do you see that?"

Questioner: "Yes, thank you very much."

White Feather: "God bless you for that."

Returning again to the topic of reincarnation the next question once more reflected the concern which many people experience in regard to whether or not our loved ones will be awaiting us when we ourselves are promoted to the higher life:

Questioner: "When people reincarnate or whatever, some people may take years before they reincarnate. But it has been said that a person can pass over and reincarnate very quickly afterwards. Now, if that happens......supposing that in the same........

White Feather: "I know what you are going to say!"

Questioner: "Supposing that in the same generation......how could the family of that spirit get in touch? How could they come back to them if they had reincarnated?"

White Feather: "I know what you are saying, yes.......and you shouldn't worry about that because it won't happen to you. It is far rarer that this happens than you would think. It does happen but it is a rareity rather than being the norm. Don't think that when you pass into my world your father and mother will have reincarnated and you will be searching for them when they are back on the earth! That won't happen. There are laws that govern every aspect of life and it would not be right for you to find when you pass into my world that your beloved family have reintroduced themselves into the body of matter. That would not be just. It would not be fair. There are laws that govern that. Where it does happen.......and it does on occasion........you will find that more often than not it occurs within circles, races upon your earth, in certain eastern races, where the understanding and belief in reincarnation is far more prominent than it is in the western world and there is a deeper understanding of it and it is more accepted in certain areas.

There you will find that on occasion it can happen for specific purposes and reasons and that is perfectly acceptable. Nothing is written in stone in that respect. There is not an alloted time that you have to spend in my world but where there are family ties, particularly in your western civilisations they have to outwork themselves before one can reintroduce into the body of matter. So don't concern yourself too much about that. Does that help you?"

Questioner: "Definitely!"

Obviously enjoying his conversations and the questions being asked of him White Feather once again added a note of humour into the evening:

White Feather: "Are you glad I turned up?"*[Laughter from audience]* I nearly didn't you know, because the one through whom I speak couldn't find this place!"

Questioner: "Good evening White Feather. Although we have a concept of time in the physical, can you tell us if there is such a concept of time in the spirit world?"

White Feather: "There is such a thing as time but it is different than your linear experience of time. You know, I've heard it said many times in your world, even by learned people 'when you go to spirit you know, there's no time'. Well, I'm sorry to disappoint them but there is time, but its passage is different than your linear time.
What is time? After all, time is a subjective experience in one sense. An insect in your world, a bee or a bird, will experience time differently than you do. There are creatures that live only for a day in your world and yet that day to them is like seventy or eighty years to you. So they are within the same linear time frame but their experience of it, which is subjective, is different than yours.
In my world for example, if I speak of myself, I am aware of the passage of time but not in the same way as you are. I know that I have been operating through this medium for a certain amount of time because I know that I can work in a way now that once I could not. So therefore, time must have passed.
What I will say to you is that the more spiritually evolved you become, the quicker your vibrations, the closer you become to perfection, the closer that you become to the Great Spirit and the divine within, the more that you have awareness of past, present and future being one. Because at the very highest levels in my world one can have an experience of all of these 'past, present and future' being one whole. Rather like a balloon, in your world that balloon is opened up, it is spread out like a pathway and you experience time in the linear sense of the word, which is a different experience to my world. Do you understand that?"

Questioner: "Hmm, yes......."

Sensing that the gentleman in question was having difficulty understanding his answer White Feather pressed him further, striving to provide him with a more concrete answer to his enquiry:

Questioner: "Hmm, yes......."

White Feather: ".......but?"

Questioner: "It's interesting......yes"

White Feather: ".......but?"

Questioner: "Explain to me about that balloon again and I can try and catch that."

White Feather: "Yes. If you think of.......and this is a simple analogy to what refers to a more complex reality.......and I am struggling for words because I have to operate through your language which cannot do full justice to the thought process.......but if you think of time and all of creation and everything that is, for the purposes of this illustration, as being like a balloon and you are somewhere at the top of that balloon, rather like being at the top of a mountain, as you look over the balloon you can see everything that is - past, present and future all together in a globe or sphere. Then when you come 'down' the vibrations to the body of matter upon the earth, it is rather like bursting that balloon and stretching it out like an elastic band so that time has its elements of past, present and future.
Rather like the roads upon which you drive so frequently. So time is experienced differently. That is what I am trying to explain to you."

Questioner: "So what you're saying is, there is no beginning and no end then?"

White Feather: "In real terms there is no beginning and no end. I know of no beginning and I will have no end because the Great Spirit has no beginning and no end. That is of course a difficult point for many to accept in your world because in your world everything seems to have a beginning and an end. That is the nature of matter after all. Even the physical universe as you know it, had a beginning in its now, current structure. But when you speak of the Great Spirit or God, you cannot speak of beginnings or endings because there are none."

The debate continued when the audience member asked a further question regarding the existence of God:

Questioner: "You talk of God......so there is a God then is there?"

White Feather: "There is a God, absolutely. I refer to God as the Great Spirit. That is just a label which I choose to use. It does not matter what label you put upon God, but God exists. God has always existed and you are all parts of that existence. God works through you all, in degree. But do not think of God or the Great Spirit in a personal sense. Even though you can have a personal relationship, do not think of God as being a man or a woman or any gender. The Great Spirit is everything that is. The Great Spirit is beyond form and yet comes through form in order to express itself. That is what you have to try and grasp. Do you see that?"

Questioner: "Thank you."

Amanda: "The lady over there."

Questioner: "Why do so many cruel and evil people seem to prosper on the material plane?"

White Feather: "Because the law does not appear to outwork itself upon your earth. However, let me justify that by saying that ultimately it does. Because the law is perfect. It cannot be cheated, it cannot be abrogated. If the law or any aspect of it were imperfect, then the whole fabric of life - your universe, my world, everything, would cease to exist. Laws are made by the Great Spirit. The Great Spirit is within them and they are perfect in their operation. In your world you don't see the whole picture. You have to look with the eyes of the spirit to recognise that those who perpetrate acts of cruelty and violence borne out of ignorance, upon their brothers and the lesser bretheren of your world, do not ultimately escape the consequences of their actions. Because what is sown has to be reaped and even though they appear to escape punishment, they appear to escape justice on your world, ultimately spiritually, they do not.

The richest of the rich in your world can be the poorest of the poor in mine. They can be spiritually bankrupt. So try to look with the eyes of the spirit and recognise that in eternity the balance is addressed and that what you do to others you do to yourselves."

Questioner: "I can understand it with people, but what about animals. There are millions of animals slaughtered every day. How can this be allowed to carry on?"

White Feather: "I know the sorrow that you have in your heart regarding this because it brings great sorrow to myself and many in my world also. Man's cruelty and inhumanity to those over whom he is given temporary charge in your world.......and you say 'how can it be allowed to be perpetrated? How can it be allowed to carry on?' There are many injustices in your world which are allowed to carry on because we cannot interfere with man's freewill. What man sows he will reap. Try to understand that where you see pain and suffering inflicted, let us say upon an innocent creature, for the purposes of material exploitation, that creature and its race, the group to which it belongs, the species of which it is a part, are ennobled through that suffering. They do not lose out from it. Their spirit gains from it. That you must understand. Pain and suffering, even though they are suffered in innocence and silence...... nothing is ever lost. And that race, the soul of that race, the group soul, is compensated as a result of the actions of those ignorant minds. That may sound a contradiction but it is a fact."

At this point the spirit guide surprisingly revealed an insight into his past life as a native American by disclosing that his 'race' was the victim of abuse by the white race of man. He said this, not in a discriminatory way, but to emphasise the point that forgiveness is always better than revenge:

"Let me say to you this; I belonged when upon your earth, to a race that was persecuted by the 'White Westerners' who came to my country. And yet I choose now to come back and speak through a 'White Westerner'. Why do I do that? Not because I have anger in my heart. Not because I seek revenge. But because I seek to show the wonderous power of the spirit that operates through the very individuals who were called 'savages', who were disregarded by many in your world. I seek to demonstrate to humanity through the power of love, the power of the spirit and that man is ever poorer by his actions borne out of ignorance. You will do the same. When you have understanding, which I know you have as I speak, you won't want to injure or hurt those perpetrators of violence and pain, you will send your thoughts out, you will feel sorry for them. But even more than that, you will want to educate and help them and you will do all in your power to bring that about. And that is the mark of an evolved soul."

The lady thanked him and commented that the wisdom contained within his answer was a comfort to her.

Questioner: "I listened with interest when you spoke about people in other parts of the world and because of their belief in reincarnation they can reincarnate quicker. We have those within my own family with certain spiritual or religious beliefs and they hold on to the belief that there are certain members of their group who are elitist within that group and that the rest of them, when they pass over shall remain asleep until the great day of judgement. I say this with a great deal of respect because it is their belief. How will my friends and my family be received into spirit?"

White Feather: "It is one thing to have a belief you know, but it is quite another to have a truth. One can have a belief that is based upon falsehood and it does not matter in the great scheme of things ultimately what one believes. What matters is the truth and even though there are those that would seek to bend the truth to fit in

with their beliefs and their ways, the truth does not bend. The truth is eternal, it is infinite. Otherwise is would not be truth. If it was true yesterday it is true today and it will be true tomorrow. For example; there are many people who believe wholeheartedly, with all of their being that when they pass into my world they will be met by the one called 'Jesus'. So much so, that the power of their thought which has more expression in my world than it does outwardly in your world, manifests that form for them. So that when they pass they are met by that form which they expect to be there. That is the power of their thought and their belief. But ultimately they come to the realisation that they have created that through their own minds and they have to reassess their thinking and their understanding. So belief in itself, as powerful as it is, does not alter the truth.
I respect the beliefs of all because I am not so dogmatic and so all knowing and all powerful that I will seek to impose my views upon others and say that they should discard everything that they have come to adhere to. What I do say to them is that this is the way that I see it and think about it. Enable it if you will to modify your own beliefs if you are ready to do that and perhaps you can see things a little differently. If not, then put my beliefs to one side and hold on to your own beliefs until such time as events and circumstances enable to to reassess them and perhaps change your views. Do you understand that? Does that help you at all?"

Questioner: "I am still concerned."

White Feather: "Yes.....it is one thing to be concerned you know, and it is good that you are concerned because I know from looking at you that in your heart you have love for them. Send your thoughts to them. Ask for guidance to come and perhaps that little tiny seed that finds its way into the tiniest crack of granite will germinate there and when their time comes to pass it will grow into a wonderous flower and they will remember your words, which at one time they discarded."

Questioner: "White Feather, if ten years have past by since two people should have come together and they still haven't come together and they would have had a child on the fourth year of meeting does that child reincarnate straight away if they come together or in a hundred years time, or whatever the cycle is?"

White Feather: "You have personal experience of this?"

Questioner: "Could be....."

White Feather: "Hmmmm.....well let me say to you that there are laws again, that govern all aspects of relationships and no one meets by chance. Chance and fate and luck do not occur in a universe that is governed by natural law. If individuals do not gravitate together when they believe they should have done then the chances are that the laws have operated in such a way to keep them apart. Sometimes you know,

what the heart desires the soul denies and it may be that when the time is right there will be such an attraction of magnetic proportions that no barriers, no distance or any other material obstacles will keep them apart.
As to the introduction of another, through that union of souls, again there is a time and a place and you know, so often in your world you place emphasis on time. You say that you have a time for this or there has to be a time for that. Or perhaps you don't have enough time and you rule your lives by the great clock on the wall. But time, as has already been addressed, is a wonderous thing and what doesn't occur in the time frame that you would like it to will occur in the greater time frame that is goverened by natural law. Everything is as it should be. In the universe of the Great Spirit there are no mistakes, there are no errors. You are *where* you are meant to be, you are *who* you are meant to be, you are *what* you are meant to be. You cannot be other than that. So trust in the operation of the law and when two souls are meant to be together or they are meant to be joined by a third, then nothing in your world can prevent that from happening."

Questioner:"If people do get damaged that does prevent people coming together.......well it's the same question........If two people have been told they should have met and then did not........"

White Feather: "I'm a little concerned though you know, about two aspects to your question son. Firstly, when you say people are 'damaged'.....the *spirit* is never damaged, it is only the physical form that may be damaged, or perhaps the ego may be damaged. As to being told, you know you can be told the same thing from many sources but it does not necessarily follow that it is meant to be that way. You may say 'well, that sounds a bit strange, that sounds a bit of a contradiction.' But you know, where one holds a desire in the psyche, many will pick up on that and many will sense it and feed it back to you. I'm not saying that is always the case, but it can occur. Trust in the law, understand the law, not merely with blind faith but with a recognition that you know the way that the law operates. I reiterate son, that what is meant to be, will be. If you try to take the apple from the branches before it is ripe, it is a bitter apple. But when it is ready you only have to hold out your hand and it will drop into your palm. The Great Spirit knows what is in your heart. It knows what is ahead of you. Understand that the Great Spirit is perfect and all will be as it is meant to be."

Having received a 'taster' of what White Feather once was whilst upon the earth, the next question came from a gentleman who wished to know more about his background. However, before giving his answer the guide picked up on a simple slip of the tongue by the questioner which gave him cause for mirth and also allowed him to delight the audience with his comical response:

Questioner: "White Spirit, could you please tell us when you were here on the earth plane and what Indian tribe you associated with?"

White Feather: "Well you know, I've been referred to as many things, but never White Spirit! [raucous laughter from the audience] However I understand......."

Questioner: "My apologies."

White Feather: "......I understand......son I do not mock, I merely take advantage to lighten the proceedings. I belonged to the Blackfoot tribe of Montana and let me say that I lived in that body of the Red Man, of the native American many, many hundreds of your years ago. I don't very often give details of myself because who I am is of little consequence. It is the message, not the messenger that matters. But if it helps you, that is the race to which I belonged. I come back through the astral body that I have held, of that race, for purposes which enable me to link with the medium in a more beneficial manner, but I do not consider myself to be a Red Man. I am spirit. Spirit is beyond race, beyond colour, beyond religion, beyond tribalism, beyond all cultures in that sense. I am who I am and I come merely as a messenger of the spirit to enable the truth and the light of the spirit to be made available to all who would listen."

As the evening came to its end Amanda brought proceeding to a conclusion by turning to the guide, who had laboured long on behalf of those present:

Amanda:"On that note, as we've raised the vibrations quite a bit, may I say on behalf of everyone here how grateful and privileged we feel that you and your colleagues in spirit have chosen to come here to help us this evening. It is always a pleasure and we thank you greatly for the philosophy that you have imparted and the teachings and truth that you have brought through. God bless you."

White Feather: "But you know Sunflower, as I always state; the greater pleasure is mine. Because as I look out upon you all I can see the same thread that binds you all together, that unites you all regardless of your gender, your creed, your colour, your understanding, your age or any other material differences. When I look out upon you I don't see your physical bodies, I see your spirits. But more often and more importantly than that, I see your hearts and I see that within your hearts there is goodness. The goodness of the spirit. I hope that what I have been able to bring to you tonight will touch your hearts and I hope that what you have given to me I may take back, because it has touched my heart.
So we have, as I have said before, 'a fair trade'. I thank you for this opportunity and I pray that the power and the light of the Great Spirit may be with you all, whoever you are, wherever you go, whatever you may become and until we meet again I say God bless you all."

"You can take light into a darkened room and the darkness is vanquished. But you cannot take darkness into a room which is of light. Light is always greater and the power of the spirit is always greater than the power of matter."

one2one *In Search of Answers* 6

Having previously encountered White Feather when he spoke in a home circle to which we were invited Tracey came into the one to one sitting with the knowledge that the spirit sage would do his utmost to answer both her personal and more general questions. Her enthusiasm for acquiring spiritual knowledge was evident early on during the sitting with a wide variety of questions covering a range of topics. As the evening progressed Tracey felt confident enough to ask questions of a more personal nature, particularly those relating to her son Callum who has an autistic spectrum disorder. This area of questioning also interested Amanda, who was also seeking confirmation of the same diagnosis for her own son, at the time. The guide began with a question of his own:

"Can you hear me Sunflower? Very well. I am pleased again to join with you and for you to join with both myself and the hosts of disenfranchised souls who gather here tonight. It is a joyful union, it is a glad reunion. For whenever we have the means to communicate in this fashion then it is because the bridgeheads have been forged, the barriers have been overcome and the thin veil that separates our two states of being has been drawn aside to enable this wonderous power of the spirit with which I am so familiar and privileged to be able to assist, to flow into your world, bringing with it as it so often does, all the richness and beauty that the spirit has to offer humanity. I never tire if this task for it is a labour of love. However, I never quite know what to encounter or what to expect because every communication, be it of this deeper kind or of a more lighter, quicker frequency, is to some extent experimental. When I link with this instrument it is rather like putting on a pair of old shoes with which one has become familiar. Sometimes they are more comfortable than others but nevertheless I gladly step into them for a little while even though it means sacrificing some of my own progress. It is something which I do gladly and freely and unabated. For it is more important that we should, in our linking with your world strive to touch souls, to reach out unto hearts and minds and to try and liberate those who are captive to their own ignorance, their own fears and superstitions, because if between us we can help but one individual then perhaps in reality we will reach many.

Because make no mistake what transpires here tonight, as on many other previous occasions, reaches far beyond the confines of this little temple. Hearts and minds with whom you will have little contact at this level of being will be reached. Souls will be touched, minds will be awakened and you will have played your part in that, and that is a wonderous thing in itself. For I know that in your lives there are difficulties. I know that just as we in my world have to make sacrifice upon sacrifice to return to speak with you, so you also are called upon to make sacrifice upon sacrifice in terms of your own spiritual development, sometimes your freedom and your time. That does not go unnoticed. We know the difficulties that can transpire for you upon the earth, but you know, adversity is good for the soul. Even though when you are in its midst, you think not and you will do all in your power to avoid it and to escape it. That is of course by virtue of your very human nature, the way that you are built and what you are. That is understandable. But the soul knows more than the mind upon the earth. The soul knows all about you and more than your conscious awareness makes available to you at this level. And you know it almost seems a contradiction in terms, but it is not, that you come into circumstance after circumstance which test you. Which cause you great discomfort and disharmony, which test you to the limits. And you say sometimes in your anguish, your pain, your suffering and your prayers 'why me? Why do I have to undergo this?' But you know if you see the bigger picture, which I know is difficult at times, but if you can raise your thoughts and your mind above the level of chatter to which you are so accustomed, if you can see through the stillness, through the mists, the real picture, then you will recognise that it is the soul that has placed you in this situation out of love and that you, yourself chose this pathway. In reality, adversity should be celebrated not reviled. Pain is your greatest teacher even though it seems at times that it is your worst enemy.

Very often you know, you will find the exact opposite, the antithesis of that which you are, which faces you. The meekest of the meek who find themselves in situations where they are called upon to rally themselves, to stand up against a foe, against an enemy, to use their courage and their guile against the mighty. It seems almost, upon the face of it, unfair. But there is no unfairness in the eyes of the spirit. Just as there is no chance, no fate, no luck. All is ruled by perfect law and order and you will find time and time again that the very opposite of that which you are at that moment in time, you will be called upon to face so that a change can be brought about from within. A quickening, a development and spiritual unfoldment. In real terms it is *that* which is of the greatest import. Not the momentary flurries and scurries, battles which may be won or lost, an unkind word here and skirmish there, a difficult moment here and uncomfortable time there. These are but passing moments, little landmarks if you like, upon the pathway. What is of the greatest import is the journey and the goal that is reached and in that sense you cannot fail. Even if the qualities, the gifts which the soul is trying to unfold within you by putting you into this counterbalance situation, even if the gifts are not brought to the fore, the experience itself will enrich you. Nothing is ever lost. Nothing is ever wasted. So try to understand this. Try to get a grasp that even in the most difficult, dark moments, the light of the spirit is there within and progress is being made."

The spirit helper, knowing intuitively that his guest was eager to begin her discussion with him paused for a brief moment before deciding that the time was at hand to open up the evening to questions:

"Now I'm not going to take a great deal of time in my opening gambit tonight because I know that there are questions to be asked which deserve answers. I only hope, as I always do that I am befitted to answer them. Because I am not the fount of all wisdom as you well know. But perhaps I am privilaged enough to have acquired a little more understanding and also have access to the many liberated souls who stand at my side, some of whom are far greater than I. We come as always as messengers of light, seeking to impart a little of this light into a dark world and most of all, a little love into your hearts. So I give you the opportunity now to ask whatever you will."

Tracey: "First of all I'd like to thank you for allowing me here today and to have the privilege to talk to you. I do appreciate that."

White Feather: "The privilege is mine."

Tracey: "My first question is, for what purpose did God make man?"

White Feather: "Try to understand that man *is God*. Man is a part of God. When you say 'make' it almost gives the implication that in some way man is separate from God. That God in some way decided one day to 'make man' in order to outplay and outwork some directive or other. What must be understood is that *man is God*. Everything is God. The Great Spirit IS. There is no separateness. Everything is but an expression of being. Everything that is, whether it is animate or inanimate, complex or simple, mighty or minute is part of the Great Spirit.
The Great Spirit however, seeks to unfold that divinity through whatever form it manifests and it does that through imperfection, that through imperfection that individual spirit can learn through the many lessons of life. The highs and the lows, the good and the bad, the negative and the positive and so on and so forth. It can learn what it is, its own nature, and so can return to the source from which it emerged. If you think of you as an individual, as a stone sent skimming across the waters of life by some unseen hand that launched you, then you will perhaps

recognise that over that time you are moving farther and farther away from the *source* that sent you skimming across the water. You touch, like a stone bouncing upon the surface of this world this experience and that and you glimpse certain lessons, certain experiences, and then you slow down and you sink into the depths. And it is here that you truly begin to experience the stillness and the quietness and you begin your return journey. Having emerged from that source and yet never having been separated from it. Always connected. You begin your journey back, rather like a boomerang that is sent spinning through the air only to cycle its way back to the hand that cast it forth. So, through the experiences of life you begin to quicken. You begin your inward journey. You begin to gather momentum. You begin to throw off the heavier grosser bodies which you have accumulated over many, many centuries of experience, begin to outwork Karma, to purify that which has become tainted and you return slowly, imperceptibly but most certainly to that higher realm of the spirit to a union again, with the Great Spirit, although perfection I have to say, is never reached. There is always a striving, but it is this theatre which is life itself. This is the play, this is the narrative of life which is forever unfolding and this is why the Great Spirit created form. Not just man but many other forms, animal, bird, fish, insect and many other forms upon other worlds not dissimilar to humanity, so that his wonderous majesty could outwork itself in this infinity of form, in this infinite play of the one upon the many.
It is a difficult, complex question in itself and yet you know, like most things of the spirit the answer is essentially a simple one. This is life. This is what God is."

Tracey: "Thank you, I understand that. I understand how you've explained it. My next question is; Is your destiny already laid out for you? If it is, is there any way we can change it?"

White Feather: "Yes, you know I have been asked this before but it is always a delight to answer it. There is not shall I say, a preordained life. Life is not preordained in that sense. There are certain patterns that unfold, there are certain landmarks within an individual's life which are set. Some before that individual enters into the physical body, some predetermined by the nature of the physical body itself, certain genetic markers and pointers that determine certain attributes and to that extent the soul which is coming into a form has to contend with that. Certain patterns are known by the higher self, by the soul, before its entry into form. But we cannot exclude freewill. Freewill always has to operate. Were there no freewill then life would be a mockery. One could do, think or say whatever one desired and it would have no impact upon one's destiny and that quite clearly, could never be so. So you have a degree of freewill - never total, *never total* freewill - but a degree of freewill operating through certain parameters that are predetermined. Together this makes up the individual and determines to an extent their earthly sojourn. Freewill however, can alter things dramatically. You cannot lengthen your life but you can shorten it. You can for example, take your own life through an act of suicide, which some choose to do, and that alters to a great degree the plan that should have outworked because it is never within the scheme of things that one should take one's own life. That is a matter for freewill. So you see how you can change things?"

Tracey: "Yes......it was as I thought but I wanted it confirmed if you understand?"

White Feather: "It's good to know that you think on the right lines."

Tracey: "When we return to spirit, are we aware of things there as we are here......do you understand what I mean?"

White Feather: "If you mean 'are you aware of the world of spirit around you?'......"

Tracey: "Yes, yes."

White Feather: "Of course. But it is never a total awareness. You see, here now upon your earth you could say to me 'well I'm aware of my environment', but how aware are you of your environment? You can be aware of certain things but you are never aware of the totality. You never can be because the physical environment itself exists upon many frequencies and there are for example, even now, filling this of your temple many things of a physical nature which you cannot sense, you cannot see, you cannot hear, you cannot touch. Yet they are very real and they compose part of the fabric of your earthly domain and the physical universe.
The same applies in my world and it is more marked in a sense because one finds oneself in accordance with one's spiritual development and one's thoughts, one's nature. That opens up a great vista of potential which one was previously unaware of whilst on the earth. But it is never total. Never a totality. There are always things which we cannot sense because we are not yet opened up to them. We have not yet earned the right to see them and to sense them and to feel them.
So in a sense, the same law applies in my world as it does in yours but on a different frequency."

Tracey: "Ok, thank you. If we are 'spirit', then how does evolution fit in?"

White Feather: "Because the spirit has to work through the body of matter which presents itself to it. In a sense, there had to be a degree of physical evolution taking place upon your earth for example, before a greater, higher and finer degree of spirit could manifest through it. Now try to understand this because it is a complex teaching; when we speak of matter and spirit, we tend to think of them as separate but in actual fact they are part of the same. It is a matter of degree. But for simplicity's sake let us think of spirit as being the higher vibration and matter the lower vibration. Now, for the spirit to 'enter in' to that matter there has to be a point

of contact somewhere. There has to be a means for it to express itself and it was not until evolution brought about a more complex material form that the higher expression of spirit could manifest to the point where it *gained consciousness*. Where it could *express consciousness*. For example; there was a time when there was no animal, fish, bird or insect life whatsoever upon your earth. Going back way before what you sometimes refer to as the caveman in prehistoric times. But gradually, there emerged through changes in the 'primordial soup' which was referred to as the ocean of your early earth, many changes at sub-atomic levels that gave rise to the simplest creatures, the single celled forms. Gradually these grew into more complex forms. Not by chance, not by accident but because the spirit was beginning to enter and work its way within their evolution. Over many thousands of millions of years, great epochs of time, vast aeons of time which you cannot comprehend, the physical form grew and evolved and diversified into many species. But still, there was not the ability for the spirit coming through it to gain *consciousness,* to have *reason*. To think, to ask 'who am I? What am I?'
A tree cannot know it is a tree and the fish does not know it is a fish. The bird does not know it is a bird. The insect has no way of knowing that it is an insect. And so evolution continued as it is today continuing until the point where spirit could come through that form which had developed a brain, which had developed a nervous system and which was equipped for the spirit to express itself through mind, through reason. It could think. It is for that purpose, that is why evolution occurs. If there is no evolution then the spirit is inhibited, it cannot express itself beyond a certain level. Do you understand that?
There are planets in your solar system, in your universe on which there is no 'life' as you would recognise it and the spirit cannot express itself there as it can upon the earth. You have to have this evolutionary pathway, this evolutionary track before the higher can express itself through the lower. Does that help you?"

Tracey: "It does yes, I understand. Can you tell me 'have I been here before, on the earth as another spirit within another person?"

White Feather: "You have.....you have......but you've not been as *another spirit* because you are what you are....."

Tracey: ".....sorry......I mean as another person......."

White Feather: "......but you have come, as you all have in this temple, through different individualised vehicles. You must remember that with each separate visit, with each incarnation you take upon yourself a different personality. Be it male, female......be it this race or that......endowed with this quality or that, this belief or that idea, and you will find that the spirit that comes into that form has to contend with that personality and all that goes with it. Do not confuse the *individual* with the *personality*. You are an individualised spirit. You may come through many personalities in different lifetimes, in different forms, male and female. Each one with their own unique stamp or unique fingerprint if you like. But that is not *you.* That is just a vehicle through which you express yourselves. The individualised you, which is the facet of the diamond continues and will always continue and always has been and always will be from lifetime to lifetime."

Taking the bit between the teeth Tracey was eager to discover who or what was her 'real' self and pressed the guide further:

Tracey: "So how can I find my true spirit then, my true 'who I am' if you like, other than the individual that I am now?"

White Feather: "Well you know, in time you will come to recognise the other facets of your being. When you pass into my world you will not automatically gain recognition of your past lives. This is why some spirit teachers do not speak of reincarnation because they have no recall of it. That does not mean that they have no knowledge. It does not mean that they are ignorant, it just means that they have not yet earned the right to have reached that level where they can have recall of their past lives and their other facets.
So it is not God-given that when you pass to my world you will gain access to that knowledge but in the fullness of time, when progress is made and development occurs, then you will earn the right to have access to these past lives. There is a very good reason for that. You know, if you had full awarness now of what you once were or had been, it would come as a great shock to you. You could not take it and I say that to all who listen to me now. Your soul could not take it. You have to be strong enough, spiritually. You have to have achieved enough development and sufficient growth to enable you to withstand that. When you have done so then you can have access to it. Is it making sense to you?"

Tracey: "Yes you're answering all my questions thank you."

As sensitive as ever to the fact that Amanda was also an important part of the evening White Feather comically enquired if she was still present before his guest continued her interrogation.

White Feather: "Are you still there Sunflower?"

Amanda: "I am!"

Tracey: "What happens......I understand that we come back to learn our lesson or to learn lessons to be able to go back to the divine and with those lessons learned to make him, or to make everything pure if you like, but when I have learned my lesson will I then die or do I learn my lesson and then carry on to the end of my life if you understand what I mean?"

White Feather: "Are you talking about learning a lesson here upon this earth?"

Tracey: "Here at the moment, yes."

White Feather: "Well you know, you never stop learning lessons. I mean, you can learn a lesson when you are five years old and live in the physical body to be eighty or ninety. It does not matter in that sense because what is important is that the lesson is learned. And the lesson will only be learned when you are ready to learn it. The fruit can only be picked when it is ripe. If you pick it earlier it is a bitter fruit and when you have learned the lesson, then it may be that you can learn other lessons or also that you have come to render a service because you don't come here upon the earth just to learn lessons you know. You come here to render service, to help others, to perhaps pay a Karmic debt, to help another with a Karmic influence. So there are many reasons why you come here. Not just to learn lessons. What matters is that the lesson is learned. Whether that is when you are eighty five or when you are five, it doesn't matter."

Tracey: "That leads me to my next question......"

White Feather: "I thought it might!"

Tracey: "What happens if you don't learn your lesson? I understand that we come back but do we come back again for that specific lesson to be learned?"

White Feather: "There some lessons which have to be learned at the place of origin. Where the difficulty was born, where the Karmic debt was created and you cannot learn them in my world. Pain for example, of a physical nature, has to be born and endured in the physical domain, so it is essential that the soul, or a facet of it comes back to that level to learn that lesson.
If by chance - that is not a very good phrase because there is no chance, but to use your terminology, if you do not learn the lesson then you have to come back. The opportunity will present itself again. It may not be directly in the next lifetime, it may be in a future existence upon the earth but it will present itself again. These things don't go away, you cannot just bury your head in the sand or 'sweep it under the carpet'. You have to learn it, there are no short cuts......"

Tracey: ".....I was just going to say, there are no short cuts....."

White Feather: "People try to make short cuts. They think there are but there are no short cuts. And you must understand as well that it is not a question of punishment. It is a question that the soul, *you,* the individual soul, recognising that it cannot move on unless it has learned that lesson. It cannot move on in my world to higher frequencies of greater expression until it has learned that lesson. So it chooses voluntarily. Wisely, it chooses to return to another time, another body and another set of circumstances to facilitate a similar experience to that which it had prior to this one but did not take the opportunity to learn."

Feeling that many of her more general questions had been adequately dealt with by the teacher, Tracey felt confident enough ask the guide questions of a more personal nature, beginning with one about the identity of her spirit helpers. White Feather's answer was not about to reveal what she had requested.

Tracey: "These now are personal questions for myself. Are my guides here and are you permitted to tell me who my guide is, or my guide that I can learn from or I can talk to? I sometimes tend to talk to nobody with a name if you understand what I mean, because I don't know who they are."

White Feather: " That's very good and I am pleased that you don't know the name! That sounds a contradiction I know, to you. But let me say that there is a very good reason for that and that is why I am not going to give you the name even though I could and it is within my power because it is a matter for the individual guides through their own wisdom, who work with you, to show themselves to you, to give you a name if they choose to or if they are ready to. Now you may say 'well this is very unfair. I want to know who is with me, I want to see them, I want to be able to greet them in person.' But you know, sometimes this is a stumbling block, it is a hinderence to those who work through you. Let me say that in my own personal experience it was several years of operating through this instrument before I revealed to him my name and identity because it would have been a stumbling block had I done so earlier. When you are ready, even though you think you are ready now, but when you are truly ready, your helper or guide will step forward to give you whatever information they choose and it would be remiss of me to take that privilege away from them."

Tracey: "Can I just ask you another question about my guide. Have I seen them if you understand what I mean, because I believe I have but I don't know if it is them.......because I have seen this person in my dream.....twice....."

White Feather: " Well, let me say firstly that you have more than one. The one that you have seen, you have seen correctly but is only a facet, only one of several and should not be focussed upon as being *your guide*. Try to avoid using the term if you can, it is not a pleasurable one. Remain humble and recognise that there are many who seek to work with you. They are not greater than you. I am not greater than the instrument through whom I work. I am not greater than you, I am not lesser than you.

I have a little more knowledge and access to far more knowledge but that does not make me a deity or a saint or greater in any way. You will find that those who work with you are the most humble of souls. They require no praise, no thanks, no gratitude, no plaudits. They do not require putting upon a pedestal or heaping with praise. They require only that they can seek to serve through allowing themselves to operate through you to help you, to assist you in your own development and so then in turn to reach others who come into your orbit. That is how it works. I have always said, and I repeat 'it is the message, not the messenger that counts'. Who I am is of no consequence. I only give this name because it helps in certain circumstances for individuals to identify with it, but who I am is of no consequence. What matters is the truth that I impart. Always remember that."

Tracey: "Now I know that you can't tell me about my son Callum but is there anything that you can tell me to give me peace of mind, to know?"

White Feather: "Yes, there are several things actually that I want to impart to you and to you also Sunflower. But let me address you first. Whether this is of comfort to you I don't know but take some comfort from the fact that the soul of your son, the individual soul, has chosen this pathway. 'Callum' is only a personality that has come through you. It is only a personality, it is a vehicle that the soul of Callum is using. 'Callum' as a personified form has certain distinctions which are the result of the genetics of you and your husband who have created that physical vehicle and also the incoming soul or a facet of it that has come through it. That is what makes the individual. But what you must remember is that the soul has chosen at this time to come through you into that form to experience what it is experiencing with all of the difficulties. Let me say to you this; it is a great, great privilege for you that he has chosen to come through you. It is a great privilege. As difficult as it is, it is a great privilege that you can assist this soul in its development. He could have chosen to come through another. He did not. He chose to come through you. Why did he choose to come through you? Because you have the necessary qualities that attracted him in the first place. You did not *create* Callum. You created the vehicle, the vessel that you have named 'Callum'. You did not create the soul that comes through it. The soul that has chosen to come through it has done so because of the attraction, the magnetic attraction to you, the circumstances and the vehicle that equips that soul with the necessary means to learn its lesson, however difficult that may be. That is a tremendous privilege and also a responsibilty, I concede that. But a great privilege. Do you understand that?"

Tracey: "Yes."

White Feather: "So take comfort from that. Take comfort and use the knowledge and wisdom that you have, as difficult as it is at times. Use the knowledge and wisdom that you have to help this soul and to recognise also that, that soul is helping you, for there is no teacher who is not also a pupil or pupil that is not also a teacher. There is a trade-off here of experience. There is no growth of one without growth of the other. So you are both learning from this experience, try to understand that and take some comfort from it.

Now, you may say to me, both of you, that 'this is all very well but how do we learn to adapt ourselves, how do we learn to cope with the difficult circumstances that this condition *[Autistic Spectrum disorder]* [1.] brings?' Is that not what is in your hearts? Are you with me on this Sunflower? Have I not said to you about 'working from the top down'? Let me reiterate that. If you have a stream that is pure, crystal clear and you take a cup and fill it from that stream and then you put into that cup, let us say yellow and blue to make it a muddy green, that water is no longer pure and clear. It is a muddy green. How do you then change that? You say 'I don't want it a muddy green, I want it yellow', so you pour more yellow into it, but you can never quite get it to a pure yellow because there is so much discolouration and contamination. So how do you change that? If you pour it back into the great stream that is flowing you will find that the stream remains clear. It may be muddied for a little while but it remains then clear, because the muddiness dissipates into the crystal water. Or if you take the crystal water and pour that into the muddied cup which then overflows, you will see the same result.The muddiness disappears and clarity returns.

So what then, is the moral of this story? It is to take it back to the higher. You cannot always treat it from the lower. You have to take it back to the higher or you have to bring the higher down to the lower. Do you see what I am saying with this analogy? Now, you may say to me 'this is all very well, it is a good descriptive, a good narrative, but how do we do it in practice?' You know, if you have a broken arm as I am sure you are familar with of late *[Amanda's younger son had recently broken his wrist]* then you have to treat it by physical means. You have to put it in plaster. That is the best way to treat it. You *can* give healing to it, but it is best to set it so that heals. You have to treat it with plaster, to set it to enable the bone to knit together. You cannot do that with things of a mental nature. You have to treat them differently. Emotions have to be treated differently still. So you have to adapt."

At this point the spirit guide decided to impart some important information in a unique way and asked if those present could assist him by closely following his careful directions:

"Now, have you got a pencil and paper? I am going to give you something. I've never done this before but I am going to give you a model."

The sage slowly described a 'working model', taking care to ensure that each step was correctly transferred to paper by Amanda who was diligently scribbling away in the semi-darkness of the room. After some five minutes of descriptive dialogue the illustration was complete and the guide began his explanation of its significance:

Fig 1.

White Feather: "This model *(see Fig 1.)* that I have given you can be adapted but I have given it in this particular way because it applies to this condition with which you are both familiar. The circle on the right is what is required as a means of assisting and healing the individual to enable them to cope with their map of the world and for you to cope with dealing with it. What you have to try to do is to focus your energies into that right circle, not from the lower material self but from the higher spiritual self using the qualities of the soul, bringing the qualities of love, compassion, empathy, kindness, tolerance, understanding into those structures, into those disciplines. To give the individuals concerned a structure, a discipline and a self knowledge and by that I mean a knowledge of themselves and of their condition which in itself will bring about a greater insight and understanding. They require structure, they require discipline very, very much so in their lives. This will bring about an easement and a comfort to the way they they operate and it will also help you. But you have to do it through the soul. From your soul to their soul. From spirit to spirit."

Amanda: "Can that be done through absent healing through the sleep state, rather than having the physical in the way, as it were?"

White Feather: "That can be one aspect of it, one facet of it. You know that many tributaries run into the same stream and one can approach this task in many, many ways. Spiritual healing can be done in the sleep state or the waking condition and is always beneficial but I am referring also to operating from the soul level, of soul qualities. Let me give you an example; when we speak of discipline, one can discipline with love or discipline with fear. You can bring that discipline from two separate directions. You may still achieve the same result, or perhaps not, but it is far more potent to bring discipline allied with love and kindness that is understood than to impose it through fear. So many do it out of fear and sometimes through frustration, sometimes through anger or even despair but that is the test for you. That is the test for your soul and if you can do it as I have said, from the higher to the higher, always from the top downwards, like taking the paintpot back to the clear waters then you will find, in my opinion and those with whom I have consulted, that is the way to approach this.

The difficulty I know that is there for you is that you seek to find a cure. Sometimes there is no cure. Sometimes it is because as I said earlier, the soul of that individual has chosen that pathway, has chosen that lesson. Who are you to deny them that lesson? Ah, but you say 'I want to heal them!" But the soul may not want to be healed. That may be part of the plan. The soul has come to learn that lesson and has chosen you to help."

Amanda: "Our difficulty is, at what point do you let go and let them learn what lessons they have to from their own perspective when you as a mother are overwhelmed with love and a desire to protect the child......"

White Feather: "That is always the hard part and is always the dilemma, but then it is every mother's dilemma anyway. When does the eagle know when to push its offspring out of the nest? *That* is a dilemma. Because it does not know whether or not the bird will plummet to its demise or whether it will spread its wings and fly. How does it make that judgement? It does so because it uses its own instincts as a mother. Be it a bird, it still has instincts. It still has a knowingness and it knows when to leave that chick in a nest, when it should fly, when it should abandon it, when it should caress it. And you as mothers must strive to use every ounce, every facet of your in-built feminine wiles, instincts, spiritual knowledge......everything that you have at your disposal. Use it wisely and you will find that you will be richly rewarded."

Amanda: "The other thing I'd like to ask......and I take your point, I'm very grateful, we both are, for that model, because I think it will be something that will help a lot of people..... we also have to deal and live in a world of matter. So in order to get to 'fight' if you like, for our children and their needs and their rights, we have to sometimes work very, very hard with the 'powers that be' down here either to get a diagnosis or the help and education they need and one wonders why sometimes that is so difficult and are we right is pursuing it? That sometimes tires us, drains us of energy, but is something I know instinctively that we should do because we know it in our hearts to be right. What is'spirits' view on that and why is it so difficult?"

White Feather: "Because here of course you are venturing onto another agenda totally. It is one of which I have spoken before and which is to do with control by certain individuals over the masses. Your particular predicament is indicative of a greater malaise that is afflicting humanity as a race. Where the spirit, or its expression, is being stifled or crushed, inhibited, prevented by certain individuals who think they have power over it and who seek to deny its expression upon the earth. That is like a cancer that is growing daily, by the moment and it is right in my view that you should strive to oppose it, to fight it, to overcome it in everyway possible other than by violent means.
Again you must recognise as I know you do, that the lesser cannot overcome the greater. You can take light into a darkened room and the darkness is vanquished. But you cannot take darkness into a room which is of light. Light is always greater and the power of the spirit is always greater than the power of matter. This is what those that seek to enslave humanity through whatever means do not fully comprehend. They are taking on a giant, in the spirit, of which they have no comprehension of its power and might and they do so at their own peril. All that you can do.......... you may think that you are humble, insignificant beings but you are an essential part of the machinery that is the universe, you are an essential cog in its outworking. Were it not for you, for all of you, the universe could not exist. That is how important you are. That is why for every effort that you make, be it in the quiet sanctuary, be it in the darkened room, uneard, unseen, untouched, unknown except by the spirit, everything is known. This is why you must never cease your tireless struggle for what is right and what is true. Truth will ultimately endure. Man can hinder, man can delay but man cannot prevent the truth from expressing itself because truth is light and light is stronger than darkness."

Amanda: "Could I just ask then, on a very personal matter.....as I have to take Matthew [Amanda's son who has since been diagnosed with Aspergers Syndrome][1]. to see someone who will make an assessment of him in this world......I fully take what you said and I will wholeheartedly do what you suggested about going from the top down, but I also need to have, to help him in this world, unfortunately what we might call a 'diagnosis'. Could I be helped in the person I am seeing actually knowing what I feel in my heart and agreeing so that I can get on and help Matthew and Tracey can help Callum in the best ways we can. So that we haven't got to use all of our energies in fighting the system, because that is so difficult?'

White Feather: "Naturally it is helpful and beneficial if you have others on the same side who are trying to help you rather than oppose you. Unfortunately they are in the minority and that has been orchestrated in that fashion by those who put money before anything else, who put material wealth and control above spiritual growth and spiritual virtue. That is what you are up against. Whatever the outcome what I would say to you is that it does not change what is in your heart. What you know to be true. If someone said to you that black was white it would not change the fact of what you know would it?"

Amanda: "No."

White Feather: "So when we come to add everything together, to weigh up, ponder and consider our lot in life, what is of the greatest import is what we know within ourselves, what we know to be true. Because if we align ourselves with truth, if we align ourselves with the light, then we are aligning ourselves with a power that is far greater than any diagnosis and any words, any certificate, and report, any speech from any individual or collective. That is what I have to get across to you."

Amanda: "I understand that. Unfortunately supposed 'learned' people in the world of matter wrongly in my opinion, have a say that's far greater than they actually deserve and that can and will blight our children's development."

White Feather: "That is so. But let me say this to you both. You have both modified your behaviour. You particularly Sunflower, have modified your behaviour despite the absence of what you call a diagnosis by anyone in officialdom. Why have you done that? You have not done it out of any other purpose other than the fact that what you *know and sense*, not only as a mother but more importantly as a *soul*, as a *spirit*.......has modified your behaviour. You have done it because you love that individual you call Matthew. That is why you have modified your behaviour, to enable you to deal with the situation. Not only from your own point of view but more importantly from his 'map of the world'. You have done that without any help other than your own initiative, your own enquiring mind and your own discernment and that is a tribute to you. That is the very point I am making. You have judged and you have trusted your insinct. So whatever the diagnosis it will not change what you know to be true. How often have your heard me say 'the truth is the truth is the truth and I am not changing it for you!' I know that you won't change what *you* know to be true upon somebody's diagnosis. I know what you're saying - it helps if you have them on your side. But in a world that is upside down in its values, in its morals, you cannot always rely upon the outworkings of others. You have to rely upon what is within here and perhaps Sunflower, this is the lesson that you have come to learn. To trust what is within, not from others. Others will not paint you as you are. You will only paint yourself as what you are."

The guide then came out with a disturbing revelation when anticipating the meaning behind Amanda's next question:

Amanda: "Are you permitted to say to us.......because of the knowledge we have about conspiracy theories and those trying to control others through misinformation etc.......do you know whether.......and there are a lot of children these days, I'm not just talking about ours......."

White Feather: [interrupting] "The answer is yes."

Amanda: "It has been done deliberately?"

White Feather: "Yes. It is part of, and it pains me to say it, a greater scheme, an undercurrent that is unfolding from the deepest levels of man's psyche. From the ego state of his being. And it is this with which we have to contend in our operations and our dealings with humanity. It is a battle in which we are engaged of light against darkness, truth against ignorance. There are battles that are fought. Some we 'win' some we 'lose' but the 'war' if you want to call it that - a term which is so often used these days upon your earth - the war will be won by the truth because the truth is the most powerful force in existence. It cannot be denied."

It seemed that the guide was insinuating that there is a deliberate effort by some to manipulate events in order to bring about changes that conform to a hidden agenda - something of which he has spoken many times before. Indeed one only has to witness other wordly happenings to realise that attempts are currently being made to orchestrate the way in which mankind is controlled and policed, a worrying scenario for those who truly understand and respect that humanity is essentially spirit, with a collective and individual freewill that cannot be shackled to the desires of the few whose motives seem to come from the lower mind. These issues may be thought of by some as mere 'conspiracy theories' but the evidence is overwhelming to the acute observer that something deeper and more sinister is unfolding and the fact that spirit guides such as White Feather are also commentating on these occurances should not be dismissed lightly. This point having been made, the sitting progressed with another question from Tracey:

Tracey: "This applies to Amanda as well.......our children, they've come to the earth and they have chosen us......I have asked you the question before......we stay within that 'family link' so how can I put it.......they came as they are but did they help us before?"

White Feather: "Were you linked before? Yes, that is so. That is so. It is not always the case let me add, but that is so in these links to which you refer. You have experienced life here upon the earth together before and have chosen to be reintroduced together again. Be it under different circumstances, through different vessels in a different time period, to outwork, to help each other, to fulfill. That is why you are here and it is a great privilege for you both and a great and wonderous opportunity that you have presented to you now, to quicken your souls and to fulfill your destiny."

Tracey: "I'm sure you Amanda, will want to know this as well, can you tell us......will Matthew and Callum be independent as they get older or not?"

White Feather: "Independence will come. It does not emerge as swiftly and as naturally as with some because the condition precludes it, but independence will come. They will always be on your pathway. You know it is perhaps human nature that a mother would like their son to be 'tied to their apron strings', that's what you say isn't it? But you know, the greatest service that you can give is to loosen those strings when they are tugged. That will come later rather than sooner......."

Tracey: "Will they be......"

White Feather: ".....let me finish please. They will always be tied. They will always be linked. There will be no separateness, no separation and that in itself should be some comfort to you. You were going to say......"

Tracey: "I was just going to say I understand about loosening the apron strings but what I wanted to know is will they be OK. That's.......you can loosen the apron strings....BUT....is it the right thing to do?"

White Feather: "What is your estimation of OK?"

Tracey: "That they won't be taken advantage of, that they won't be hurt in anyway."

White Feather: "I cannot guarantee that and I will not promise you that. They will be hurt as you have been hurt. They will be taken advantage of, as you have been taken advantage of and if you look with the eyes of the spirit you will have it no other way. The eyes of the mother, the love of the mother would have it *any other way*, but the wise soul would *not* have it any other way. Because it is through adversity and this is where I began, I think tonight.....it is through adversity that the soul learns. It is from darkness that one emerges into light, it is from captivity that one comes into freedom and it is from ignorance that one finds truth. And it is natural that a parent wishes to protect it's offspring but the soul knows more than you do. The soul knows that these things are necessary for growth to take place. All that I would ask you to do is to trust. Not a blind trust, not a blind faith, but a trust in the power of the spirit that has never let you down and has never deserted or neglected anyone or anything in the whole history of life itself. The greatest power of all whose wisdom and love and light is beyond anything you can know."

Tracey: "Thank you."

Amanda: "Can I just ask one more question.....is forgiveness a spiritual or material attribute?"

White Feather: "In essence it is spiritual. It is divine. Forgiveness is divine, but as in all things of the spirit it manifests through matter also. Have you not heard it said 'as above, so below?' What you have to learn, all of you, me too........ is to bring what is above down into the great below. To bring into manifestation upon your earth the qualities and the gifts of the spirit. Forgiveness, kindness, love, empathy, sympathy, compassion, tolerence, understanding, beauty, richness, all the qualities of the spirit, to make them manifest through your lives in all that you are and all that you think and all that you do. That is the challenge. It is a mighty, mighty challenge. Are you up for it? For if you are, you will find that the rewards are beyond measure.The richness and progress to be gained are sublime, supreme, magnificent. Strive in all that you are and all that you do to imbibe the qualities of the spirit. If others criticise you and they jibe at you and they hurt you, give them love. I know you say 'well of course we get caught up in the moment and we have to respond, sometimes in anger!' Sometimes it is necessary. But also, try to understand with the eyes and the mind of the soul, that there is love in your heart. If you can do that then you are upon the pathway to becoming a great, great soul."

Amanda: "Sometimes the difficulty we have is that in trying to do that we feel that we don't 'hit the mark' as it were. That even with our best intentions we don't actually seem to get the results that we want."

White Feather: "Because you are imperfect, as are we all. But let me say this to you: if you look at the index of an evolved soul you will find that even though that soul has all but eradicated anger, temper, violence........you will find that in the index of that soul those things have existed somewhere. There is no great soul who has not also touched the very lowest depths, who has come through despair and grief and suffering, pain, anger, violence and hurt, all the things of the lower order. They are never eradicated in the sense that they are always there. But you will find that the difference is, in that greater soul they have been transcended, they have been transmuted from the lower into the higher. They have 'taken the paint pot back' into the great stream of purity and clarity and it has cleansed. That is the difference."

Amanda: "That's why when we look at and hear you we have the greatest respect because I know that when you have answered difficult questions you have not been phased by it, you have not insulted anybody, you have not got angry and sometimes we're not as good as that! We get it wrong a lot of the time."

White Feather: "But you know, I have no anger but I have been angry. I have walked in your footsteps. I have walked in your shoes. The only difference is that I have been able to transmute that and that comes only with experience, only with time, only with spiritual growth. One thing it does not make me however, is better than you. Nor will it ever."

Tracey: "I've just got one more question although I could be here all night and I'm sure you have other things to do! But you said about souls getting over being angry, is that for all souls? Because my understanding is that there are lower souls or malevolent spirits. Will they eventually evolve to be good, if you understand me?"

White Feather: "Absolutely. There is no difference, it is only a matter of degree. There is no difference between the highest of the high in my world and the lowest of the low in my world or in yours. No difference other than the degree of expression of the spirit. Those of a lower order, of a lower mind or malevolent mind, of an evil mind or whatever you want to call it....... it is only that the light of the spirit is not expressing itself as it should. It has been overcome, overtaken temporarily by the ego mind, by selfishness, by greed, by avarice, by violent thoughts, whatever emotion or whatever label you want to put upon it. But there is a thread that joins the highest and the lowest together. The golden thread of the spirit which is never severed. The tiny spark is never extinguished, even in the darkest mind. It is still there. And those who are down in the depths of my world will stand side by side with those who are at the moment, at the summit, at the zenith of unfoldment. I hope then that what I have given you has been of some help?"

Tracey: "It has yes. Can I just say thank you again for letting me talk to you and for answering my questions."

White Feather: "It is always a privilege. It is never a hardship or a difficulty and I have all the time in the world, and beyond. It is you that struggle with time because you have to obey the great clock that ticks away mercilessly. But even that is an illusion.
I thank you then for this opportunity and I thank all who have laboured on my behalf, who have not spoken directly to you but who have nevertheless helped to generate the atmosphere of love and kindliness that has prevailed. Thank you all and may the blessings of the Great Spirit be with you until we speak again."

It seemed that the evening had been an emotional but successful one, with many questions being asked and answered. The guide's often anticipatory answers seemed to help provide an understanding and insight into dealing with the autistic spectrum disorders that affected both Callum and Matthew and his compassion and love for all present shone throughout the proceedings, the hallmark of all true spiritual communications.

1. Aspergers Syndrome and related conditions are autistic spectrum disorders which are characterised by often servere and sustained difficulties in social interaction, development of restricted and repetitive patterns of behaviour, interests and activities which can result in clinically significant impairment in social, occupational and other important areas of functioning.

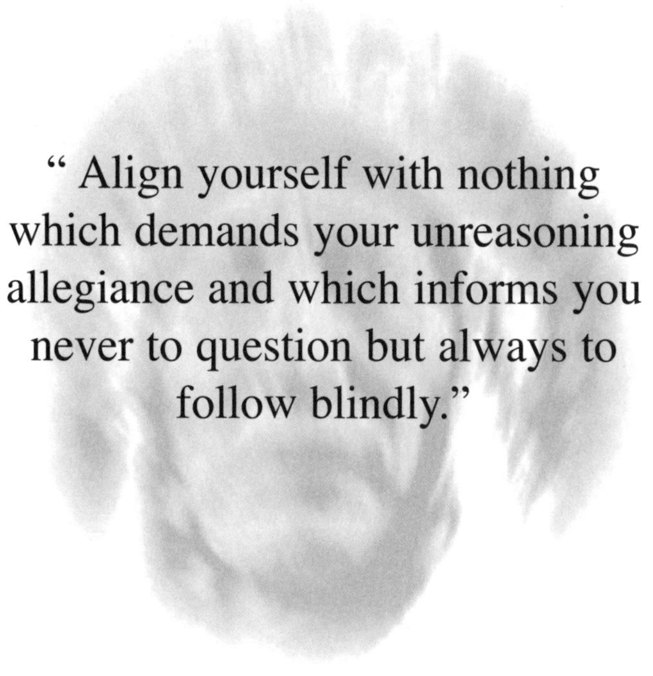

" Align yourself with nothing which demands your unreasoning allegiance and which informs you never to question but always to follow blindly."

Knowing the Illusion 7

Many individuals are blissfully unaware that their lives are anything other than what their five senses inform them. Happy to conform to the status quo and to believe what they are told is 'reality' and 'truth' they go about their daily lives unaware of any deeper significance or greater dimensions to existence. Souls of this nature are often, although not exclusively, some of the most kindly, generous and spiritual people on planet earth, seeking nothing other than to live their lives carrying out what they see as their duty to society and to others. They are no trouble to anyone. Some might call them the 'salt of the earth'. Others however, encompass such closed minds that they not only have no real awareness or interest in anything beyond their immediate local environment, particularly if it is of no personal advantage, but also do not wish to know. Their minds have become shut to anything which lies beyond what they consider to be the 'norm' often to the point where they become vociferous in their attacks on alternative thinking, preferring to adhere to what mainstream science and the 'official line' tells them is reality. They appear comfortable in their small world, which to them offers all that they need. According to this philosophy, why seek change?

More increasingly however, there are emerging individuals who not only recognise that this world offers a completely false sense of 'reality' but who are actively taking steps to open up their minds to greater understanding. Whilst taking note of what scientists reveal to them, they are also aware of more esoteric thinking which in truth, informs us in different ways what mainstream thinking is attempting to prove through its regimented, well defined procedures. The fact is, that as we move more deeply into the realms of the intangible, the more we recognise that those boundaries are shifting and what once appeared concrete and immovable, is no longer regarded in the same light. The previous chapters in this book covering 'The New Physics' and 'Synchronicity' are in part, a response to that shift in understanding with

eminent spirit teachers such as White Feather responding to the 'new thinking' that is emerging within sections of humanity. The growth in communication through inventions such as the internet along with more natural phenomena such as the previously discussed 'collective unconscious' of mankind can only further this knowledge and make it accessible to yet more minds on a global scale. Rather like a snowball gathering momentum and size as it rolls down a hill, so awareness is beginning to emerge that our physical universe truly is illusionary and that 'reality' lies at deeper levels of perception. White Feather touches upon these revelations whilst rightly pointing out that what we think of as belonging to ourselves is only something which is borrowed for a short while:

White Feather: "Once again the blending of our hearts and minds has resulted in the divine link between our two states of existence being established. It is across this bridgehead that the almighty power of the spirit can once more transcend the barriers of your material world to impart its richness and beauty to you. The work which we always try to undertake is essential because there is a need for truth and light at all times, especially for those engaged upon this evolving journey with its many pitfalls and difficulties. Not only this, but we recognise that perhaps long after the medium through whom we speak has departed the material world and we have completed our work through him, these words will continue to be read by seekers of knowledge and understanding. Thus it is that we seek always to address the most intricate and deepest issues, never seeking to shy away when difficult questions arise, but always endeavouring to answer in a forthright and honest fashion. For an enquiring mind deserves only the truth, nothing more, nothing less, because it is the truth that both inspires, uplifts and liberates.

If ignorance is man's jailer, it is truth which sets him free. If ignorance is man's greatest enemy then it is truth which is his staunchest ally. If it is ignorance that brings about darkness and despair then it is truth that opens the door to enlightement and joy.

Man for all his physical, emotional, mental and to a degree spiritual development, still has a long, long way to go upon the pathway of freedom and illumination. It has to be said that at times the physical dimension which offers the soul many great experiences and innumerbale lessons, also hampers its progress. It may seem a contradiction to say this and you may think that I call into question the wisdom of the Great Spirit that has devised such a universe in which the higher spiritual aspect experiences through the lower material existence in order to quicken and to evolve, but the difficulty which arises at times upon your world and which the individualised soul has to contend with, is the reliance on materialism to the exclusion of the higher spiritual aspect. For make no mistake, the world in which you live is not what it appears to be. It is an illusion and many individuals fail to grasp this fact because they are so reliant and comfortable within their surroundings which they think of as being their possession.

The truth is that you own nothing of a material nature and that which you think of as yours is only something which is borrowed and utilised for a short time. Even that which you think of as yourself when you look in the mirror, when you awaken in the morning and dress yourself or go to your place of work or place of worship, is but an illusion. Only that which lies in the unseen realm, which endures beyond time and space and matter, constitutes reality. You think do you not, that the chair upon which you sit, the floor upon which you walk, is solid. It is not. It only appears that way because the vibrations of the atoms of your body cannot easily penetrate the atoms of the chair or the floor. Therefore it appears that they are solid. Because you cannot see into the microcosmic world of which matter is composed you do not realise that what you are witnessing is not 'solid' at all but for the most part, emptiness."

Einstein himself stated that the atom appeared to be virtually empy with the nucleus appearing the size of a pea when compared to a building the size of St. Pauls cathedral whilst modern thinking refers to the atom and its component parts as being quanta of 'energy' whose position and location are impossible to accurately predict. White Feather's confirmation that one of the greatest illusions of all is 'solidity' bears this out. The guide continued by addressing whether or not it actually matters if we are aware of this knowledge or not:

White Feather: "You may say that this does not concern you, that you have enough to contend with without having to think whether this is real or that is illusion. But try to understand that at some point there has to be a realisation that the portal of the five senses upon which you rely is only a very small part of the overall picture. When you begin to realise this then you also recognise that many other things around you may also appear as an illusion. Knowing this begins to set you free from those things which would hold you back and imprison you, temporarily. You begin to understand firstly that you are not beholdant unto matter but have a degree of control over it and secondly that you are an eternal, infinite soul who has a latent divinity that transcends all time and space.

Remember that the body which you now have, which has a gender, which has certain physical characteristics and possesses a personality which is the result to a certain extent of your genetic inheritance, is only a temporary vehicle. *You the individual* existed before you came into that body and will exist long after that body is no more. Yes, the personality will persist after death as long as it is necessary for it to do so but the individualised, multi-facteted diamond of the soul exists above and beyond all personality."

Touching again on the 'conspiracy' theme White Feather commented on his sadness that those in positions of government are not the wisest amongst men:

"It saddens me at times when I see those in your world struggle to adhere to man made principles and laws, regimens, doctrines, creeds and ways of being which often do a great disservice to the wonderous power that seeks to express itself. Those who should be advising you, who should be guiding and counselling you are often the ones who mislead you the most. Those whom you elect to the positions of office in government, those who have temporary control and power to make decisions that affect so many lives worldwide should be the ones who are the wisest and most caring and yet so often they are mere puppets to a materialistic system that demeans freedom. The elevated soul, the liberated being, which is beyond materialism, recognises the illusion and witnesses the weaknesses of the materialistic systems that apply to the majority of your world and which deny the spirit its true expression.

Adhere to nothing that demeans the soul. Align yourself with nothing which demands your unreasoning allegiance and which informs you never to question but always to follow blindly. The very nature of your being is to question, is to seek truth and understanding. Throughout the ages of time man has followed one illusion after another. For so long he was and still is to a degree, fearful of death, which is the greatest illusion. Added to this he has created his own illusions based upon religious belief, political opinion and social demands and pressures, with historical tampering. All of these aspects have added to the overall illusion in your world. It is only when you begin to see through all of this that you will see the innermost dimensions wherein lies the true nature of being. It has to be said that the pathway of the soul is one that takes it from the purity of existence through the muddied waters of ignorance and back again to the refined clarity of life. The soul has to undertake this journey because it cannot become aware of itself and its divine nature unless it has witnessed all aspects of that which is. How can it know light unless it has known darkness? How can it know reality unless it has been within illusion? How can it have understanding unless it has been ignorance?"

The sage went on to reveal, perhaps surprisingly to some, that even in his world illusionary aspects are still evident due to the nature of the personality and its apparent ability to temporarily delude itself:

"Even in my world it has to be said that there are still levels of illusion. For the spirit operating through mind creates and builds around itself, through the power of thought, that which it *thinks* it is. It creates, it becomes that which it *believes*. So even after death when one finds oneself in the vehicle of one's creation, one is still not free of some of the trappings of the illusionary existence.

There are for example, those in my world who still adhere to religious practices, who still undertake certain habitual actions with which they have become accustomed because they think that is what they should and must do. Those upon the lower realms of the astral planes exist within even larger illusionary states brought about partly by their individual actions and thoughts whilst upon the earth that still persist long after they have vacated the physical body. Thinkers amongst you may say 'if the Great Spirit is all love and light and wisdom, why does he allow so much illusion? Why does he express through these states?' It is because this is the pathway of life itself. As I have already said, one must move from the lower to the higher, from the confined to the expansive. It is only by undertaking life's many experiences that one comes to the richness of spiritual truth and understanding and the illusions, the many layers, fall away, to reveal what lies at the heart of life itself."

The spirit world visitor also went on to mention another aspect of the psyche which can at times create inner disturbances and that can give rise to further delusionary states:

"I must mention also, the ego, which is that part of man's mind that so often seeks to decieve his higher spiritual self. The ego acts if you like, as a kind of counter-balance to the higher mind. It does have its role to play within mans constitution. For without the ego aspect some would find it difficult to move forward at times into situations that demand presence, in a very public way. For example; those who speak upon stages, who are within the public arena very often can do so because the ego aspect of their being is at the forefront of their nature. The problems arise when the ego becomes overbearing and important. Then it seeks to feed itself and its own self importance takes presidence over all else. It becomes cunning, devious, self protective, manipulative. It engages in a kind of inner battle with the higher aspect of the self. So one must be wary of the ego for it is a contributor to the illusion of the self in your world.
How often have you heard it said 'he has an ego, or she is such an egotist?' You find that individuals who aspire to fame and fortune in your world, often to the exclusion of all else and are not afraid to trample over the needs of others, are driven by the ego facet. The enlightened soul however, has transcended the ego and become selfless, humble and recognises that it is the higher qualitites that endure and reflect the divine within."

White Feather completed his short talk with a confirmation of the oneness of all facets of creation and the unique place that we have have in the grand scheme of life:

"Try to understand who and what you are, and who and what you are to be. Never forget your connection with the divine. As I have said so often you are part of the Great Spirit. You *are* the Great Spirit. You have much to unfold, much to develop, many imperfections to iron out over time, but above all the latent divinity of the Great Spirit within, seeking always to express itself and to reveal to you that which is, through that which is not. Whatever horizon you reach, seek to go beyond it. Whatever barrier you find in your way, seek to climb over it. Whatever doorway is shut, seek to open it. Whatever window is closed, seek to look through it. Whatever imprisons you, seek to free yourself. Let no one and nothing hinder your progress or add to the illusion. Remember that which lies within, forms the basis of the real. It is that which lies without that is often the illusion. Seek to apsire to the highest within yourself. Accept nothing less. Yes, you will stumble, you will fall but will always pick yourself up because you have the driving principle that inspires you to greatness and all things are possible to the individual who recognises its true self."

"I have looked already into your hearts and I know that there are many questions that not only require answers but deserve answers. For what good is a question if it does not provide an answer?"

one2one From the Mouths of Innocents 8

In what was a first for White Feather (as far as we know) the encounter with two young boys John and Matthew, proved to be as entertaining as it was informative. We had always wondered how the spirit messenger, so used to dealing with complex questions asked of him by adults, would accommodate two young, eager and enquiring minds. Having been asked so often, difficult questions covering every imaginable aspect of life both here and beyond, could the wise old sage deal with such complex questions as 'how old are you? and 'could I be a footballer in the spirit world?' In truth, the questions provide an insight into the thoughts of two young boys approaching their teenage years and the answers demonstrate the wonderful way in which White Feather can both simplify and convey even the most profound truths in a manner which can be understood by the developing adolescent mind. The gentle brother began by reassuring the youngsters that no harm would befall them:

White Feather: "You have no need to be afraid, concerned, apprehensive in any way for I bring only the love of the Great Spirit and those in my world to speak to you. All that I ask on my own behalf and those who stand at my side is that you welcome us with the same respect as we afford you. It is always an honour to speak to anyone regardless of their age, the colour of their skin, their gender, their spiritual or intellectual awareness or any other determining factor. For my words are always directed to help, to guide, to uplift, to educate and to inspire and I know that the purpose of this talk with you tonight is just that.

For I have looked already into your hearts and I know that there are many questions that not only require answers but deserve answers. For what good is a question if it does not provide an answer? What good is it to have a mind that thinks and reasons if it cannot expect that reasoning to provide it with solutions? So without further ado I will invite you, in your own good time to put to me any questions that you believe deserve answers."

Matthew: "Err..............................."

White Feather: "I don't bite you know!"

Matthew: "What's it like in the spirit world?"

White Feather: "Well it depends where you are you know. I could say to you 'What's it like on the earth?" and you would say to me perhaps 'well it depends where I am, what I'm doing, who I'm with, what the weather is like' and all manner of things that influence us in our daily lives. In my world you know, it's not so different to your world. As to what it is like, that depends upon who you are and where you find yourself. Everyone in my world is where they are meant to be. You cannot be other than where you are intended to be because you actually place yourselves there by your actions and your thoughts and the things you do in your daily lives. They determine where you find yourself when you pass into my world. I am fortunate to find myself in a place that befits my own understanding, my own needs and desires and thus it is that I am surrounded by many, many good friends, people with whom I have come to share an affinity, whom I love and with whom I can share knowledge, discussion and humour.
My world is not so dissimilar to your world. We have flowers, plants and trees, rivers, streams and oceans, mountains to climb, valleys to walk amongst.......we have all manner of music, laughter, animals, children, adults, buildings, libraries, theatres, concert halls. We have great orchestras. We have writers, we have artists, we have painters. We have all manner of learned people and from this great variety of souls we have a world in which there is plenty to do, plenty to occupy us and a great deal of enjoyment and learning ahead of us. Does that help you?"

Matthew: "Yes thank you."

John: "What happens when you die?"

White Feather: "Well again you know, it depends upon circumstances but quite simply when you die the silver cord that joins your spirit body to your physical body, that is the body which you now have, which you think of as 'yourself', which you can touch and feel.....the body of the spirit is joined to that body by a silver cord, much as in the same way you were joined to your mother at birth......and when that cord is cut then 'death' occurs and you will find yourself in my world no longer having the physical body that you now have and think of as yourself. But you will be in your spirit body. You will still be 'yourself', you will still be John, but you will have a body that is without any pain, that is more refined and more beautiful than the one you now have and that is the body that will take you forward into your spirit life. Do you understand that?"

John: "Yes, thank you."

White Feather: "Are you happy?" [*Yes*] Good. You know it's good to be happy because you know, with happiness.......happiness breeds happiness. Where you have happiness, you create happiness around you and where there is happiness around you then that happiness comes back to you. So what you give out, you get back. So it's good to be happy."

Matthew: "It's a bit of a personal question but, how did you die?"

White Feather: "I have died many times! It depends which one you are referring to! I do not like to elaborate too much about past lives because I have died many times, as will you. Death is nothing at all. It matters not, the circumstances of one's passing, but what one does in one's life, the way that one lives one's life. That is what matters. That is what befits the soul for the journey that lies ahead of it and death you know, is nothing at all.
Do you remember Matthew, when you came in one night and you had been in the rain and your coat was wet and heavy with water, and you took it off......and as you took your coat off you felt lighter because your coat was so heavy? That's what it's like when you discard the physical body at death. It's like taking off a heavy overcoat or raincoat. You feel so much lighter and so much more refined. That's what death is about, being able to remove the heavy overcoat of the physical body to be left with the lighter, much finer refined form that is the true you, the spirit."

Being something of a film buff John then enquired of the guide if the Hollywood fim 'The Matrix' had any basis in reality:

John: "Is there such a thing as 'The Matrix"?"

White Feather: "It depends what you mean by 'The Matrix'? What do YOU mean by 'The Matrix'?"

John: "There's this film on DVD and there's this computer thing......I just wondered if there was such a thing?"

White Feather: "I don't know a great deal about computers. What I do know is that there is a kind of a web that joins everything together. The world in which you live is a type of matrix in that, it is not reality. It is not real. You think of it as real but it is an illusion, rather like the matrix of your film is an illusion. It is something that you step into as you come upon the earth. When you came through your mother, you came in to an illlusion. But to you it is real. It is only when you step out of it and come back into my world that you realise that my world in the real world and your world is the illusion. Think about that!"

Matthew: "If you had an illness when you were on earth, such as cancer or something and then died and went to the spirit world would you still have it in the spirit world?"

White Feather: "No. In my world there is no illness, no pain. The only illness is that which the mind thinks that it might have and it creates a temporary condition, a kind of illusion if you like, but that is very seldom, very rare because the spirit body cannot be ill. It carries no disease, it carries no pain. These things are, by and large, peculiar to your world. You have them in your world, not as a punishment from God but that you may learn through them. When you pass into my world all traces of illness and disease and disharmony that you once had in the physical body dissolve away and you are in the spirit body which is abundantly healthy and filled with wellbeing. So you need not have any fear or concern about that."

John: "Can I put one in......?"

White Feather: "Put one in by all means!"

John: "If I was a footballer when I was older and I died, would I be a footballer in the spirit world if I wanted to?"

White Feather: "Whatever you are now you will be when you die. If you die tonight you will be as you are tomorrow but in my world. If you die seventy or eighty or a hundred years from now, whatever you are then you will be when you pass into my world. Do you understand?"

John: "Yes."

White Feather: "If you happen to be a footballer in your world and you want to play football in my world then I won't stop you!"

Matthew followed with a somewhat deeper question concerning the nature of the creator which gave White Feather the opportunity to put a question of his own in order to prove a point to the youngster:

Matthew: "Who or what is God?"

White Feather: "How long have you got? That's a very good question and one which many learned minds and deep thinkers have pondered over for many aeons of time. There are many concepts of God, many ideas, many formulations, many thoughts apertaining to what the creator is. To me God is everything that is.

Everything that you see around you, everything that you are. The seats upon which you sit, the clothes that you wear, your body, the table, everything is God. God has many forms, but you know, the greatest expression of God is through you and I when we enable him to work through us in our lives.
How do we do that? By helping others. By giving service to them, by being kind to them, by giving them love. By helping them. That is when God really appears because he works through us.
Matthew, you play instruments, am I right?"

Matthew: "Yes."

White Feather: "What do you do when you play an instrument? You create a sound. That sound is a kind of expression of you, through that instrument. You are creating that sound through that instrument. You are making that music through that instrument. If you think of yourself as an instrument then God makes music through you, that others may hear it. That is a wonderful thing. So next time you play your trombone or piano or whatever instrument you take up and you make music through it, just remember my words and allow God to make his music through you by your kindliness, by your gentleness, by your helping others."

John: "We used to have a pet hamster Pip, but he died and I just wondered if he was OK?"

White Feather: "He is perfectly fine.......I haven't spoken to him recently but I can assure you that he is well because no creature in your world is ever extinguished at death. They live on in one form or another just as you will when you die and because you have had personal contact with Pip, because you have been able to give him your attention and your love then he will retain that form in passing to my my world, which he already has and he will one day return to you and you will see him as he is and remember him and recognise him because he cannot die."

Matthew: "Ben, one of my friends........his Grandad died and he gets very upset about it at school and everything.....I just wondered if he was alright?"

White Feather: "I can assure you as I already have with Pip that all who pass into my world are fine. They are taken care of, they are looked after. No one suffers in that way and you can reassure your friend Ben, if you choose you when you next meet with him, that all is well, all is fine and he has no need to concern himself with anyone who has passed because they are still there, they are still close. They are still the same person that they always were and again, one day when the time is right he will be able to meet with him and they will converse in the same way as they always did. Tell him not to worry, he will see his beloved Grandfather again."

John: "If I died and went to the spirit world, could I come back and see people?"

White Feather: "Yes indeed you can. You will go to the spirit world, in fact you are already in the spirit world although you don't realise it. You know, what happens is that it is like eating an orange. When you peel off the skin, what is left inside is the real orange that you eat and enjoy. When you die it is rather like peeling away the physical body and being left with the inside piece, which is the spirit. When you are in my world you have.....I won't say unlimited powers......but you have powers that you cannot express here upon the earth. You can travel to distant places merely by thinking of them. You can fly if you wish, through the air. You can fly through space. You can visit anyone, within reason, that you choose, as long as you have earned the right to do that, but you most certainly will be able to come back and visit any loved ones or friends who still remain here upon the earth. Even though they may not necessarily be able to see you, you will be able to see them.
But the best part is that you can, if you choose to, send your thoughts to them either directly or through a medium rather like the one that I am speaking through now to talk to those people on the earth, to let them know that John is OK, John is still alive. John is still the same cheeky boy that he always was! And you know, that is a wonderful thing to be able to do that. [Laughter from John] You see, I am making you laugh now. I must be doing something right."

Gaining confidence in the spirit guide and also in their own ability to formulate interesting questions each of the boys moved swiftly to enquire of the teacher when their turn arrived:

Matthew: "You know there are famous people here on earth, well would they still be famous in the spirit world but on a wider scale?"

White Feather: " Fame doesn't mean anything in my world Matthew. In your world famous people are pictured in the media, in your newspapers on your television set, they are spoken of, they are photographed, but in my world they are not afforded the same fame as they are in your world because what matters is not how many photographs or newspapers they are in, but what they are really like in here [White Feather points to his chest] what they are like as a person, that is what matters. There are some famous people in my world but they are not the same famous people as you have in your world because they are famous for a different reason. They are famous for the service that they have given whilst upon your earth. The people they have helped, the souls they have touched. You have to remember, all of you, that it is the spirit that matters, not the physical body. Not that someone has been a footballer, has acted in films or is seen to be this or that. What matters is what they truly are. That is what counts, that is what means everything in my world."

John: "Is the spirit world like our world today?"

White Feather: "The spirit world is very much like your world today but you have to understand that it has many levels, rather like the rungs of a ladder. The first rung after your world is called 'The Summerland' and that is very much like your world. We call it The Summerland because it is as if it is always summertime, rather like it is now in your world, where the sun is shining, the birds are singing and everything is light. The higher you go up the rungs of the ladder the more beautiful it becomes. The higher you go the less it looks like your world and the more it looks like my world. My world has so many things that your world does not have. Shall I tell you one of them?"

John: "Yes please!"

White Feather: "We have colours in my world that you don't have in your world. Matthew, you like pencils don't you?"

Matthew: "Yes."

White Feather: "Next time you look at your box of pencils, with all their colours, all the colours of the rainbow, try to imagine a colour that isn't in that box of pencils. You may find it very difficult, but I can say to you John and Matthew that there are colours in my world that you don't have in your world. They don't exist in that box of pencils or that rainbow. That's a wonderful thing and you will only discover those colours when you pass into my world. There are other things also that you don't have. We do not have sufficient time to list them all but I will tell you one! John, you like music don't you?"

John: "Yes."

White Feather: "When you put your music on, you put your headphones on and you listen to that range of music, the voices and the instruments and the sounds........in my world there are sounds that you can't hear in your world. There are sounds much deeper and much higher, much broader, much more of an enriched sound. Even the flowers have a sound. When you look at a flower, it has a colour but it also has a sound. It has its own music. You can reach out to pick a flower and as you do so, that flower will turn its head toward you and it will give off the most wonderful scent of perfume and the most delicate sound. It something that you don't have upon the earth. These are things of great beauty that await you but you will only discover them when you are ready to do so."

Matthew: "Is there a man called Jesus and is he really God's son?"

White Feather: "I don't refer to Jesus in the same way that your Bible refers to Jesus. I speak sometimes of the Nazarene who *is* not, who *was* not, the son of God. You are all the sons and daughters of God. You are all part of God, the Great Spirit. The Nazarene was one who came upon your earth and around which have been built many lies, many falsehoods, many stories and many myths that have elevated him to some kind of 'God' who cannot be touched, who is portrayed by many in your world as being unique, as being the son of God. He never wanted that. He never intended that. The Nazarene is not, was not, cannot be, unique. You are all special, you are all unique for you are all the 'sons of God'. What the Nazarene did, or in your language, what Jesus did Matthew, you can do. He didn't create miracles. What he did was within the laws of the spirit, that he understood how to operate. You can do the same if you choose to."

John: "Is your day like ours?"

White Feather: "I doubt very much that my day is like yours John. I have much to occupy me. For one thing you know, I don't stay in bed until lunchtime! [much laughter]. Let me say that I have a great deal to occupy me. I have a lot of friends with whom I have great conversations and laughter. I too, listen to music. I too, read books. I too, go to concerts and places where I can learn. I too, like to study and I too, like to visit different places. So I have a great deal to occupy me. We have no time to sit idly back, there is so much to do, so much to learn, so much to discover, so much to unfold. We are never bored, never tired. Always there is some new challenge or new exciting thing to discover."

Matthew: "Today we went to Portsmouth Old Harbour and I wanted to go on the Mary Rose but it was too expensive, but I just wondered if you knew anything about it?"

White Feather: "I know about history, if that is what you are referring to. There are many, many pages written in history throughout time. If you could put history into one volume or one book it would span from here to eternity, but what you have to remember Matthew, and I know you are an advocate of learning and that history is something that interests you, is that the history that is written in your books is not always the real history. You have to learn to sift through and find the truth. There are two kinds of history you know, there is the history that is recognised in your world as being the 'official' history that everyone is told and learns about, then there is the real history that is written upon the pages of time and life itself. Upon what is referred to in my world as 'The Akashic Records'. These are records of the real history as it happened, not as it is painted by scholars in your world.
So, as long as you remember that you have to use your reasoning mind and sift out what you consider to be inaccurate and what you consider to be accurate then you will find, more often than not, the real history. Do you understand that?"

Matthew: "Yes."

It was evident that the White Feather was enjoying the discourse as much as the two young boys and was taking every opportunity to take a simple question and expand upon it to encompass aspects which the children had not thought of, something which he often does with adults too! The questioning continued after the teacher enquired of the boys health and temperament:

White Feather: "Good. Are you happy still? I'm not boring you am I?"

Matthew and John: "No!"

John: "Do need to drink like us?"

White Feather: "I can have a drink if I wish to. I can eat if I wish to. I have no need to. You have to eat John, you have to drink because if you did not, your physical body would not grow and eventually you would find yourself passing into my world before you should do. In my world, I don't need to eat and drink because my body does not have the same internal organs as yours does and I get my sustenance and my energies straight from the Great Spirit. However, if I desire to pick a fruit from a tree and eat it, provided the tree has given me permission, I can do so and that fruit is so wonderful. It fills me with energy. It fills my whole body with colour and light. Sometimes I do that not because I have to, but because I enjoy doing so and let me tell you this John, when I pick a fruit from that tree, that tree sings to me. That tree is so grateful that it offers me that fruit. As I reach out my hand to the branch, so the branch reaches out to me and says 'take me, take me' and that is a wonderful exchange from one form to another. So if I want to do that I can, but I don't have to."

Amanda: "Have you got any more questions?"

Matthew: "Yes......yes."

White Feather: "There's no stopping them!"

Matthew: "Could you send something to earth?"

White Feather: "Could I send something to earth? In what form? Do you mean an object, a thought or.........?"

Matthew: "An object."

White Feather: "It is possible but I have to employ the use of certain energies to enable me to do that and the conditions have to be right. I have done that before with the help of those who stand at my side. Sometimes you know, the one through whom I speak and Sunflower witness a form, a feather, sometimes in their house or on an item of clothing or wherever I choose to place it and it has come from my world to their world. So I can do that if I wish. The object that I choose and its movement from my world to your world has to be done very carefully because nothing happens by chance and the energies that we use have to be very carefully calculated and orchestrated, in order to enable the object to move from one dimension to another. You have a programme don't you, in your world, called 'Star Trek'?"

Matthew: "Yes."

White Feather: "Am I right? You see I am very switched on to these things! In that programme it is possible for one person to dematerialise in one place and appear in another place, kind of 'beaming from one place to another'. It is rather like that with what we call 'apports' when we are able to beam an object from our world to your world, or from one place in your world to another place in your world, or even from your world to my world. Do you understand that? So we can do it. I don't choose to do it very often because it is a complex procedure and I don't need to keep proving to Sunflower and to this instrument the spirit reality because they already know of it."

Amanda: "Do you want to ask something else?"

White Feather: "I think you do......."

Matthew: "You don't have to.......but could you do it now?"

White Feather: "I cannot do it at this moment because as I said a few moments ago, it has to be carefully planned and now is not the right time or circumstances. Perhaps at some point in the future we will arrange something."

John: "Do you need and do you have money to buy things?"

White Feather: "We don't use money in my world because when we want something, provided it is appropriate, provided we have earned the right to receive it, provided it does not harm anyone or ourselves then we can have it. We have merely to think and it is there. It is our thoughts that create it. If, for example, we want to build a house or an extension to our house, we can first of all think in our minds, that which we wish to have. Then by consultation with those who are more adept in these matters than we are, we can choose the design and the materials and by the power of thought that is brought into being and it is built, just as a house is built in your world. So we can have things without money. We don't have to pay for them. But you know John, in real terms everything has a price. Everything has a price and we have to earn things. If we haven't earned them or the right to have them then they do not become ours and the law that governs this is that the more that you give to others John, the more that it comes back to you, rather like a boomerang. John, you like football.......when you kick a ball against a wall what happens?"

John: "It comes back."

White Feather: "It comes back to you.......and that is what happens with your thoughts. When you think a thought it comes back to you. Always remember that. You don't always think of it there and then, you are not always aware of it but whatever you do, whether it is a nasty thought, whether it is a loving thought, it comes back to you. It's worth remembering."

The next question from the younger of the two boys, evoked an eloquent response from the spirit visitor when asked his age:

John: "I don't mean to be rude, but how old are you?"

White Feather: "I am older than the hills, older than the blades of grass. I am older than many things that you see around you but you know, despite my advancing years I am younger than you. There's a riddle! You do not have to measure time with age in my world because in truth John, I am ageless, you are ageless. You cannot remember John, what you were before you came through your mother, before you were born. You have no memory of that now. You cannot remember the last time that you died and there will be a time when you will be able to look back in my world upon all your past lives, all the things that you have gone through, all the experiences that you've had and they will stretch out like a road, a railway track into the distance. As you look back you won't be able to see where they start because they go back so far. That is how old you are. You're older than I am! You're older than I, do you know that? But really you are younger because you're only as you truly are, as you create yourself. The wonderful thing about being part of the spirit is that you never die. You never reach the end of your existence. You never reach the finish and there is never a time or place where you cease to exist. If you had a candle here now and you lit it, you could with your fingers, just snuff it out and its flame would be no more. You cannot do that with the tiny spark of the spirit. It has always been alight within you and can never be extinguished. Do you understand that?"

Matthew: "Can you see into the future?"

White Feather: "I can see a little further than you because you see Matthew, you stand at the moment in the valley and I stand a little way up the mountainside. So I can see a little further unto the horizon than you can. It doesn't mean I'm better than you, it simply means that I can see a little further and you know, in real terms Matthew, the future, the past and the present are all one. They exist in the same moment. Now that is something of a riddle for you. It is something for you to think about. Let me put it to you this way; if you take a piece of string and put it out upon the floor, it has a beginning, it has a middle and it has an end and you can think of that as being like time - past, present and future. If you take that string and put it into a circle, into a loop, then where is the past? Where is the present? Where is the future? They are all there at the same time. Do you understand that? And that is what it's like in my world. We are able to see all things, to a point - past, present and future and the more refined we become, the greater evolved we become, the more of the circle we can see, the farther into the future we can see. It's all a matter of where we are and of who we are at any moment of time." *(see overleaf)*

White Feather seldom speaks of his earthly incarnations, but the final question teased a somewhat revealing reply that gave the guide the opportunity to weave a tale relating to his last life upon the earth:

Matthew: "Where was your favourite place when you were living on the earth?"

White Feather: "I have many, many favourite places, but I will share a secret, just with you. In one of my last incarnations, one of my favourite places was a river that was surrounded by trees and it had a wonderful grassy bank that swept down to the water. The river itself was very still here even though the waters were moving and we could see into the depths below, although the water wasn't that deep and we could wade out into it. I remember even now, walking into the water in my bare feet and standing there and feeling the water moving between my legs. The coolness of it......and listening to the rustle of the wind as it passed through the leaves of the trees. I remember looking and seeing how the sunlight dappled through them and how each little leaf seemed to dance with the wind that passed through it. I looked into the water and I could see the fish swimming. They would swim between my legs. I could touch them. I could put my hand there and feel them. I could stroke them. This was a wonderful place to be and it was a place of great peace. A place where I used to go when I was troubled of mind and you know Matthew, you should have a place, it can be anywhere you want it to be. It can even be in your own house or it could be somewhere else. Where you can go when your mind is troubled and you can just be relaxed."

Recognising that the session was reaching its conclusion, the spirit teacher issued forth his thanks to all present and bade farewell to the small gathering. Both the youngsters seemed to have enjoyed their chat with the wise spirit

messenger and for days afterwards they referred to things which he had told them. As so often happens, the words of White Feather linger on in the mind like seeds planted by a loving hand, one day to germinate and grow into something even more profound and beautiful.

It could be argued that today's young people would gain considerably more from broader spiritual teachings than those imposed by manistream doctrines within the education system. It is interesting to note that following this sitting John in particular, whilst taking part in classroom discussions questioned what was being taught as 'truth' by his teachers. We are pleased to note that the enhanced knowledge John received from the spirit mentor has taken his thinking to a deeper level of understanding.

Fig 1. **Linear Time**

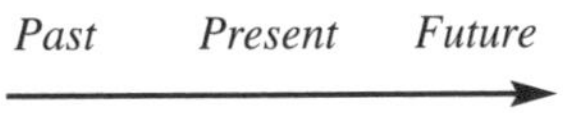

Fig 2. **Radial Time**

Past, Present and Future combine to prdouce an 'eternal now'. Where does one end and another commence?

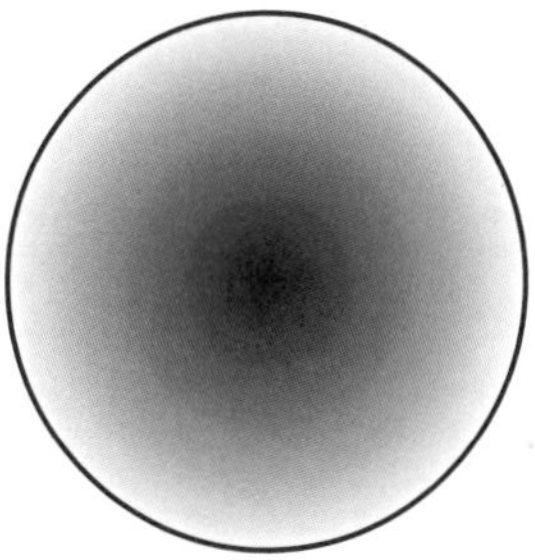

Concepts of Time

These simple illustrations may help to explain the point that White Feather was endeavouring to make when he spoke of past, present and future being one. Upon the earth we live in linear time (Fig 1.) but spirit world time, particularly at the higher levels or planes combines all three aspects as an ever present 'now' (Fig.2). It is as if time itself broadens as we ascend to higher dimensions rather like an upturned cone. (Fig.3)

Fig 3. **Conical Time**

In this 3D model of Radial Time, Linear Time (Earth time) is represented by the line along which the cone moves and the cone itself is Radial Time with the broader diameter representing the eternal 'now', scaling down to a singular point where past, present and future stretch out.

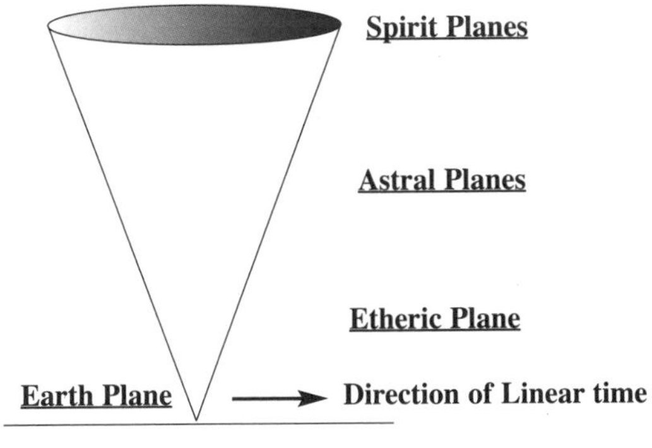

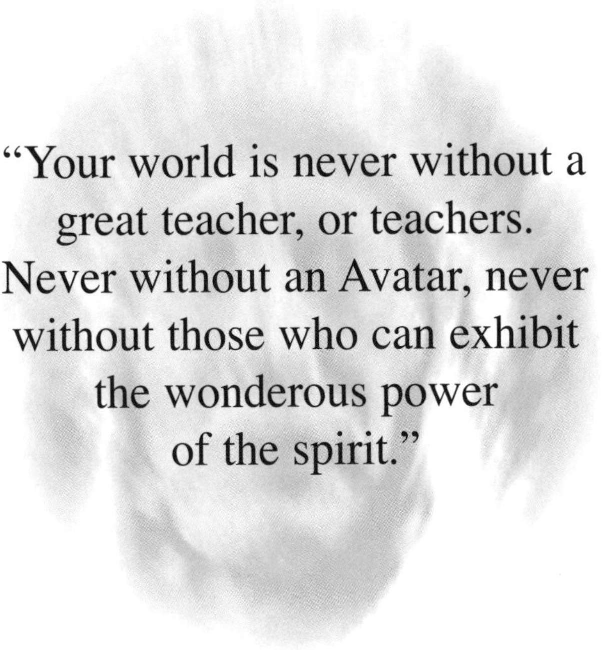

"Your world is never without a great teacher, or teachers. Never without an Avatar, never without those who can exhibit the wonderous power of the spirit."

Laughter and Illumination 9

White Feather is seldom anything other than his usual calm, considerate, humourous, eloquent and wise self. But on this warm spring evening in a rural setting, facing a small but enthusiastic audience of eager minds he was truly 'on form'. Dispatching wise words and deeper teachings he weaved a spell of delight across the assembly with a mixture of wit, gentle teasing and profound revelation to provide those present with a wonderful demonstration of the true power of communication with the spirit world. He began in his customary way, with a short address:

White Feather: "I thought that I would give you as much time as possible tonight to ask the questions that you have but I want to say just a few words if I may as I commence my talk with you. You know, you receive information in a variety of ways, upon many levels. Not only through the five physical senses with which you are familiar, but also on many other levels of your being, some which are completely unconscious to your conscious awareness - you have no immediate knowledge that you are receiving that information. Nevertheless you do so and even in my world we receive information in a number of ways. But you know, observation which again is existing upon many levels is a wonderous gift with which you are endowed. The ability to observe, whether it be through your eyes, through your ears, through your senses of touch and smell and taste or even through your other senses which are referred to so often as being psychic or 'sixth senses', but which nevertheless are perfectly natural parts of your being, enable you to have an input of information which you then have to decipher, unravel, toy with, reason and wrestle with in order to make some kind of judgement or assessment of what it is you are receiving. And even in my world we have to employ the methods which are not too dissimilar to the ones which you do in that we bring to bear our reasoning minds upon that which we encounter. You will find that this process of thinking, reasoning and analysis allied with your own ability to sense, which is beyond intellect, beyond mind, offers you the opportunity to come into deeper levels of understanding and awareness.

I want to just begin tonight by referring to a number of experiences which I myself have encountered, not only when I was upon your world many, many years ago but also in my world, through observation. And it is through this that I want to point out tonight a deeper principle of which you may not be immediately aware. Let me explain myself further. You know, I recall once a memory of when I was upon your world watching creatures, I think you would refer to them as beavers and they were doing what beavers do best - they were building a dam. Their ingenuity, their skill, their awareness, their capacity to construct a bridgehead across a flowing river was something at which I marvelled as I watched them tirelessly, ceaselessly, day upon day, week upon week construct this fortress across the river, which eventually lead to it being dammed to the point where that which was beyond it ceased to flow with such ferocity and came to be a gentle trickle.

I watched these creatures and I thought upon their work and in much the same way I have watched spiders weaving their web and wondered at their immense ability to create something so fine and yet so delicately strong as to withstand the greatest storms, the greatest winds. So refined, so clever. And through this I had the thought; what is it within these creatures and indeed within all forms that almost compels them to do this? Is it just instinctive nature? Is it just the remnants or the hereditary traits of evolution? Of course that is part of it but far more important than that, and the same trait which I have observed within humanity is this of aspiration. Now what is aspiration? What is it to aspire? Aspiration is an essential part of the spirit and if ever you want evidence that life is indeed endless, that you are all endowed with part of the Great Spirit you have only to look at aspiration. Because every creature, every form upon your world aspires to greater things.

Now you may say to me 'well of course there is no link between the aspiration of a beaver building a dam to one who is aspiring to be a great teacher or a poet or a painter, but there is because it is part of the same innate desire to better the self. And if you look and examine the principles within aspiration they are essentially the desire for happiness, the desire to better oneself and the desire to grow into something greater. You will find that even in the most simplest forms there is a desire, there is an inherent trait to aspire to something greater than itself. Even if it is watching a termite build its house or watching a beaver, or a spider build a web, you will find there is some measure of aspiration in that.

In humanity there is a greater ability to aspire because man has the ability to think and to reason, to examine, to question, to analyse and also to unfold his divine spiritual nature to higher things. In man, that aspiration finds an even greater tool to express itself. Now you who have enquiring minds may say to me 'well this is all very well, but what of the one who does not aspire to anything? What of the 'evil' mind? What of the one who is so engrossed in putting down others, in trampling upon them, who is filled with hatred and evil? This may shock you, but let me say to you that even these minds.........even hatred is but love which has not recognised itself and operates on its negative aspect. If you think about this, the one who is purportrating hatred towards another does so because in some perverted, misguided way they seek to change their world into something that they desire, something that they want at the expense of another. I am not saying this is right, but it is a fact. And you will find that at the root of even negative behaviour, even behaviour which comes from the ego self, the lower mind, is the higher aspirational force seeking to express itself and yet being somewhat thwarted by that individual. It becomes turned into something which it is not. It becomes the opposite of that which it seeks to express.

Now I realise that perhaps this is very deep teaching for you and you have to think upon it but that is what I always ask you to do, to think, to reason, to examine it. Because anything that we say to you, if it causes your reasoning to revolt, then of course you must put it aside until such time that you can perhaps reconsider it. But you know, if you look at everything around you and this is all that we are asking you to do, you will find that always there is that desire for betterment and every one of you, whatever your situation, whatever your plight, whatever your life at this moment, if I say to you 'what is it intrinsically that you want?' the answer inevitably would be that you want to be happy and happiness is an intrinsic part of aspiration, which is essential, which is of spirit. You *are* God, and the true state of your being which you have not yet reached, is one of pure bliss. Of happiness, of joyfulness, of knowledge, of truth and of light. The fact that you don't have that is only because you have not yet reached it and have not yet remembered what you already know. Think upon these things and you will find that what I am saying to you is fact."

Sensing that there were many questions waiting to be asked, the spirit wasted no time in prompting Amanda to invite the first recipient to make their enquiry, which as it turned out was quite a complex one:

Questioner: "Good evening White Feather and thank you for being with us again. As usual I've got more questions than answers! In your culture and many primal cultures on earth, the concept of the divine feminine is often portrayed in Goddess form. How important is this concept to humankind at this time and how can we contribute to the demise of the patriarchal system in which we have our being?"

White Feather: "Hmmm....you're the thinker aren't you? I've spoken to you before! It is also a pleasure for me and a delight to have that opportunity again because I always seek to address enquiring minds.

I think the essential part of the Goddess syndrome or concept is that it offers man an alternative, a balance to the male dominated society in which you live where over-emphasis has been placed upon the male form and the male energy for many, many centuries of time much to the detriment if I may say so of the female energy. As to the usage of the term 'Goddess', that is only a semantic term, although I am aware of the implications behind it. The danger in all of these restrictive, narrative terms is that one should keep a sense of proportion. It would be equally wrong to place emphasis on the female to the detriment of the male as it has been to place emphasis on the male to the detriment of the female. So one has to always strive to get a balance. Terms such as male and female themselves and 'Goddess' and 'God' are of course semantic terms that can often create something of a confusion because the Great Spirit is neither male or female and yet works through aspects of both, each which have their own particular affinities, their strengths and their weaknesses. One should always strive in my opinion, to obtain a balance between the two. To recognise that each of the species, each of the forms has gifts to offer the whole but not divorce oneself from the fact that the Great Spirit *is as it is* and is neither male nor female yet expresses through all.

As to breaking down the traits that have been built up over centuries, that is something which will require a great deal of time and patience and effort. Knowledge of course, and truth, are the energies which one must seek to bring and to employ, to break down the old ways of doing things and the old ways of thinking. But you know yourself that 'old habits die hard' and with the institutionalised religions that have been built up over centuries it is difficult to change this overnight. There has to be a change but it is slow in coming. It is only through those who can seek to liberate, to harmonise both aspects - the male and the female and to go beyond religion, to go beyond dogma, beyond creedalism, beyond ceremony, beyond ritual to embrace the totality of life in all its glory and richness, only these individuals and only by these means will this institutionalised religion be gradually chipped away and replaced by something that is more holistic in nature. I wish it could be so tomorrow, but it cannot. We have to realise that it is a slow process. But I think in some ways, despite the materialism that is unfolding daily around you, there is an undercurrent of change in the air and man has the opportunity now if he takes it, to bring this about."

Questioner: "Greetings White Feather. In eastern philosophy it is believed that the aim of the incarnated soul is to escape the wheel of death and rebirth and merge completely with the creator. Another school of thought says that we should be glad to keep reincarnating because we will ultimately be absorbed into the impersonal consciousness and our individuality will be gone. The question is; should we be happy or dissapointed to find ourselves reincarnated?"

White Feather: "I think there are aspects of both. But one must recognise that it is not a failure to be reincarnated because when that facet reintroduces itself into the body of matter it does so for a purpose. It is not a question of failure, it is a question of opportunity and every reincarnation presents that soul with the means to quicken itself, to outwork a Karmic debt and to emerge more purified, refined and enlightened, so that when it connects with its higher self the lesson has been learned and it can go on in my world to higher things.

The cycle of reincarnation, of birth and death and birth again, is not an endless one. There will come a time when there is no need for any facet of yourself to be reintroduced again into the body of matter and that will be a joyous occasion for then the body of matter and the physical universe will have served their purpose and you can continue to experience life and to progress in the higher realms of the spirit world.

As to the question of individuality, do you think that the droplet of water loses its individuality when it falls into the ocean? There are some who may think this is the case but it is not. There is no loss of individuality. I know of no great soul, however evolved they have become, however far they have progressed, however enlightened, who has lost their individuality as they have merged closer to a union with the divine. Rather, that individuality is strengthened as all the facets become known and recognised as one whole.

So do not fear loss of self, loss of individuality, but rather a refinement of it, a greater awareness and development of the spirituality within. Does that help you?"

Questioner: "Yes it does White Feather but I was wondering then, following on from that should the incarnated soul be actively working to try and perfect the imperfections that they have?"

White Feather: "Well this again is perhaps a deeper question than you may have first realised because the incarnated soul - let us speak now of your conscious awareness whilst you are in the body - may not at a conscious level be aware of why it has come and may not consciously, actively be able to participate and pursue that pathway of enlightenment. However, the soul knows. The greater self, the higher self, the soul, knows why that facet has come and it is the soul that will pursue that directive through that lifetime. Whether or not you become aware of it consciously within that lifetime does not matter necessarily. The fact is, you will be following that pathway which the soul has directed. Indeed let me say to you that very often the opposite is required. Because if you were aware of the need to pursue a particular pathway that may negate your undertaking certain experiences which you may regard as negative or painful, or harmful. But it may be those very experiences that equip the soul with the necessary impetus to be quickened. Do you understand that?"

Questioner: "Yes I do."

White Feather: "This is why individuals go into circumstances which cause them great pain and suffering, sometimes unwittingly, sometimes deliberately. You say 'why would they do this? If they had full knowledge they would not go surely, into the jaws of despair and pain? But the soul knows. The consciousness does not. The soul knows and that is why it is important that they undertake that experience, to learn from it and to be quickened. Do you see that? Does that fulfil your thirst?"

Questioner: "Oh yes I do. That's fantastic. Thank you very much White Feather."

The next question concerned the nature of angels but it appeared that the lady who asked it was not altogether happy with White Feather's reply:

Questioner: "Good evening. Can you tell us about angels?"

White Feather: "Well, I can speak about angels but it may not appeal to some minds here. Because to me the angelic is not the same as it is sometimes portrayed in certain fashionable quarters upon the earth. There is a great desire at the moment in some areas to proliferate the story of the angelic realms, to personalise them, to offer symbols that are angelic in nature and in some way to almost deify them. But to me, I have never yet encountered an angel with wings in my world! Nor do I expect to. But there are many angels who are not as you would think. They do not have wings but they are angels within their hearts and their minds because they are beloved souls. They are great souls, great teachers. They inspire us and they inspire humanity. They are Avatars. They are the teachers of light who come to draw close to your world, sometimes through a group soul, sometimes to individuals, sometimes to nations upon your world, to bring light, to bring healing and to bring guidance. It is a pity that man has to individualise them and personalise them to suit his needs.

But if it is that man seeks to think of angelic forms in this way and it helps him, then so be it. If it brings him closer to the truth, if he finds comfort, if he finds understanding, if he finds healing, if he finds light through it then so be it. Who am I to say no? Do you understand that?"

Questioner: "Hmmmm...."

White Feather: "But you are not happy with it?"

Questioner: "Do angels not walk on earth?"

White Feather: "Of course they do. But they don't have wings. They do walk upon earth. There are many angels upon the earth who belong to no creed, no religion, who have no recognition in a public sense. An angel could walk into this room and you would not be aware of it. A great soul could be sitting next to you on a bus or train or an aeroplane and you would not know it. But they are a great soul.

You will find that the greatest souls are the humblest. They do not find their way into governments, into being a president of this or a leader of that. They work in the stillness, in the quietness, unseen, unheard and yet they reach many souls. Those to me are the greatest angels of all."

Knowing that the silence which greeted his answer was indicative of disagreement the guide launched a cynical attack upon the more commercial aspects of the 'new age' movement:

White Feather: "Ask yourself this sister, ask yourself this........what is it, this building up within this new age philosophy of the angelic realms? What is it of this that leads to so much financial gain for so many? That may perhaps be a little cynical but I have to say to you that many of the 'ism's', many of the movements, many of the creeds even in your modern age have their basis in egotism and financial gain. I am not saying that applies to everyone within them but in certain areas this is the case and you must have a discerning mind to decide whether or not to accept something or to reject it. It is not for me to tell you. It is not for me to say that you must believe my words and not believe in angels. I would never do that. What I am pointing out to you is that the angels with wings as they are portrayed in your world I have never encountered in my world. But you must decide for yourself which pathway you seek to walk. Many paths you know, lead to the same place ultimately and there are many ways to find truth."

Questioner:"Can I just clarify, when you said 'they walk the earth', are you saying that they are invisible to us or do they take a human form?"

White Feather: "Both. There are many invisible forms. There are many here, now in this sanctuary. You think that your seats are only half filled and yet I see that this place is overflowing with forms. Let me say to you this, and I have said this before; I haven't counted them by the way, but I know that there are over a thousand people here in this of your temple and yet you see but twenty or thirty with your eyes. So there are many drawn. Not all of great knowledge or understanding. Some of ignorance. Some come as teachers, some come to learn, but nevertheless they are here. Some of a higher mind, incarnate into your world in the physical sense. Your world is never without a great teacher, or teachers. Never without an Avatar, never without those who can exhibit the wonderous power of the spirit. Humanity is never left alone, never cut adrift. You must always remember this, the links with the higher are always there."

Questioner:"I would like to ask what is the nature of mind and what is the difference between mind and consciousness?"

White Feather: "You have to remember that semantics comes into operation here and what one may refer to as consciousness and mind another may think of in a different light. Try to recognise that you are in essence, spirit. You *are* spirit. That is part of the Great Spirit that has always been and always will be. That spirit, that energy, that light, that love, that wholeness which is everything, comes through mind and that mind operates in a physical sense, through a physical, material body. Within that it gains consciousness and so becomes aware of itself. Now, by consciousness, let us say that even in the 'lower forms' of life as they are often referred to......the insect or the fish or the bird......there is consciousness because they have the ability to think. But they cannot reason in the same way that man can reason. So man has a higher degree of consciousness because the physical brain of human beings facilitates a greater expression of mind within it and gives rise to a greater consciousness, an ability to think and reason, analyse and question. And so you have spirit, operating through mind resulting in consciousness in degrees. An amoeba, a sub-atomic particle, does not have the same degree of consciousness as an evolved soul and yet they are still linked. They still have spirit within them, they still have mind within them but they do not have the same degree of expression of consciousness. So you have to understand the meanings of these words in the context of which we are speaking. Does that help you?"

Questioner: "Yes it does."

White Feather: "I like questions like that because they are very deep, as are they all tonight and that pleases me. Thank you."

Questioner: "Welcome, it's a pleasure to be here tonight. As I walk my pathway upon this earth plane I come across many beings, spiritual beings who do their best and work for your creator. Could you just help me to understand why so many of those spiritual beings who give of their time, of their love, of their energies to be who they are, why they are hurting so much within their physical bodies?"

White Feather: "You know, very often you find this pattern repeats, where you have one who is enlightened, so generous, so giving, so loving, so kind, so thoughtful, who attempts to unfold and express the divine within them in service to others and who themselves suffer. There are many, many reasons for this. Suffering in itself of course is not a punishment in any form but by its very nature it brings out the divine. It quickens the soul in that it enables that individual to dig deep within themselves and because they themselves have been hurt and touched by pain, so their desire is even more intense to serve.

You will find for example, that there is no healer who themselves has not felt pain, who has not been hurt either physically, mentally or emotionally and it is that this is the catalyst if you like. It is this which is the crucible, which contains the greater desire to serve. It is this which brings it about, this very suffering, this pain, this hurt. And this we find repeated time and time again. It is also if you like, a way of demonstrating to humanity that even though they have these wonderous gifts of the spirit, and can demonstrate clairvoyance, healing, philosophy and all the gifts of the spirit, they are themselves only human and they are not gods.

Man has a tendency to place anyone with any ability upon a pedestal and worship, as was the case with the Nazarene and many other great prophets and seers who have been placed upon these pedestals and worshipped from afar as some kind of gods. They are not. You will find that those who are the greatest servants themselves are the ones who are very often hurt and who demonstrate their fallibility and that is a message to humanity.
So it is a lesson if you like, that is applied upon many levels to help humanity to come into an understanding of its own nature. Does that make sense to you ?"

Questioner: "Very much so."

Following a slight dip in the energies the spirit communicator once again introduced a note of humour into the proceedings with a question for the audience:

White Feather: "Am I fullfilling expectations? Am I coming up to the mark?"

Audience:[laughing] "Yes!"

Questioner: "Some of us believe, either rightly or wrongly, that before anything comes into manifestation it has to be created by thought in the realms of mind. Is this correct and if so can you explain the process and its importance to us?"

White Feather: "I know what you are inferring. In the strictest sense I have to say no, but I know what you mean and let me justify that by saying to you that the very nature of the spirit is beyond *even mind* and the spirit can create. The spirit can create without mind. The spirit can bring into being *without the thought process of mind, without the intellect of mind, without the direct application of mind.* The spirit can bring into being spontaneously. Now I know that may be difficult to understand in itself because everything that you do seems to be channelled through mind in some way but it is possible in the truest sense to go beyond mind. You must recognise, and I refer to the previous questioner, that spirit operates through mind and one can through pure *beingness* create. It is the spirit that is the ultimate creator, not mind. But I know the context in which you frame your question in that everything in the tangible world, the material world, has to have first been created in the unseen before it can manifest and there is a degree of truth in that. I myself, have said the phrase 'everything that is around you has been thought of' and that is because in the world in which you live you are partakers in creation. Those of you who have any knowledge or understanding of the sub-atomic world, or quantum physics as you refer to it, will understand and have a grasp of the concept that 'the observer and the observed are linked'. As man observes, as he thinks, as he brings into being so he creates in the material sense This is a difficult concept if you do not understand the operation of nature through the sub-atomic levels and if you are clinging to the old school of thought that the universe around you is in some way separate from you. It is not. You are an intrinsic part of life itself and man's unconscious processes, even the unconscious mind, brings into being matter, brings into being 'reality'. This is what your scientists are beginning to discover and reveal to you in some quarters. But man has yet to grasp fully and comprehend the importance of this knowledge."

Amanda: "If I could just ask a question here, talking about quantum physics and how the observer might be able to change what they are observing, is the difference of what might be changed in that operation the 'intent' behind it and if it is, is that from the spirit element of that person or can they from a mind perspective, actually change what they are looking at?"

White Feather: "It is the intent that plays a greater part than the mere operation of mind. It has been found I believe, in some experiments that your scientists have undertaken where an experiment can be recorded and observed in one place and yet it is different in another, even though the same criteria has been applied, because circumstances are subtly different and the experimenter themselves may be different than the original. So even though, through the tenets of science for something to be proven it must be duplicated and provable time and time again, when you are dealing in the realm of quantum this is not always possible because the different nature of the experimenters affects the results. It is not always their minds directly, but their *intent* behind it. That is what is important."

Amanda: "If that is an explanation for absent healing then for instance, does the intent of the giver and the way that the recipient is open to it make a difference in the quality of the healing?"

White Feather: "It can do to a degree but it is not the be all and end all. Naturally the one who is giving the healing, or the 'healer' as they are referred to even though the energy very often comes through them, not from them......the very fact that they have that ability means that they are of a particular constitution. They have compassion. They have the desire to serve and to heal. That very often is constant, it is unchanging. Whether or not that healing is effective depends upon many, many factors. If we take for example the case of healing that is given to a child or an animal who has no conscious awareness and grasp of the principles, who is not even aware that the healing is reaching them, yet it is successful......that is one application where faith alone does not come into the equation. It is not necessary. The fact is, if you have one who has the ability to tune in to the healing force, whether that is the natural force that is around all of life, or whether it is the healing spiritual force that comes from the Great Spirit and is channelled through helpers in my world, if they have that ability to tune into it then it will go to its recipients if the recipient has earned the right to be healed and there is no blockage or prevention from that healing power."

Considering that the trance evening was taking place in a predominantly Christian area of the country, it was no surprise that a question about Jesus and the Bible was forthcoming. Equally, the response of the guide was not entirely unpredictable as his views on orthodox religion are well documented:

Question: "Is Jesus at present re-writing the Bible and was it the Christ who was crucified and not Jesus? Are they two different people? No one seems to know."

White Feather: "Again, I am not happy about 're-writing the Bible' because it wasn't particularly written very well in the first place! *[loud audience laughter]* Why repeat the same mistakes! But in all seriousness, what I refer to as the Christ energy is separate from the Nazarene or the Jesus as you refer. The Christ energy is a spiritual energy that operates and has operated through many upon your world, the Nazarene being one, even though that individual has been deified and placed upon a pedestal and worshiped out of all proportion to what he actually was and there has been a great deal of distortion and myth surrounding that story. But the Christ energy is a higher spiritual energy that seeks to operate and does operate through many. Even now in your world, it operates and seeks to make itself manifest to humanity in the form of enlightenment and healing and wisdom. So you have to separate the Christ from the man. They are not the same. They have become merged in the confusion and the myth over centuries of time."

Amanda: "Do we have any questions at the back there?"

It seemed that the audience were still taking in the guide's comments as stillness decended momentarily upon those present. White Feather however, was unperturbed by this and seemed to be sensing that someone at the back of the hall had a question they wanted to ask but was perhaps lacking in confidence. Gesturing through the medium's hand he directed Amanda to an area on the right:

White Feather: "......and yet Sunflower there is a question there.......but it is not ready like the bud, to open yet. Perhaps before the end of the proceedings it will come forth!"

Questioner: "Could I ask a personal question? Good evening White Feather. I wonder if you could help me with my pathway........I seem to be stuck, in your words. Do you have anything you could tell me about it?"

White Feather: "I'm not going to answer it in a personal sense because that is not my intention in this setting. But let me say to you that I'm glad that you are stuck because when you're stuck it means you have a desire to be free. When you are confused it means that you are at the commencement of understanding. When you are in darkness, it means that there is light awaiting you. So it's good to be stuck, because through that you will find that you come into a state where you are free from that which now holds you back.

Try to understand sister, and I'm giving you this answer in all seriousness, that every condition that you go through......and I talk to you all with this......*everything* is temporary. Nothing in that sense, in terms of experience, in terms of material possessions or environments or experiences themselves, is permanent. Everything is in a state of flux, in a changing environment, in a state of flow and movement. So you will find that where now you have obstacles, where now you have difficulty, where now you are captive, tomorrow you will be free. Tomorrow you will be unchained and you will see things differently.

You may say to me 'that's all very nice, that's all very well, but how about some hard advice as to what to do? How about telling me what to change in my life?' and you know, always the answers lie within. Not externally. Not in changing this house, or moving to that place or reading this book or moving away from that person, or taking this tablet or doing this or doing that, but looking into the self. Because ultimately that is where all answers lie and when you begin to change the self you change the outer, you change the external. It may not be overnight, it may not be tomorrow but it will come nevertheless.

If I can refer you to my initial talk about aspiration, ask yourself what it is that you aspire to and if you aspire to that, if you hold that thought, if you give it energy, if you give it wings, it will fly and you will find that you are one step closer to bringing that into being. That is the greatest advice I can give you."

Questioner: "In this century, many people tell us that we are entering a time of great change and some authors suggest that we may be making a shift into a different dimension. Would you agree with that and if so can you tell us something about it?"

White Feather: "Yes, movement of course has always been so upon the earth. If I can refer to my last answer, nothing is permanant. There is always movement, there is always change. As to whether man is moving into another dimension, I am not happy with the term dimension. I would prefer to use the term consciousness or awareness because there is a deeper shift in awareness which is underlying the apparent descent into materialism in your world. On the surface it seems that humanity is heading into the deeper waters of materialism where he is more reliant upon the things of matter than he is of the gifts and the qualities of the spirit. But underneath that, there is underpinning that a deeper current of energy that is seeing a greater awareness on a worldwide scale beginning to emerge and this is because the unconscious collective of humanity is becoming aware of the higher teachings of the spirit, even though in some areas this may not seem apparent. It is so. There are more minds who are beginning to ask, who are beginning to look, more minds who are beginning to question, who are beginning to seek more deeply the ways of their true self. So you have this apparent contradiction, this paradox between the material on the surface and the underlying spiritual trend that is unfolding. So in that sense there is a shift taking place, but it won't be in your lifetime, in this generation, in this expression through the physical body. It won't be in such a short space of time, but you are beginning to see the commencement of it. I would also add, and this might interest you Sunflower, that with this shift there is an emphasis on a different ray configuration which is coming about to humanity, where more interest, more desire will be shown on the esoteric, spiritual front to the exclusion of the material. Man will eventually move out of the materialistic framework in which he lives his life in his reliance upon matter and he will move into a more spiritual, esoteric frequency, but that will take generations. There are those who are seeking to stop this happening, who are seeking to imprison humanity, who are seeking to hold it back, but they will be thwarted eventually, ultimately, because the higher is always greater than the lower and you can imprison the body but you cannot imprison the soul."

Questioner: "The question I was going to ask was that same question! But if I could carry on from there with a few fragments......could I ask a few questions?"

White Feather: "Please do."

Questioner: ".....the angel one, the bit about the angel question......would I be right in assuming.....I understood that there were Divas, great spirits that worked with groups?"

White Feather: "That is so. I refer to them as Avatars, you may call them Divas, others may call them angels. That is so."

Questioner: "Ok.....that's that one........"

White Feather did not want to let this question go so easily and decided to expand a little more on this subject, feeling that he needed to make a point:

White Feather: "Let's just stay with that a little moment longer, because you have to understand that although you are individuals apparently existing in isolation to some degree from others, of course there is no isolation and as individuals you connect with everything and everyone but you gravitate and are part of a higher soul group. Each of you is part of a higher soul group which you may or may not be aware of and each soul group is itself part of a higher group and at the higher levels of groups there are.......I don't like the term 'leaders'.....but there are enlightened souls such as those to whom you have referred who have charge over the energy of that group, over the ray of that group, over the direction of that group.

It is these souls who are sometimes referred to as angelic. But they are evolved souls, they are no greater than you or I and yet they have a wonderous knowledge and express a greater divinity than do we, of the spirit. And yet we are still linked with them and it is their directive, their charge if you like to influence the group soul from the higher down to the lower, to filter the energies down to the earth. So it's worth just mentioning that to you perhaps."

Pleased that the teacher had taken the time to answer the question in more detail the same lady cheekily asked if she could ask another of the guide, who in turn gently teased her before consenting to his request:

Questioner: "That's lovely, thank you. Could I ask just a little one?................"

White Feather: "Another one?!!!"

Questioner: "......I know it's naughty........"

White Feather: [turning to Amanda] "Is that allowed Sunflower?"

Amanda: "I should think so, just a little one!"

White Feather: "Set the clock!"

Questioner: "The lady over there asked about evolution and somebody told me the other day that there was going to be a great explosion or something was going the happen in the core of the earth which would cause vibrations to change on the planet which would affect human beings......"

White Feather: "Who told you that?"

Questioner: "......probably a nutcase! I just wondered if you could enlighten all of us as to whether that is likely to happen?"

White Feather: "Not in the short term, I have no knowledge of this. Let me say to you that there have been such predictions and forecasts since humanity first learned to walk, to think and to reason. There have been those who have been predicting such events and of course there have been cataclysmic events from time to time, but I think the overriding thing to say in this matter is that whatever befalls your earth, life will persist because it is part of the spirit plan that life will persist upon your world, whatever befalls it. There has been a great deal of evolution which has taken place, a great deal of advancement and that is not about to be wiped out and whatever man does, whatever natural events transpire - and let us understand that the earth will not go on forever in the physical sense, there will be an end, there will be a finality to its existence - that is not about to happen yet and life will persist. I know of no such imminent threat to humanity or to your world as we speak."

Questioner: "I've heard of the universal mind. If there is such a phenomenon, what is it?"

White Feather: "Well again you know, I think we have to consider semantics here and the use of terminology. I know of the Great Spirit which is sometimes referred to as the universal mind, the universal consciousness and many other labels and forms. That mind of the Great Spirit exists throughout the universe and *is everything that is*. There is nothing which is not the Great Spirit. The Great Spirit is in degree of expression however and operates through many vehicles, through many forms, through many levels, some more enlightened than others.
What you may be referring to, I don't know.......is a kind of 'natural intelligence' that operates throughout the universe, which is still part of the great spiritual mind but operates upon a kind of a sub-strata level. Let me relate it in a way that you can understand it, to your earth for example. You may have heard of the term 'Gaia' which was initiated by one in your world whom I believe instigated a publication about it. Now what he referred to as Gaia could be referred to as the 'intelligence' of your earth. The intelligence of nature to operate and to pick up the spiritual mind that works through it. It is not a question of someone directing the wind or bringing about the waves or creating an earthquake or bringing about night and day, and yet there seems to be a pattern does there not, within this? There seems to be some kind of intelligence that creates balance and harmony and if you look within nature you will see that there is perfect balance. Even through upheaval, even through cataclysm, even through change there is ultimately balance and it is this overriding principle which is the intelligence of the planet.
The planet is not an individualised soul as some like to think. They refer to the planet being a 'him' or a 'her' or a 'this' or a 'that'. But there is an intelligence that operates around and within nature that is part of the Great Spirit and part of the universal intelligence that operates at this level of being.
Now whether that is what you have heard or are referring to I don't know, but that is my explanation of it."

Questioner: "Good evening White Feather. I'd like to say 'Welcome Brother.' My question concerns the astronomers looking for other worlds in other solar systems which would perhaps hold life such as ours. Have you any evidence of any such existence of life like ours or similar to ours in a physical way on other planets?"

White Feather: "Yes I do, but not within your immediate solar system. But certainly within your galaxy, which itself contains many such worlds, many stars around which circle planets similar to yours, some a little different, but certainly within your galaxy which itself is one of many billions within the universe and which itself is far greater than your scientists realise or can 'see'. There is undoubtedly life, which I have knowledge of. Some which is similar to yours both in appearance and in the level of development, some which is more advanced and of course some which is less advanced. It is difficult for me to give you direct evidence of this or even describe it because of course you do not have the means even through your telescopes or your spacecraft to justify or quantify it. But it is a fact because your universe is teeming with life and your tiny world which is but a grain of sand upon a beach of many billions of grains of sand, is but one aspect, one facet of this expression of the Great Spirit."

Questioner: "Can I ask a second question?"

White Feather: "I thought you might!"

Questioner: "It's to do with your work and how you react to those individuals who are asking more questions of you. Which part of a congregation or group of people do you least like to be facing?"

White Feather [turning to the audience who are laughing]: "He likes to be controversial! It is not a question of that which I dislike because I welcome all-comers. I welcome everyone, whatever their degree of intellect, spiritual progress, or lack of it - all are welcome and I treat them all, I treat *you* all with the same respect and love. I hope that comes across, and what is important is that whatever lies within your heart, whatever the question that you ask, whatever you seek, you should receive the same degree of respect and answer that is befitting your intelligence and your need to know. So I treat you all the same.

Of course it is desirable in some ways to speak to minds that are open, rather than minds that are closed because where you have a closed mind it is difficult to enter into it, rather like seeds that are scattered and find difficulty in obtaining a lodgement in rock. It is better if they have a fertile soil in which to settle. So it is more desirable in that sense that I can speak to minds and hearts that are open and receptive. But I repeat, that I give you and I afford you all the same love and respect. I could do no other because you are all parts of the Great Spirit."

Question: "I thank you for that White Feather. Could I just ask a supplementary question?"

White Feather [turning to Amanda]: "Do you think he's working to a script?"

[Audience laughter]

Questioner: "I'll ask it later!"

White Feather: "Ask it now."

Questioner: "I'll wait until later."

White Feather: "That's your prerogative."

Amanda: "Anyone else have a question they'd like to ask?"

Questioner: "My query is that a few years ago in this world we had what was known as a population explosion with many new souls. Where did they originate? And the other part of the same question is, if this planet is no more, where are the incarnated souls going to learn their lessons?"

White Feather: "You're learning fast you know, how to ask two questions in one! To take the first part of your question; yes there has been an increase in the physical sense in your world, in terms of the numbers of population, the explosion of population. But you must recognise that first of all those who are returning to the earth may not necessarily be what you call 'young souls' or 'new souls' but older souls reincarnating. As to where they came from, you must understand that the Great Spirit *is* and you are part of the Great Spirit as I have already said. You have no commencement in terms that you have no beginning and no end, but the spirit comes into an individualised form and when it does that it can come through humanity and it can express itself through the body of man. When it passes at death into my world it may go on or it may return again to come through another physical body in a different reincarnation. But in terms of new souls being created it is not quite as clear cut, as simple as that. It is merely that the Great Spirit has always existed but comes into individuality and expresses itself through the vehicles that are presented to it.

I've used this analogy before but I think it's a good one so I'll repeat it; if you think of the Great Spirit as an ocean and you take a cup and you fill that cup from that ocean, that is *you the individualised spirit*. If you then fill a spoon from that cup, that is *you the personality*, a facet of that individualised spirit that has come into a physical body. You are still connected to the cup, you are still connected to the ocean, even though you are separate in the sense of the expression of degree. But you are still part of the whole. You are still part of the ocean of the Great Spirit. That may give you perhaps an illustration of what we mean when we say that the Great Spirit individualises and comes into form. So it does not matter how many are upon your earth. If your population currently was to triple and your earth could sustain it, there would always be enough souls because the Great Spirit is infinite and the Great Spirit has an infinite number of expressions.

As to the second part of your question 'what would happen if the earth were to be destroyed or come to its natural conclusion' as it will one day, of course that would necessitate that the Great Spirit and those souls who had even begun their expression would have to experience upon another world, of which their are countless billions. You must recognise that the earth itself, in cosmic terms is not special. It is not unique. It is not so important that its loss could not be compensated. It is only a planet of expression. It is like the physical universe itself, a means to facilitate the spirit to work and experience through it. To gain lessons, to learn lessons and to quicken itself. So when the earth comes to an end you will find that the spirit will express itself in other ways, through other forms, upon other worlds. Even as it does today."

Questioner:"White Feather, further to the question on reincarnation and in the light of what you have said can you tell us about the decisions and preparation a spirit soul has to undertake before entering into the physical world to continue upon their pathway of spiritual development?"

White Feather: "It depends upon the individual, upon the level of spiritual development they have reached, on the expression of freewill that they are permitted or that they have unfolded, their spiritual awareness and what they have earned the right to express in terms of choice, because not all who reincarnate are afforded the same degree of choice as more evolved souls. Where there is choice then the soul will look at the whole scenario, the whole picture. Rather like rolling out a map of life. Rather like unfolding a film if you like, that contains many captions, many pictures. The soul can see the whole and it chooses the experience through the parentage, through the line of descent, through the social and moral fabric of the society into which it allows that facet to enter, that it knows will equip it with the means to learn that particular lesson. For example, it may not be to the advantage of the soul to enter into a particular race or a particular culture upon your earth that would perhaps decry and inhibit the expression of mediumship, the gift of healing or perhaps the gift of music and so the soul would choose, so that, that facet would come into a line of parentage that would bring about about the physical body that was sensitive enough to enable mediumship or musicianship, as is the case, to emerge and to flourish. The culture itself, the country, the race would facilitate the means of expression that would allow that. So what I am saying to you in a broad sense is that the enlightened soul has choices, informed choices which it makes. It chooses very carefully the means for that facet which is about to incarnate to do its work, to unfold itself as it should, to pay any Karmic debts that may need to be addressed, to render a service to humanity or to itself and to generally enable itself to be quickened. And all of this takes a great deal of consideration and time and the enlightened soul will choose very carefully the vehicle into which it comes.

There are of course determining factors as well as other things which can change. Nothing is certain. Nothing is absolutely set in stone because if it were that would rule out any measure of freewill that may occur. So we never quite know totally what will happen. But where we have an overall picture we know that, that individual will undertake certain things within that lifetime even though it has freewill, that will enable that lesson to be outworked, that service to be rendered and that whole life experience to be a worthwhile one."

Amanda: "We are coming to the end of the time that we have for questions, so can I just ask the gentleman at the back because I know we have a question there."

Questioner:"What is heaven and hell? Is there such a thing as hell?"

White Feather: "Not in biblical terms. There is no place where the fires burn and where individuals are cast into oblivion for eternity. But there are lower planes, make no mistake, where individuals through their own actions will have placed themselves. Not as a punishment but as a way that they can come to terms with their actions, learn that particular lesson and so move on. So that I suppose you could refer to as hell. But again, it is not God created, it is man created. It is man's own ignorance that puts him there and if he chooses to move from it then that choice is available and he can be helped.
Heaven on the other hand again is perhaps not quite like it is portrayed in your world, but to me heaven is the unfoldment of the enlightened soul. The ability of the individual to express the divine within, unfettered, unhindered, untainted, purified. That is heaven, because to that soul there are no limits. There are no limitations whatsoever and all things are open. All things are available and that soul moves beyond form, beyond the physical form into the realms of pure being in which enlightened bliss is a normal state not a momentary one which you sometimes experience if you are fortunate on this level. That is heaven and it is something which you will all reach, whatever you think at the moment. You will all reach it because you are all parts of the same Great Spirit."

With the evening reaching its finale Amanda was preparing to bring the proceedings to a close, but White Feather still insisted, as he had previously that there was someone who had not yet asked their question:

White Feather: "Now what about this question over here?"

Amanda: "The supplementary one?"

White Feather: "No, I'll leave that one until last. I want the silent voice, the one who won't speak. I'm not going to bite you know!"

Amanda: "Is there anybody who hasn't asked a question......the lady at the back?"

White Feather: "I'm looking at her now........you have the courage?.........then perhaps I will have to speak to you in your dreams. Now where's the troublemaker

......is he still here!?"

[Audience laughter]

Questioner: "I've got three questions now!"

Amanda: "Oh no.....we haven't got time for that now!"

Questioner: "Ok. The question I have is not the one I was going to ask before, it's a better question I feel. Do you work through another channel as well as the one you are using or if the current channel went to another country would you speak in the natural tongue of that country?"

White Feather: "No, because that requires a special type and development of mediumship which requires in itself a certain constitution, a certain type of medium. So I would not be able to do that. If this individual moved to another country as you put it, upon the earth, I would still operate through this individual but not in the native tongue of that country, although that is possible through certain individuals who have an aptitude for that level and that type of mediumship.
As for speaking through other individuals I do not, as an individualised spirit. But I am part of a greater group of souls that does operate through many mediums under a similar banner, but it is not I. It is part of the group soul. It is part of the energy that works through others. Do you understand that?"

Questioner: "I understand. Thank you."

White Feather: "Does that help you? Are you sure you haven't any more?"

Questioner: "I have one which I will ask, which is easily answered by you White Feather, and this is my original question. We often see written down or through instruments of a similar type to yourself, but not perhaps on the same level, those who do not believe in reincarnation. But I firmly know, inside, that it happens."

White Feather: "Yes. Let us link this back to what we said earlier about going beyond mind, that you *instinctively* know. It is your *being* that knows. It is a fact. As to why some spirit guides in my world do not speak of reincarnation, it is because they have not yet come into an awareness of their past lives. You must understand that when you come into my world you do not become enlightened overnight. You do not reach the status of all-knowingness in an instant. There are still many things in your past that you do not have recognition of. Reincarnation may be one of them. That comes with the unfoldment of spirituality in the fullness of time. All the facets have knowledge of themselves and of their other parts and it is then that you will find that the topic of reincarnation will be reintroduced and that individual will speak of it. That is not to decry the teachings of those who do not speak of it because they still have something of value to offer humanity. It's just that they have not yet recognised and earned the right, if I may say so, to see their past lives and the other facets of themselves. That's why they don't speak of it. In fact they are not allowed to. I can only speak of what I know and what I have experienced, not what someone else has told me. That is a law that operates and that perhaps explains to you why."

Amanda: "In conclusion then White Feather, could it not be said that if we are beyond mind and beyond the physical body, if there was something for us all to take away from tonight it would be that if we followed our instinct, that which is at the very heart of our being, we really cannot go very far wrong. Would you agree with that?"

White Feather: "I couldn't have put it better."

The controversial, laughter filled and informative evening had reached its natural conclusion with every questioner being afforded the same respect and every question answered in the only way the guide knew how, truthfully and without compromise. With a few final brief words, the messenger from beyond this world rounded off his work with words of encouragement and thanks:

White Feather: "Thank you all. There is none so greatly enhanced as I because whenever I link with you I am filled with joy, I am filled with love, I am filled with light. It is always a pleasure to have this discourse with enquiring minds and I thank you for this opportunity. I would also thank you Sunflower and thank all who have operated in my world, unseen perhaps by yourselves but who nevertheless have played an important role in linking with us tonight. May the light, the power and the love of the Great Spirit be with you all until we meet again. God bless you."

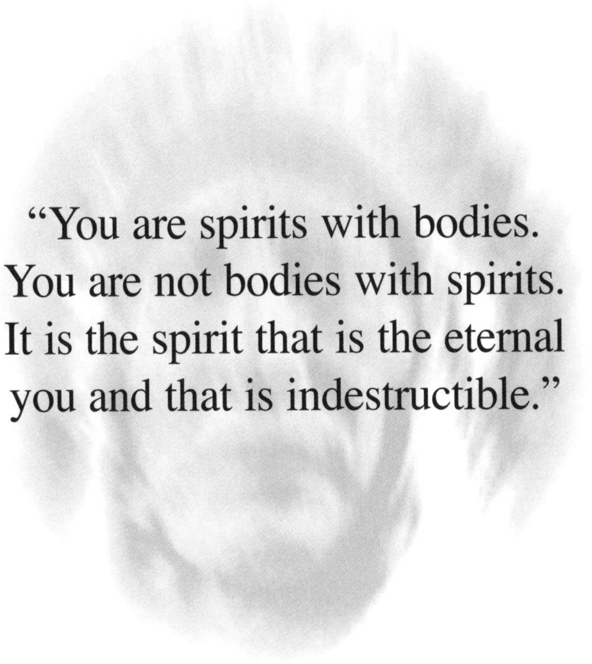

"You are spirits with bodies.
You are not bodies with spirits.
It is the spirit that is the eternal
you and that is indestructible."

one2one

A Gathering of Spirits 10

At times in life, particular events and happenings stand out from others as being unique, memorable or simply special. The evening that was spent at a house of some new aquaintances in the Clent Hills proved to be all of these and more. Invited to join two ladies, M'halleta and her daughter Sandra in their quiet sanctuary in order to allow White Feather the chance to communicate, the evening began with the gentle sounds of Silver Wings playing softly on tape, awaiting the arrival of White Feather through his medium. The guide did not disappoint, announcing his entrance in his usual style:

"May I greet you all with the divine light of the Great Spirit. Just as the gentle breeze of nature caresses the chimes that sit beyond your window so I enter into this holy temple upon the breath of the spirit. That in some small measure I may caress your reasoning minds into a deeper understanding and awareness of the true nature of reality which encompasses the rich vein of spiritual truth that seeks ever to play upon the heartstrings of those who are its seekers. The truth, as I have said so often, is the liberator of the captive soul. It is truth that enables individuals and humanity as a collective to reach out to the highest plateau of spiritual verity and to leave behind once and for all the grossness, the heaviness, the pain and suffering that the body of matter affords the spirit. For matter, even though it has its distinct place in the soul's growth and evolution is only a stepping stone and should not be thought of as being anything of permanance. It is but a transient state which the individualised spirit employs for its various needs. To outwork its Karma, to fulfill its destiny, to render service and above all to learn from the great spectrum of experiences that the world of matter gives.

As I say very often when I link with your world, I am but a messenger. It is the message that I seek to impart that is of the greatest import. Like you I am not infallible. I have a great deal yet to learn, to unfold, to develop, but perhaps where there is a difference is that I am free of the heavy overcoat of matter which so often cloaks down the expression of the divine. That does not mean that I am in any way superior. Only that I do not have to express through the physical body as do you in your temporary sojourn upon the earth. This facilitates access to a greater, broader spectrum of knowledge and although I am not the fount of all wisdom I have access perhaps, to understanding which your world has yet to grasp and for that I am privileged.

I thought I would say a few words before I invite questions, as I like to do. Are you all happy by the way? Good. It is good that we can link together in this fashion and I pay tribute to the energies which have been already assembled, built over many ages in this temple. It is a credit to those who have sat here, who have passed through and who have left traces of their vital spark of the spirit in the atmosphere itself. It is something which makes our work a delight, a pleasure to perform.

You know, a young pupil once asked a great teacher 'where do I find the path of illumination?' The teacher looked at him deeply before uttering the words 'son, you are already standing upon it'. You know, every pathway, however humble, however great, however complex or simple, however diverse, is a pathway of illumination. And even though you think at times that life has dealt you a cruel hand or that you are in the midst of turmoil, suffering or difficulty, never lose sight of the fact that you are spiritual beings upon a spiritual pathway and that every lesson in life has something of value. Every experience has something of worth to offer. And the true acolyte is one who accepts every life experience as one from which wisdom can be gleaned. In my view there is no bad experience. There is only experience and from that the soul can equip itself for its eternal journey to illumination.

I thought I would say a few words tonight however, concerning some aspects of that journey, regarding in particular what I refer to as symbolism. Because you know, symbols take many forms, not merely pictorial. Not merely the more recognisable forms with which you are familiar but also words can be regarded as symbolic. Shapes, colours, they each have their own energy. But what is important is not the symbol itself but the meaning attached to it and the intention residing within it and around it. Symbols you know, are often regarded with great awe and just as some individuals are unwittingly and even purposely placed upon pedestals that they may be worshipped, so symbols also can be addressed in this way and in my view whilst they have their role to play one should not become so attached to them that one cannot move beyond and see anything else.

Symbology has always played a role in humanity's development but what has to be recognised is that they are only there to facilitate, not to be assimilated within the understanding to such a point that they become irrevocably a part of that individual's philosophy. Let me give you an example of what I mean. There are some in your world who place great adherence to the cross. Particularly those within organised religion. Those of a Christian belief for example place great homage and adherence to the symbol of the cross. That is as it may be if they choose that and they gain something from it. Simply by viewing the cross or thinking of it or linking with it they have a certain awareness and understanding attached to that symbol. But in another culture, in another time, another age, the same symbol may mean something completely different. Because a different meaning and intent is attached. For example, in your last great conflict there was the sign that was referred to as the Swastika, which was employed by certain factions of humanity that were warring against others and that symbol became recognised and adhered to something of a negative nature. Yet you know, that symbol is far more ancient than those who adopted it during that conflict and it once held a different meaning than it did during that time.

If we extend this teaching beyond the boundaries of your world you can understand perhaps that what is symbolic in your culture now, to an alien race upon another world may have no meaning whatsoever. The reason I am telling you this is that truth is beyond symbolism. Truth is beyond culture. Truth is beyond language. Truth *is*. It has always been and always will be. And yet truth needs to find an expression. It needs to have a vehicle to express itself. In the case of humanity that vehicle by and large, although not exclusively, is language. When we speak to you we can do so in thought, which is beyond language and yet to communicate with many we choose to employ language. We work through a language of the modern age which you can understand, hopefully in terms with which you are familiar. But the language of the world is not the truth. Just as the cross or any other symbol is not the truth. It is a means of expressing a facet of truth that is eternal. Truth is a thread that is universal. There are those on other worlds, in other universes that appreciate and imbibe the same truth of the spirit as you do and yet you are poles apart in your use of language and symbolism. And yet the truth is constant because the truth is the truth is the truth. What is true today was true yesterday and will be true tomorrow. It does not alter. What alters is the manner to convey it. The messenger if you like, may change, the language employed may alter but the essence is infinite. And when you can go beyond and simply be one with what is, then you have transcended all boundaries, all barriers, all language, all symbols and you have become one with the infinite. That truly is the spiritual pathway to which you should all aspire.

Now, I know that within your hearts and minds reside many questions. Questions which you have already formulated, others that have yet to arise, like the wellspring coming up to the surface. What I have to say to you I hope will be of some help and guidance. I have no prior knowledge as you are aware, of any questions that you may ask me and that is as it should be because all true mediumship and communication with the spirit is always a spontaneous occurance. We do not rehearse because all that is of the spirit is a flowing movement and that is as it should be. So Sunflower, you are familiar I know with the way that we work. I will now hand over the reigns to you and perhaps you can orchestrate proceedings, not only for those of you who are gathered here in this temple in the 'seen' but also in the 'unseen'. Make no mistake, your room is overflowing with souls who are drawn here to participate in this wonderous experience."

Amanda: "Would you like to start?"

M'haletta:"Well, at first to thank you White Feather for the beauty of your expression that has certainly touched a chord in me because the word is the means of expression that I employ and that I feel, not only with my heart and I have some understanding with the mind, but I feel the word to be a part of me that is alive. Often on a page, if one reads words they feel as if they are flat, without the spark of life. It is my joy, when I find words that can be linked together to produce that spark. Could you speak perhaps a little more of how the light of the divine can be brought through in this medium of expression of the word?"

White Feather: "You know I have often said that your language, as wonderful, poetic, artistic as it can often be, is still a somewhat clumsy medium to express the true beauty and divinity of the spirit because we have to cloak down to a degree the expression of the spirit when we communicate with your language. But we always seek to employ it in a way that befits the beauty of the truth that seeks to express itself and we labour long and hard to cooperate in a way that we can work through the mediums that we have at our disposal to give full justice to that which we seek to express.

I often liken this to the music that seeks to express itself in your world through a musician using an instrument. The music itself is a wonderous thing, but it has to rely upon the skill of the musician and the instrument which that musician is playing. The greater the instrument, the greater the musician, the more wonderous the music that can play and the more exquisite the sound that can reach the ears of those who listen.

When referring to the spoken word, it is a very powerful medium. We can speak a language that can be heard and recognised by the minds of those who are in its presence, but the spoken word as powerful as it is, is as yet not even as powerful I think, as the written word because the written word can reach out to many. Just as a stone dropped into the centre of a lake radiates its ripples far and wide so the written word can be carried faithfully if it is reproduced in that form, to many, many hearts and minds who would not otherwise have come into contact with that teaching. Faces and people whom you will never contact directly can read the teachings that are given. I am speaking now not particularly of myself but of you also and others who have been able to put those words into a printed form. And the words contained, have a great power. They can touch minds, but more importantly they can touch hearts. They can invoke emotion. They can bring healing. They can bring enlightenment and understanding and long after the author perhaps, has passed to higher realms, the written word remains here to bring enlightenment to others. That to me is a wonderful thing. There are books that have been written in your world many centuries ago and yet that knowledge is still available to those who seek it. It has not been lost. It is still there. Thus, teachings which are being imparted today from many sources will be like seeds planted in the

soil of life, for tomorrow's children to reap the harvest. That is a wonderful thing. So I always pay tribute to the power of language and to the written word in particular for it has a great role to play in the world.
One word of concern, is that one should not perhaps rely too much on the modern electronic technologies. There is nothing finer than holding a book in one's hands!"

The next question touched upon a subject of which the guide very seldom speaks, 'the rays' which are featured in the spiritual writings of Alice Bailey amongst others. It gave the sage the opportunity to give his own version of their significance:

Sandra:"I'd like to ask a question about the 'rays'. We're struggling to understand, I'm struggling to understand the seven rays and how I can best use them in the work that I do?"

White Feather: "Perhaps my understanding of the rays might be a little different than yours or that which has been purveyed in your world."

Sandra: "I thought it might be. We've only got one resource, that is our problem."

White Feather: "That is the difficulty and if you don't mind me saying so, and I hope I cause no offence by this, one perhaps should not adhere to information, as expansive as it is, that results from one source without applying one's questioning and reasoning mind. Now let me tell you a little about the rays as you refer to them and their origin in my world. Perhaps you will already be familiar with the understanding that the spirit domain or dimensions are many faceted. There are many levels, just as the teaching that was once given that said; in God's house there are many mansions. So in my world there are many frequencies, many levels of unfoldment, each level corresponding with the minds and the souls that dwell therein, and indeed which are partly created by the minds that dwell therein. Mine is a very organised world. There is no chance or fate in any form. All is ordered by perfect law in operation, that encompasses every facet of life contained within it. There are those who I would refer to as 'the illumined ones' who are more advanced than I. Who have a greater awareness and understanding of the divine source from which all life is continually pouring. Never think that life was created in a single event, never to be repeated. Life is continually evolving and being created as an outpouring of light from the source, which you may think of as God or which I call the Great Spirit. It is not an individualised deity but is the essence of all that is. Contained within that pure essence of light and love that is beyond form is every colour, every facet, every frequency. These may be understood as being 'rays' of different vitality, different power, different energy, different colour. There are those in my world whose sole charge is to help to direct the ray energy as a kind of a waterfall, if I can express it that way, that permeates through all the levels of being in my world before eventually reaching your world, in degree. Each ray has its effect upon the various bodies of man. Some are more in attunement and harmony with one particular aspect or ray than they are with another. Even whole groups of society or race in your world have more of an affinity with one ray configuration than they do with another. The rays themselves can be thought of as being an outpouring of the Great Spirit which is for the benefit of man and for all of life for that matter.

At any particular time in man's evolution, because of his mental, emotional and physical development he will attune himself to a particular aspect or particular ray configuration. We are speaking here not merely of one ray but of a combination of several, and as that understanding and development changes as man grows spiritually so naturally his vibrations change, his frequencies quicken and he becomes more attuned to a different aspect of rays, that bring to him perhaps, a particular knowledge, that draw to him a particular mind or a group of individuals that are part of his own soul group. Because you must understand that you are not isolated. You are all parts of a greater soul aspect and even with you as individuals it is only a facet of your greater self that is expressing itself at any one time.

As to the collective humanity, that also is determined to an extent by man's physical, mental and emotional state at any time and at the moment in time man is in a state of materialism. Even though he has made many advances scientifically and industrially, as can be seen by what you commonly refer to as the 'industrial revolution', and the current trend upon the reliance upon electronic gadgetry and the transfer of information, that is a part of the same configuration to which man is currently attuned. But also, man's spiritual aspect can never be discarded, for it is always there and we are trying to help man's spiritual aspect to keep pace with his intellectual aspect because there is somewhat of a gap appearing. Man has developed intellectually, but he lags behind spiritually and even somewhat, emotionally.

So those in my world who have understanding of the rays will try and impose a particular ray configuration upon those in your world to realign, to balance and to bring back into a state of equilibrium. There are no guarantees of course because man's freewill is very strong and his ego is even stronger. So we have to contend with these things. As for you who have some spiritual knowledge, there is an attraction to a particular aspect of spiritual work with which you find familiarity and that ray will be attracted to you. You will attune with it in a natural way. It is never forced. Also with that you will find that like minds will be drawn to you and through this combination and through your own endeavour to serve and help others, so you will be quickened and your own frequency will change. As that happens it will enable you to become aware of higher and greater things and so you are automatically elevated to a higher frequency.

As to the rays themselves, understand that a lot of that information which is available in your world has, in my understanding been somewhat, shall I say..........clouded, by the intellectual mind of man that has tried to place certain restrictions upon it. The truth, in essence, is simple. If it becomes so complex, convoluted and difficult to understand then it is of no value. Rather like religion that imposes so many doctrines and dogmas and creeds that its essence is lost, so the same has happened to a degree to the information that has been imparted regarding the rays. You are quite right in that its source has been an individual one, which itself is open to question. So use your reasoning mind and your reasoning capacity and you will find that the information that you feel comfortable with is that which is right for you because it goes beyond words, beyond intellect. You simply know that it is so."

Revealing her interest in the healing aspects of colour Amanda asked the visitor if intuition played a part in their utilisation:

Amanda: "Could I just then ask, if you are working with those energies and the colours that go with them and the frequencies that these draw, is it not always best, as with other things to utilise your intuition, and whatever you perceive that person to need is right for them at that time?"

White Feather: "Absolutely, and is intuition not more reliable than intellect so often? When you have a feeling about someone or something it is generally perceived to be correct. Even though part of you may be questioning it and perhaps thinking opposite. Intuition is generally correct because it is beyond matter, it is beyond mind, it is beyond intellect. So follow it."

Amanda: "I would say that the use of colours and the energies that go with them is becoming much more an integral part of the healing that we are using, whether it be words or hands-on healing or mindwork. So in the spirit world is colour as important a part of things when you're healing and learning about new things?"

White Feather: "Colour plays a vital role in healing in my world as it is becoming to in your world. I spoke many, many years ago about colour and I remember saying at the time that colour and sound are part of each other. There is no colour without a sound and there is no sound without a colour and of course colour and sound are both frequencies. They both have an energy and frequency and both play their part in life because you are in essence, energy, of a frequency. Where there is a disturbance, be it on any level - physical, mental, emotional or spiritual, then that can be healed and rectified by the application of energy. Energy upon energy, frequency upon frequency. Colour and sound play their parts in this because they are very vital energies. You do not live in a world of black and white. You live in a world of colour. If, for example, you feel drawn to a particular colour then it is perhaps more often than not that your own body at some level is lacking the energy that, that colour brings. And simply by linking with that colour, whether you imbibe it through the breath, whether it is through the clothes that you adorn or simply by looking and walking in nature and attuning with it, you are bringing harmony where there was disharmony. You are bringing balance where there was imbalance. It is a great pity you know, that there is not more taught about the power of colour and sound in your schools. They teach a great deal of misinformation, particularly about history and religion, but they give very little about spiritual understanding and awareness. You know, you have heard the saying I am sure, 'Healer, heal thyself!' and if man but realised the power to be had in colour and sound then there would be a great deal less stress and disharmony than there is in your world."

M'halleta:"Oh that was very full and extremely helpful. Very much on our wavelength, very much so. A question that's perhaps a little more personal; Our family has a sense of itself as being a group energy. Personalities are immensely diverse yet that somehow has no impact on the fact that we are aware of ourselves in essence as one group and one being. Could you speak about that?"

White Feather: "I think that is a wonderful state of awareness that you have achieved. For there are many in your world who do not perceive that reality. The fact that you have collective awareness and understanding of your spiritual links and destiny is in my view, a wonderous teaching that you have acquired, but one which is perfectly natural. For very often you will find that families have chosen to reincarnate together simply because there is an affinity between them. There is a love that enables them to work closely together over successive lifetimes. To outwork Karma, to bring healing, to bring resolution and to give service, not only to each other but to humanity and those who are drawn into their orbit.

Seldom do people recognise this fact. And yet when it dawns, when the understanding arises then it is a wonderous thing because there is a realisation that you have all been linked before and that you are indeed part of a soul group, a spiritual collective which transcends boundaries. It does not matter whether one was male or female before, or even in the future. For this transcends the boundaries of gender and I want you to understand that what you sense, what you believe, what you know, is true. Never doubt it. Those who have formed a part of your family life, here and now in this age, you have known before. Those who have passed on will be awaiting your movement from the physical body to the spirit world and that also will be a joyous reunion. And who is to say that even in future lives those aspects of your soul group who choose to return to the earth will not be accompanied by the same loved ones who link with them now.

Sunflower has the knowledge of a saying of mine which I often refer to which says that 'where there is love, there is no separation.' Love goes beyond all generations of time and space. Love is infinite. It is eternal and it is the golden thread that binds one with another. It is unbreakable. It is divine."

The next question touched upon an important aspect of both M'haletta's and Sandra's lives and brought out great compassion and love from the spirit guide.

It concerned Benjaya, the son of one of M'halleta's daughters, whose brief earthly life had made such a profound impact on the lives of the whole family, and who had left a spiritual legacy which had resulted in a book 'Benjaya's Gifts'. So powerful was the impact made by this soul, that there seemed still to be a spiritual energy that pervaded the sanctuary in which we sat, belonging in part to him. It was as though his presence was still apparent in the room, not least because where we sat was actually his birthplace. White Feather seemed aware of this and of the soul himself, whom he referred to as 'the old one'.

M'haletta: "There was a child in our family, Benjaya, who came for some great purpose that was worked out in five years of his life and he passed back at the age of five. We feel him still, as a living body within our family circle. We speak with him, we enjoy his presence and yet at the same time we are aware that we are not speaking to the boy as was......"

White Feather: "That is correct. Because he is the old one. I refer to him as 'the old one'."

M'haletta: "The old one?"

White Feather: "The old one. Not the young one, the *old* one. An older soul if I may say, than yourself and when we speak of age it is sometimes difficult because one sometimes associates age with wisdom and greatness and the one to whom you refer has a wisdom that accompanies his spiritual age, if I can refer to it that way. And yet he is not greater than you, he is not lesser than you, but he has acquired experience which follows his many lifetimes upon the earth. Let me say this to you; Do you know why he came the last time, for those few short years? Do you know that?"

M'haletta: "To teach us of love?"

White Feather: "Yes. To touch many souls. To touch many minds. Not simply those of the close family, the group soul, but to touch many minds and many hearts and you know we spoke earlier of the written word? ......then you will be aware and appreciative of the fact that the expression that had but five short years resulted in the written word going out to many souls, touching many minds. As it will do beyond your physical lifetime. And that is important because you must recognise that the length of time spent upon the earth encased in the physical body is of little consequence in its length. What matters is what is accomplished in that time. Like a stone sent skimming across the waters to touch upon life's surface, this it may do, but it is when it sinks into the depths that it truly comes in to its own. And the soul in question, the 'old one' touched your world for a short time and yet the legacy of that experience extends by far the earthly lifespan and the knowledge, the teaching, the love contained within the book will reach many souls and will render a great service to them. That is the true essence of that lifetime. That is the true purpose of it. *That* you must understand, I want you to know that. You played your part in that, all of you did. And that is a credit to you as a group soul in the love that you have between you. Do you understand that?"

M'haletta: "I do and thank you for that."

Amanda: "Can I just say at this point that I have had the privilege of reading the book you refer to and it has certainly made a huge impact upon me as an outsider. One of the things that really was very, very poignant to me was how death is addressed, especially with other children. What are yours and your colleagues in the spirit worlds' views on death from your side of life? Because this passing and the way that this was done was different to most people, but I felt that it was one of the most beautiful and lovely things.......and I'm getting quite emotional as I say this.....does it impact upon the soul that has passed, the way that the body of the child or whoever, comes to its conclusion in the material world?

White Feather: "It depends upon the knowledge of the individual. Knowledge accounts for a great deal and where there is an old soul who has full spiritual awareness then death, however traumatic, is not so impactful as for perhaps an unillumined soul and quite quickly when death has occurred to the physical body that individual who has knowledge and understanding will adapt to the new surroundings with which they are familiar in my world. That you must recognise.

Very often you know, we stand at your gravesides, in your cemeteries and your temples and watch the tears flow from your eyes. How we wish that we could lift that veil from yourselves because you know, what is a defeat for you is a victory for us. What is a loss for you is a gain for the world of spirit. It is a homecoming. For us it is a celebration where the physical body has, or should have served its purpose and that individual can relinquish it and allow it to dissolve into its primal state, having served its purpose, to reside resplendent in the spirit body that it has earned by its own endeavours, to which no one can add and no one can take away. You are as you are.

Let me say for the record that I have not read the book! Neither has the instrument through whom I speak. But I know of the 'old one'. I know of the soul to whom it refers and that is why I am so pleased that the teachings contained within it by all who have contributed, are so worthwhile. Because death you know, is a very emotive issue. Particularly when it concerns young ones, young children in your world. It causes so much grief and stress and hardship.

That is why it is important to remove the taboo of death, remove the stigma of it. To enlighten people, to help them to understand that death is an impossibility. You cannot die for the life of you! You exist because you always have and always will do. So often, and you will know this, where a young child has been taken, the individuals are so often left with that image that death portrays. But that is an illusion. It is only the shell. The spirit may long since have departed and where one sees an empty shell, that is what it is. If we can bring understanding to people, if we touch but one soul, then it has been worthwhile."

Amanda: "But what I found the most poignant was that the children who saw Benjaya after the death of his physical state, were the ones who went to see him and the parents who were fearful were led by the children! That is a teaching in itself."

White Feather: "I cannot add anything to that for it is a great truth."

Amanda: "I'm saying this because I think that in the books that we write and the things that we do it is so important for us also to address death from the point of birth to the point beyond and that actual physical passing is as important to address and to know that grief in the physical sense is part of that process."

White Feather: "That is so, but if you think, you analyse and you look at what is taught from a very young age in your world you will find that many are taught to fear death. That it must be avoided at all costs. That one must do anything to cheat it, to abrogate it and you will find that, that is a great disservice to death. Because death is the liberator in so many ways of the disenfrachised soul. The soul that is encased in the body of matter with all of its pain and suffering and hardship is freed like a bird from a cage, flying through the ether. That is what death is. It is a liberating experience and yet it is taboo in society. Society that teaches also that death is the end of everything. That has to change and until that change can come about and the stigma and fear can be removed, man will continue to be held captive by the jailer that death is portrayed to be. That is a great pity. All who hear these words, or read these words if they are published can play a part in the liberation of humanity by spreading the simple truth that you are spirits with bodies. You are not bodies with spirits. It is the spirit that is the eternal you and that is indestructible."

Sandra: "I have worked quite a bit in the past with people who have loved ones and people who have died and have gone over to the other side and it's my belief that I work as a mediator to connect the two. Is it always the case, that people are able to connect to people they were close to who have died and people who are working through trauma.......people who have perhaps seen someone who has died?"

White Feather: "In essence, to answer your question, it is always possible. But in reality and practice it is not always so because we find that barriers are erected that prevent the closeness necessary to maintain contact that can be recorded and established as being fact. So often grief throws up a cloud of despair around the one in your world that makes it very difficult for contact with those in my world to be established. This is the very reason why mediumship is such a vital link and you in your way are a medium between those in my world and those in your world. So you are able and privileged, if I may add, to assist in your work to bring the two together.

But so often you find, because of one's beliefs, into which one has been indoctrinated and which very often deny even the existence of life beyond the world of matter, it is difficult for that natural link to be maintained in a way that can be mutually fulfilling.
So you have a great deal of work to do but you know you are helped. You are never alone and there are many, many ways to work. Not necessarily in the more accepted ways of mediumship. There are many who are mediums, who are sensitives, who do not even know it, who do not even recognise it. Doctors, for example. Surgeons, who perform the most intricate surgery are helped and guided by the unseen hands of spirit doctors and yet if you were to tell them this they would laugh at you. They would scoff. The fact that you have knowledge of those that work with you, even though you may not have been given names or identities, does not matter. The fact is that your healing words and healing energies are assisted by those in my world to help those in need."

Amanda: "Any more questions............?"

White Feather: "I think we are having a very informative discussion and I must say that I am gaining a great deal of enjoyment from being in your esteemed company!"

Amanda:"The feeling is mutual."

M'haletta: "Could we speak about time. Time of course, is something here that we adhere to and my question relates to time and death. As to whether there is an optimum time to die that is registered and known? I ask that question because clearly Benjaya knew that he would not be on the earth plane beyond the week in which he died. Now, also there is a school of belief that we cannot pass until we have reached a particular point of accomplishment, but it doesn't necessarily relate to time, but more to frequency or to our actions or intentions in our lives. Could you speak of that?"

White Feather: "Let me say this; in my understanding there is a time to be born and there is a time to die in the sense that the allotted time span of the physical body is known by the soul that is coming into that body beforehand. However, because you have freewill you can interfere with that lifespan. You cannot extend your life beyond that allotted time to any degree, but you can shorten it. And if you think about this, if this were not to be the case and life was so preordained as to be known exactly from the moment of birth to the moment of death, then that would exclude the operation of freewill and it would not matter what you did or said or how you acted towards others or yourself. It would make no difference. Quite clearly that cannot be so. Man has freewill and the way that you live your life, the actions that you take, the thoughts that you think, the words that you speak, the food that you

eat, the way that you exercise in your life.......all of these things have a direct bearing upon your lifespan. If you act in great ignorance then the chances are that you will shorten that span because your freewill is interfering with what should be the natural outworking of a life of birth and death. So you can interfere in that way, this you must understand. But the soul knows before it incarnates what it has to accomplish. It knows the type of body into which it comes and very often it has earned the right to choose that body. That body, be it male or female has a certain predisposition to a genetic order of sorts which may predispose it to certain health conditions. It has a colour of hair, of eyes, of texture of skin that are genetically determined through it's parentage, it has certain mannerisms...........and all of these things the soul knows before it comes into that form. So it knows what it has to contend with. It knows its life's purpose.
Now at a conscious level, you may not know life's purpose. But your higher self does. That is what is important. Consciously it may not be necessary for you to know. That is why sometimes, individuals shorten their lives, either through ignorance or because they choose to take their own lives. That is a matter for freewill. But when the time to pass into my world, or to 'die' as you put it, is reached, there is nothing that you or anyone can do to prevent it. Your doctors may say that they can keep the body alive with a support machine but all that, that does is enable to spirit to keep functioning *if it chooses*, through it. If the spirit chooses to withdraw or the time is reached, no machine and no doctor will prevent that from occurring. Matter is servant, spirit is master. Do you understand that? Does it answer your question?"

M'haletta: "Thank you. It does."

Returning to the subject of Benjaya, whose presence still seemed to be influencing the energies of the evening, Amanda felt that she needed to know if there was any significance to the relationship between his earthly entry and exit:

Amanda: "Can I just ask you about Benjaya.......this soul passed into the world of matter through water [a natural 'water' birth] *and went from this world through water* [drowning] *is there any spiritual reason why that would happen in that way?"*

White Feather: "There is and it links with a Karmic aspect which is peculiar to the individual concerned. I am not going to divulge to you the true purpose behind that because it is something the individual themselves should have a choice over and perhaps at some point the reason for that will be made available to you. It is not for I to have that choice. But there is indeed a more spiritual, Karmic reason for that entry and withdrawal from your world in that fashion."

M'haletta:"I think actually, because of that seeming synchronicity and the similarity of the entry and the exit it made the story more significant. It was as if a great deal was carried in that fact because of mythology in which people have read that 'Gods' and mythical beings come to the earth through water and can disappear through water. So it gave it a mystical quality to people. I don't know anything about whether that is relevant to birth or death or not?"

White Feather: "But it has a great poignancy I feel and almost one could say, an elegance to it."

M'haletta: "That's a beautiful word."

White Feather: "I hope that what we have been able to impart to you thus far has been of some small value. Let me say that I know that there are many souls who stand at my side who are listening with a very keen interest to the proceedings and also to the questions that are arising from the depths of your being."

The differences between eastern and western cultures, particularly in terms of spirituality has always been in evidence, yet across the ages many individuals have taken teachings from either aspect and introduced them into the other, often with great success. True spiritual progression is after all, about achieving balance and harmony, and opposites, when seen in their true perspective, are actually parts of each other. Here, White Feather responds to a question that addresses this issue and adds his own unique insight into the opportunities that are available to those of a discerning mind who are prepared to embrace alternative ideas:

M'haletta: "There is an event that is occurring shortly in which I must undertake a journey to Thailand. Often the east calls me. I feel that I live within two cultures. Something within me is eastern."

White Feather: "That is so. Because you have had past experiences, past lives within that culture. So just as a bottle contains the residue of the liquid that has been within it, so the residue of your past lives remains within the totality of your being and when you return to these eastern shores it is as if you are returning home is it not?"

M'haletta: "Yes it is."

White Feather: "There is a comfort, there is a familiarity there and there is a joy to return to the energies that can be found there. You have no fear, it is as if you are returning to part of a family. So that is why. You have had more than one lifetime although I cannot give you direct evidence of it as I speak. But if you can take my word for now, let me say that you have had more than one lifetime in those cultures so that is why it feels so comfortable and familiar to you. But let me say this also; you have a role to play which is part of your life's journey and part of the reason you came here, in uniting east and west cultures in spiritual knowledge. You may think it is but small and insignificant and yet it is greater than even you realise. There have been others, many in the past who have come from the east to the west. There have been those who have journeyed the other way but to illustrate a point, you perhaps will understand when I say to you that generally, the western consciousness is in many ways materialistic and relies upon scientific thought and intellect to the exclusion of the right brained spirituality that is more common in the eastern cultures. The cultures of the ancient Indian races, the Tibetans, the ancient Greeks, the Chinese cultures........many of these races of man had a more esoteric outlook and understanding. That still remains in part today and if one can assist in bringing that and marrying it to the more western scientific materialistic mind or left brained consciousness, that is a great thing. Because there you have a more balanced outlook, you have a more balanced soul. The western culture is sadly lacking in that which the eastern has to offer. So if in any small way and measure you can help to migrate that energy from east to west it is a good thing and that is part of your life's purpose if I may point that out to you. You may already be aware of it and that is a good thing, so keep up the good work!"

M'haletta: "I'd like to respond to that, because that really moves me to another dimension of understanding. I have worked with understanding to blend cultures and integrate east and west at a physical level, that's been the focus of my work. But now I will link more to the written word and what you say enthuses me to be able to find a way of doing the same task at another level....... that it must be possible on pledge. I believe it is but I've tried to find a way to do that. You encourage me that it is possible."

White Feather: "Yes it is indeed possible and let me say that you have a great deal of work yet to accomplish in this way before your physical lifespan comes to its end upon the earth."

M'haletta: "That's nice to know!"

White Feather: "You can't put your feet up just yet! But wouldn't it be of interest to take a little of the teachings which you have encompassed in the books and translate them into the eastern language, so that you are taking something back as well as taking something out? There has to be an exchange. Perhaps that is something which you may wish to consider and with which we can help you. Let us see what we can do. If you are of the mind, then there are ways that can be found."

M'haletta: "I'd be delighted. Thank you very much indeed."

Amanda: "Reading Tibetan books, I have a great interest and a great draw to that philosophy. It is written in a very casual manner about the third eye, about these esoteric gifts that were commonplace. Do you think that the western culture and consciousness has meant that, in a manner of speaking, man has 'closed' his third eye metaphorically? That because of his materialistic gains he has unfortunately shut his eyes to what is there spiritually for him?"

White Feather: "That is a good metaphor. It is also more than just metaphorical. Man's spiritual gifts to which you refer have become almost atrophied by his neglect of them and his reliance and adherence to materialism. Like anything, any gift, if you do not employ it, if you do not use it then it shrivels, it stagnates, it closes down and there have been races of man that were far more spiritually and psychically developed than the current race of which you are a temporary part. That is a great sadness. But you must remember that nothing is forever in a material sense and everything of matter is transient. Spirit is eternal and endures. The spiritual qualities, even though they cannot express themselves as they once did are still there within man's constitution and await awakening and this is why, when the time is right they will do so. I have always said that when the apple is ripened, it falls into the upturned hand. You cannot force it and if you seek to pick it before it is ripe it is a bitter fruit. There are no short cuts, but the tide ebbs and flows, it recedes and it advances and there will come a time when man, or factions of man come into a more psychically and spiritually aware age than now exists. But that is some way in the future."

Amanda: "But it is said 'do not cast your pearls before swine' as it were, and a lot of the eastern philosophies and esoteric gifts that we are talking about actually are quite mystical. Do you see any virtue in actually not divulging all of those things which we think are special to those people who would not appreciate them? Does it dissipate those special energies? Do you know what I am saying?"

White Feather: "Absolutely and that is a fact. It is wise I think to keep one's own council to a degree. There is a time to speak, there is a time to be silent. A time to move and a time to be still and the wise soul keeps its own council and is guided by the fact that it knows when to give forth and when to draw back. That you will find, will come with wisdom, with understanding. The eager young mind that acquires this knowledge, bursting forth to utter it to all and sundry, does so without thinking at times and the energy and the vitality is lost. And yet if it is kept within like a fine wine, it matures and is cultivated into something of great richness. You will find that man in his ignorance, chatters. And yet the wise soul speaks in but few words but when that soul speaks, all listen. It is quality, not quantity that matters."

Amanda: "Have you not said yourself that 'people have two ears and one mouth and yet they speak twice as much as they listen' ?"

White Feather: "I've heard that before!"

Amanda: [turning to Mhaletta and Sandra] "Is there anything else you would like to ask?"

M'haletta: "I think we must just finish with a word that has so many different connotations in the esoteric world and that word for me is Shambala, and if you would say whatever you would say about the word, the energy, the place, the purpose, the force that emanates from it?"

White Feather: "Perhaps this brings us full circle to the commencement of our proceedings this evening when we speak of the power of words. A word which you uttered contains great power. The very essence of the universe, the 'om' word has great power. The word 'love' has great power. The word 'truth' has great power. All of these things are imbibed with the essence of all who have embraced them over the centuries of time and all who will come to understand their richness as time continues to unfold. Always remember that you are part of the same great spiritual family from which all life has emerged and continues to be. You are God. You *are* the Great Spirit. Whatever you perceive that to be, whatever language you employ or whatever images that conjures up it does not alter by one facet or one degree the fact that *you are God*. That you are infinite, you are eternal, you can never die."

Saving a surprise until the evening was drawing to a close, the guide asked if the three ladies would each join hands before continuing with his revelatory message:

"With that simple touch of the physical body, flesh and bone if you like, you are united in a physical sense. But you have long been united at many other levels. Your hearts and minds are part of each others. Your souls are parts of one another. Your spirits are like birds that fly together, they turn together, they spread their wings together, they ascend to the heights of the heavens in one glorious union. You have known each other before and that is the greatest surprise for each of you. And I have delighted in waiting until this moment to reveal it! So this is a kind of a homecoming for you three.

We spoke earlier and I had to 'bite my tongue', of families being a part of each other, incarnating together, you have all known each other before. That is why there is such a familiarity. A recognition came together of that which is already known. This physical touch completes that unification which unites you together physically. Mentally and spiritually you have always had that link and perhaps from this moment that which has been re-established and reunited will work together to help many souls who will come into your orbit, whom you will touch in your own unique and special ways and the power that works through the one will work through the whole, through the trinity, because you are upon life's spiritual journey and you each individually and collectively have a great work to do. I am pleased to be able to bring you old companions back together!"

The room was charged with emotional energies as Amanda, M'haletta and Sandra held each other in a warm embrace whilst the guide remained in silence, as if standing back in admiration. After a few moments had elapsed he brought proceedings to a close with some kind words for all who had participated in the successful sitting and a symbolic gesture, the significance of which was not fully realised until afterwards:

"I thank you for the privilege of speaking with you, for your listening ears, for your questioning minds, but most importantly for your loving hearts. May I take a little of that love back with me to the realms of light as I in turn leave a little of my love with those who stand at my side and with each of you. I put also into the centre of your room a purple rose which has significance for the group and for each of you, which is imbibed with the love of many in my world evolved and in the light. May the power, the light and the love of the Great Spirit be with you until we next meet for even in our apartness there is togetherness. God bless you and thank you."

<u>Postscript:</u> *After the medium had returned from his trance state and the lights were switched on, he turned to his left and commented upon the vase of roses which were sitting upon a small table. Stating that he had not noticed them when entering the room he seemed surprised that they were there. It transpired that M'haletta had actually placed the flowers in the vase along with some large white feathers which she had collected beforehand as a kind of welcoming tribute to the guide. Unbeknown to the medium, it seemed that White Feather had returned the compliment with his 'gift' of the purple rose to the group.*
In addition, Amanda took some photographs in the room following the sitting (Figs. 1 & 2) and several contained 'orbs' - said by some to be the beginning of a spirit manifestation. These are, according to the spirit teacher actual spirit individuals whose energy can be captured on camera when conditions prevail.

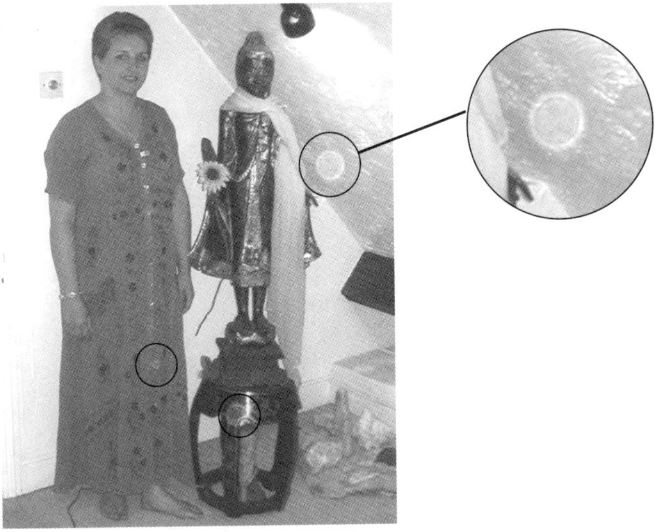

Fig.1 Photograph taken after trance evening in the sanctuary at M'haletta's house. Note the large 'orb' by the statue and the two smaller ones over Amanda's dress and the base of the statue.

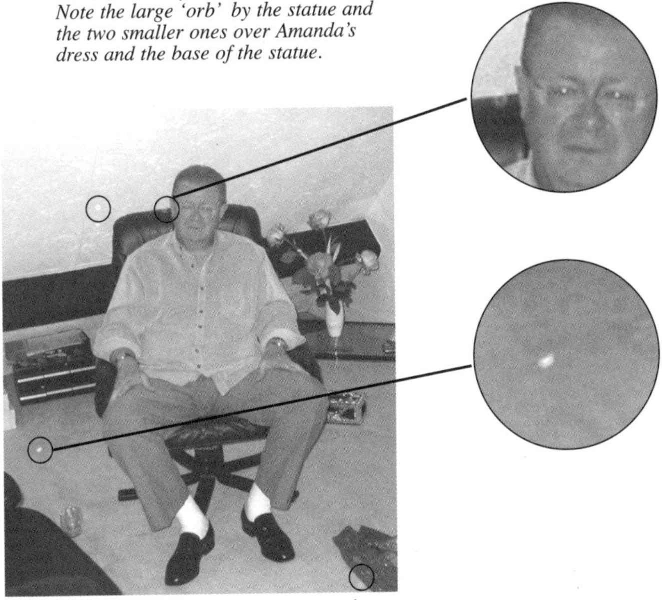

Fig.2 Photograph taken after trance evening in same surroundings. Note the various 'orbs' in evidence, particularly the two close to the mediums head. Also a small white object, which appears to be a tiny feather lying on the floor. This was not in evidence when the picture was taken and is nothing to do with the other much larger feathers in the vase.

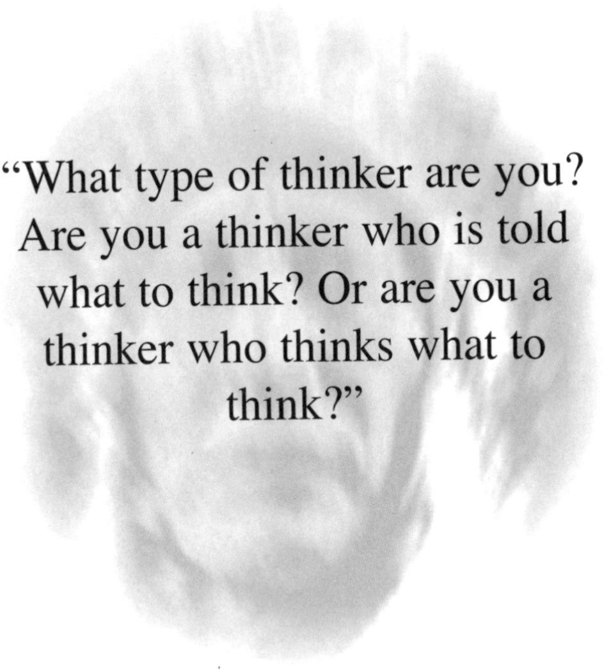

"What type of thinker are you? Are you a thinker who is told what to think? Or are you a thinker who thinks what to think?"

one2one *The Deeper Thinker* 11

We first encountered David during one of our countless 'trance evening' demonstrations which are regularly undertaken, mainly throughout the UK. Having noted that he had on a number of occasions asked questions of White Feather and recognising that he was a man who liked to think more deeply upon many subjects, he was invited to a sitting with the guide and given a free hand to ask whatever he wished. Stating that he was somewhat nervous beforehand, the guide soon put him at his ease as he introduced himself and began his welcoming address:

White Feather: [addressing Amanda who had turned on the tape recorder] "Your timing is perfect Sunflower!"

Amanda: "I've had a lot of practice!"

White Feather: "I am pleased that I have been able to have crossed the ocean of being to weigh anchor once more in the harbour of your understanding minds. I hope that what I bring to you tonight will be of some value and worth for that is always my intention. As I have said on numerous occasions, the delivery of truth to the eager mind is like manna from heaven. For just as the physical form needs food to sustain it, so the mind needs questions and answers to bring it into a deeper understanding of what it is initially in itself and in its divine links with the great spirit in order that it too can be sustained and invigorated.
I enjoy greatly these opportunities to speak at length with you, for discourse and debate are close to my heart. I am a great believer that unless one asks questions, one should not expect answers and it is good that those present tonight, and there are many in my world, are drawn here as are you because you want answers to questions.
I had a thought before I commenced my descent to you this night of a man, who

was sitting thinking about a man, who was sitting thinking about a man, who was sitting thinking........I could go on, and you know wherever one looks one finds thinkers. But what is it to think? Where does thought come from? Is it a product of the brain or is it of the mind? Or is it beyond mind? Is it of the spirit? What is its nature? What is its structure? What is its form, if it indeed has a form? What is its purpose? These are questions that a thinking reasoning mind may ask of itself or of others.

In my observations of thinking minds, of which there are many, I have come to the conclusion that thought, as it is produced by the mind, exists upon many levels. There are many kinds of thoughts, some more deep and profound than others. It is difficult to put them into distinct catagories, but for the purposes of this brief communication I would say that there are those whose thoughts are somewhat autonomous, automatic one would say. They go through their lives responding to what their unconscious processes organise for them without stopping and pausing to think more deeply. They go about their lives almost blissfully unaware of the deeper meanings of being. Almost as if they were going through the motions. A great many souls are like this.

There are those however who do think more deeply. But even here you find that, that thought is conditioned by many aspects of the individual. It is what I call 'conditioned thinking'. Those who have been schooled and educated into their role in society, into their culture. Into the fabric of their country and its ethos. Even those who have acquired a level of skill in a particular aspect and have taken employment, let us say for example, scientists.......still find that their thinking is conditioned by the framework that is imposed upon it by the very nature of the scientific model of research.

Above and beyond this group are thinkers that are tied to no one body and have no allegiance to any dogma or creed and whose thoughts truly seek to embrace the divine. These are few and far between because even here we have some degree of colouration and some degree of conditioning. Indeed, at your level of the earth plane it is difficult to fully rid oneself of one's conditioning and reflex responses. But where through the directive of the will, through discilpline, through meditation perhaps and other techniques which enable the mind to free itself somewhat from its self imposed limitations, the deeper thinker can find that thoughts are stilled to the point where they open up the mind to a broader vista, a greater panorama, a wider plateau of being. One is almost here, going beyond thought, and yet the thoughts that do flow in and out of the mind and which come from a higher frequency cannot truly be put into the framework of language.

The question I have for you, all of you tonight, is that if you aspire to be thinkers, what type of thinker are you? Are you a thinker who is told what to think? Or are you a thinker who thinks what to think, who goes beyond any conditioning and any preconceived notions, frameworks and rituals? Because at the deeper levels of being you will find all the rich treasures, all the beauty, all the lustre, all the illumination and enlightenment that is available to the liberated soul.

It is something perhaps that you can think upon. Now I know that we have within our midst many thinkers. I speak not only of those who sit here in your physical presence in this of your sanctuary but also the many in my world because I think I said to you before that like moths drawn to a flame, many souls are drawn to these events so that we can partake together in this joyous union. For each of us are teachers and students. We give and we receive. There is no one who is not a giver and there is no one who is not a receiver because we all learn from each other. So I give you now the opportunity to ask whatever questions you will of me and which I hope fall within my understanding to give you an answer that each deserves."

David: "One that has arisen whilst you've been speaking is that those people who are in the spirit world who are attached to me whilst I am going through this life.....are they aware of what is happening tonight with yourself? To put it another way, if I could see through their eyes what would I be seeing?"

White Feather: "There is awareness, yes. Particularly, more so if like yourself you are engaged upon a spiritual quest of sorts and you desire answers, then you will find that by virtue of this fact itself you will have drawn minds to you who are enlightened to a point, and who wish to help you, to serve you and to bring you into a deeper understanding. And they will of course be knowledgable about events that transpire in life and will endeavour at times to play an active part in directing you into certain avenues of thought and certain pathways that will lead you to places of discovery and experience. Of course we do not interfere with your freewill. But where we can inspire and I know that those who are around you are able to inspire you, we do so in order to help you to unfold the latent divinity that is within you. So we are aware yes, of what is transpiring.
As to what is occuring through their eyes then I know that it is very similar to what I am experiencing at the moment.......somewhat different, because I am operating through an instrument and having to be mindful of that fact, but they are aware of the fact that you are sitting in this place and they are aware of the conditions that appertain here because of the closeness that they have with you. Does that help you?"

David: "Yes thank you. I've got a few questions here that a friend of ours wanted to ask. She's a healer and she finds that when she's healing she gets very hot and sweats profusely during and after the healing session. This doesn't disturb her very much but she's intrigued to know what the mechanism is and why this happens?"

White Feather: "When the spirit power, particularly that which is generated through healers is at work through that instrument, the very nature of the energy or force itself generates a warmth, a heat with it and this *can,* although not always, at times, translate to the physical body. There is also at times, some use of the endocrine

system within mediums and this can have a response similar to what you have described. But the energy of the healing power does carry with it a warmth, a heat, and when this is put through the etheric body, because as you are aware all healing comes from spirit, through spirit, to spirit, there can be a residual effect that transfers itself from the etheric body to the physical body.
For example; when I operate through this instrument you will find that there are, were you able to measure them, changes in blood pressure, in heart rate, in skin temperature, in the skin sensitivity, in neurological activity within the brain and numerous other effects which are by-products of my linking with this medium. I think it would be useful at times for your scientists to test mediumship in this fashion..... in fact they have to a point...... to test the medium physiologically in addition to psychically and mentally, because they would find that there are many energy fluctuations within the overall constitution of that medium when they are employed by the powers of the spirit and I think it would help them to prove the case that mediumship is valid and real and not something which is the product of an imaginative mind."

Taking a personal interest in White Feather's comments, Amanda asked if there would be a measurable difference in blood pressure readings between the guide and his medium, knowing that the two men were separate people. She asked the mentor if it would be measurably different from a physical point of view:

White Feather: "Ah yes.......there are two aspects here, let us clarify this. One is the changes that occur within the physiology of mediums themselves, and we can speak here of their *own* blood pressure and heart rate as a result of the energies which we employ, and the other apsect is peculiar to trance mediumship and physical mediumship where the overshadowing of the controlling spirit is so strong that one can actually say that the blood pressure and heart rate and other such phenomena, when measured, would be those of the guide. You have to distinguish which one you are speaking of here. I was referring to the medium's own physiology and I have to be aware of these changes. It is rather, if I can use the analogy, like when you drive an automobile. When you drive your car or ride a bike or when you ride a horse, whatever vehicle you employ, you have to be aware of it. Of its limitations, of its strengths and weaknesses, so as not to over tax it or over use it. You have to care for it.
I know of certain idiosyncrasies that apply to this instrument and I have to be wary of them. But I think that where we are able to obtain a balance, were that balance not to be obtainable, then I would not function through this instrument because we cannot put any medium at risk in the sense of damaging the health of that instrument."

David: "Following on from that question, the same lady that I am talking about had one session recently where with one patient she was working on, she felt the exact opposite......tremendously calm and a wonderful sense of wellbeing throughout the time she was healing. She was really surprised by the difference on this one occasion with this one person and she wondered if this effect was coming through her and her guides or whether it was in fact from the patient and their guides?"

White Feather: "No, it was from those that work with her. You can reassure her of that. If I can open this up a little, you may be aware, those of you who have received healing or have given healing that sometimes it seems to be contradictory in that your hands can be very warm, indeed hot, and yet there is a cold power going through them and the patient or the recipient will remark on how cool the energy is and it is a seeming paradox here, between the two extremes. Equally you will find that where a particular helper in my world is called upon to help though a medium, they can bring with them their own particular energies that direct the spirit healing force in such a way that it operates in a far more distinct manner than the medium is used to. Not only that, but the very essence of the guide who is linking, particularly if they are of an evolved nature would impart itself through the auric field of the healer and its residue would be felt in the manner of a calmness, a peace, a tranquility, a bliss or any other such aspect which an evolved mind or soul in my world would bring.

Sometimes you know, we use a particular energy or a particular individual through a medium to impart a particular characteristic or a certain kind of healing power. We can do this from time to time and you will find that there is a notable difference between one and the other."

David: "Just so that I can be absolutely clear about that, in that situation I described would it be the usual healing guide working through that person in a different way on that one occasion or would it be perhaps a different healing guide working through her on that one session?"

White Feather: "When we say 'a different healing guide' you must understand that there are many within the group. You tend to be aware of one or more healers in my world that you link with and you refer to as your guides. You will find that one of those is the major controlling guide of the group, but others can still link, if not directly then indirectly through that controlling guide to bring their power and healing force into and through that channel. You may only be aware of your normal link with the one that you recognise, yet there is the healing force of another linking through them. Do you understand that? That can result in the changes that your friend was aware of. It's not as though we swap and change and one steps in and another steps out. Very often, once the links have been established then other guides within the group can feed through the main channel, bringing their power through that instrument in my world and through that instrument in your world. It's a little more complex perhaps than some in your world realise."

David: "I'm familiar with the idea with trance that there is one person on your side whose expertise is the actual linking or communication but you're saying it's the same sort of thing here."

White Feather: "Let me give you a brief example of my own circumstances; it is always I that links through this instrument when we speak in this situation and yet at times if I wish it I am able to link to others within the group who can impart through me a particular teaching that can be put into the mind of the instrument. We seldom do this in a situation such as this, especially when we speak to a larger audience. But at times when the medium sits and links with us on his own we can through me, link with other minds that impart a particular knowledge or a message or teaching that we know will feed his mind and that we can utilise on another occasion."

David: "One last question on healing. I hope this doesn't sound a bit too silly really, but why if the healing guides come through and use a physical person in this world to touch the person who needs the healing, to affect their spirit, why don't they go directly to the spirit world instead of using the conduit of a healer of this world?"

White Feather: "It is possible you must understand, for those in your world to obtain healing directly from the Great Spirit. The problem is that many people don't know how to do it. For whatever reasons, they may not have earned the right, they have no awareness, they have no knowledge or they simply don't want to. This is why, and this applies not only to healing by the way but also to spirit communication, why do you think you have healers? Why do you think you have mediums? You do so because these instruments are the channels through which healing, knowledge, guidance and philosophy can be brought to your world for those who do not know how to receive it directly.

You know I sometimes wish that mediums were redundant in your world and that we didn't have a need for them because that would mean that each of you were able to link directly with those in my world and with the higher divine source of all power to re-establish balance and harmony and to reap whatever knowledge and understanding you sought. You know it's rather like a young child looking up at a great tree and seeing the apples growing on the uppermost branches. He looks to his father and says 'Why can't I pick those apples?' and his father says 'Because you are not tall enough and you can't reach'. The parent reaches up, picks the apple and gives it to the child. When the child grows up, when it learns to adapt and it grows in stature, then it no longer needs the parent to pick the apple for it. It can do it itself. The same analogy applies."

David: "Something else I've always wondered about myself is that there has been talk at various times of whether one day there might be some form of electronic or mechanical form of communication rather than using a medium and I thought that perhaps there would be a downside to it in that people who can't accept the idea of mediumship or even a spiritual dimension have always got the 'get out' that the medium is being deluded or making it up or whatever, so they are not able to accept but they would be forced to if they just switch on a machine and speak to 'Aunty Floss' who died three years ago......."

White Feather: "Yes, I understand what you are saying. There's an old saying you know, and I've used this at times myself, that 'man takes what meanings please him' and even if you were to be able to invent a machine that bypassed the likes of me or mediumship, you would still have the doubters. Those who seek to put it down and to decry it. You will always have those minds who don't want to believe what they don't want to believe.
As to the evolution of such machinery, great strides have been made in my world and in your world together to create such mechanics, but let me say, and I've said this before that you will never exclude the need for a medium to be present because that vital energy is necessary to enable the communication to work effectively."

At this point the infamous house cat, scourge of many a sitting began making noises of a loud feline nature and whilst unperturbed, the spirit visitor anticipated Amanda's likely action to remove the unwanted guest with a humourous aside:

White Feather: "Yes you can!"

Having gently ejected the relieved animal, the sitting continued with a follow up comment from the *officially* invited guest:

David: "Yes, in fact I read about the situation where they appear to have had a very limited success but it only would occur when a technician, who was a medium, was there."

White Feather: "There you are."

Amanda: "I would also add to that, that the human element when delivering a message as it were, also relies on the discernment and the compassion of the person giving it. If someone were to 'log on' and Aunty Floss said something that was innapropriate or not for further discussion it could be very upsetting for those concerned, would it not?"

White Feather: "Yes. You will find I think, if you observe spirit communications of all forms that the greatest communications are those which involve people, whose live energies are contributing to the proceedings themselves. I've said to you Sunflower have I not, that I prefer to have dealings with an individual who can ask me a question and I can have the voice link, rather than one which is transmitted third hand and I think that is vital. You will find this in all good demonstrations of mediumship, that there is this vital spark, this vital energy which is the life force itself and which operates through, within and around all forms."

David: "Now the next question is about something that I do have quite a bit of confusion about. I understand the idea that we exist as a spirit in the spirit world and then the time comes for whatever reason that we choose to reincarnate and have a life......now in a situation where that life doesn't carry on for very long and as a child the body falls down and the spirit returns to the spirit world, I would have expected the spirit to be an adult spirit, the way it incarnated in the first place. Yet so many times we are told from the platform that the spirit of the child is growing up in the spirit world, which confuses me a little."

White Feather: "There are several aspects to this. Firstly it is only a facet of the total self, the individualised self, the diamond of the soul, which incarnates into a physical body and once that aspect, that facet has entered upon that pathway it has to fulfil its obligations and outwork that journey which it has begun. Even though the soul itself and its many facets may be 'old' and have had many lifetimes, that particular aspect which has been reintroduced into the physical body and which has lived perhaps for a matter of moments, or months or few short years, has to continue on that pathway and outwork that which it has commenced.

However, you will find that when death has occurred in your world, depending upon its spiritual understanding and unfoldment it will continue to grow very swiftly in my world to a point where it would have reached its zenith whilst upon the earth. Where it would have reached a maturity, physically, mentally and emotionally. The other aspect to consider of course is the parents, because it would not be right would it if the parents, when their turn came to pass into my world could not find their beloved child awaiting them? If that child appeared to them as perhaps someone older than they or as a form that had matured beyond recognition there would be great pain, great heartache and disturbance there. That would not be right.

You will find that even where growth has taken place that individual will continue to express as a child even though it may have moved beyond that form and it would appear as a child to its parents for as long as it is necessary for it to do so. So there are many aspects to be considered here and each case is different. You have to understand that where these personalities are involved there are degrees of understanding and awareness playing their parts and one instance may differ somewhat from another. Does that throw any light upon it?"

David: "Some, based upon what you have said. Now, the spirits in the spirit world.....for instance when somebody here has passed over we are always told that the spirits they have known will always be there to meet them....now the spirit of someone who has passed some time before......does that mean that they can actually choose how they will show themselves.....whether it is young, old or whatever?"

White Feather: "That is possible."

David: "The most appropriate to the person who is coming over?"

White Feather: "That is possible. The more knowledge and awareness and spiritual unfoldment and evolution that an individual has attained, the more that they have choices, the more that they have control over their appearance and you must understand that my world is very much a world where the spirit operating through the mental faculties can bring about an external change that is much more apparent than it is in your world. In your world, in order to change external appearances you have to undergo, if you are speaking in a physical sense, surgery to change your appearance. If you are building a house you have to draw up plans and then obtain all the materials and put them into an order that can be recognised as a building, but in my world through the power of intent, through the power of the mind you can change the appearance, but only if you have earned the right to do that. Now let me quantify that because if you have one for example from the lower order of mind, who has not earned the right, one who is perhaps evil or selfish, one who is greedy or spiteful, then it is not possible for them to change their appearance because that would be fooling others and there can be no fooling others in my world. You are as you are. But if you have earned the right and it is for the right motive then it is possible for us to appear as we desire as long as ultimately that recognition is established.
You see, we cannot, we are not allowed, nor would we wish to fool anyone. The law operates in such a way that the you cannot pretend to be who you are not. But we are not talking here of pretending to be what we are not. We are simply taking an aspect of that which we once were to appear as that aspect at that time."

Amanda: "It reminds me of a film that we watched [What Dreams May Come] where for want of a better phrase, a spirit appears in a different form and although the physical recognition isn't there, when the spiritual recognition of the soul of the individual who was upon the earth actually becomes apparent, then it is known to that person what the true identity of that person actually is. Is that what we are talking about? Is that possible"

White Feather: "That is possible, absolutely. When you wish to know, you will know. When you wish to see, you will see. That is the answer to it."

Continuing to expand on this deep question, White Feather then disclosed something about himself which may be surprising to some:

"Let me say to you, taking this on somewhat, that if I desired it I could appear to you in a different form than the one that you are familiar with. Why do you think that I choose to operate through the form known to you as White Feather? I am not in the truest sense a Red Man, yet I come back through the astral body of the Red Man which I once had. I choose to do that because it suits my purposes in linking with the nature of the mind of this instrument and also looking at the broader picture and the overall message which the group to which I belong seeks to convey to your world. But I could appear if I wanted to, as light. As a ball of light. But for you that would have, in your limited ways of viewing at this level, repercussions, because you would not be able to sense or see the personality in the way that I express it now. The identity would not be as distinguished.

Man upon the earth, is so used to labels, to putting tags upon things, to dealing with form and substance that it is necessary for our purposes to operate in the manner in which we do so that he can attach his understanding to something that is more familiar to him.

It is quite a concept actually, and I am very pleased to be able to express it to you because it is quite a deep question."

David: "That also answers a question of why so many spirit communicators are North American Indians or Chinese or whatever......you're saying that it's not so much that they are actually those people but that's the form that they feel will allow their message to be understood?"

White Feather: "Yes......but also again, referring again to what I said about not being able or desiring to fool anyone, I could not appear to you as a Chinaman for example, unless some facet of me had experienced that and I still had that awareness and that knowledge and that faculty to do so. If I wanted to appear to you as a Chinaman I would have to operate through the astral body of another in my world who was of that culture and *then* link with the medium, do you understand that? There are some that do that because again, it suits their purposes. The minds of mediums you know, are not infallible. They are like the minds of everyone. People like to identify at your level of being with particular races and cultures because it suits their purposes and it is beneficial for us to work with that thought energy if it enables us to get across a greater message, which is our directive."

Amanda: "I do think also that there is a consensus of opinion that a Red Man or a Chinaman has actually got a respect, so that the message that is actually portrayed is probably more acceptable and you gain that respect far more perhaps than if you had come as a different sort of personality."

White Feather: "That is so Sunflower, and that leads me on to one other important point which I almost overlooked, which is that everything whether it is in your world or my world, has energy within it. Bodies in particular, are living organisms. The physical body, the etheric body, the astral body......these are living organisms, living entities through which the spirit operates or has operated. Through which mind has also operated. Now, some races upon your world because of the lives that they lived, were more in harmony with the spirit. They were more spiritual races and when death occurs, that spirituality or an aspect of it, is taken up into the higher. Into the astral, into the spirit body and it is retained there. Therefore, when we come back and I employ the use of an astral body, that spirituality is still there and facilitates an ease of linking with your world."

Amanda: "Is it like an evolvement of a group consciousness?"

White Feather: "That is part of it. If let us say, we sought to operate through the astral level of a race that was very vicious, uncaring, harsh, dogmatic.......whatever label you wish to put upon it, then you would find that the essence of that race, the astral body of that race would be more harsh, more coarse, less refined than a race that was spiritual and it would be more difficult for us to operate through that and to take upon that persona to link with your world.
Matter is never destroyed. It only changes from one state to another. Always remember......and we could talk at great length upon this point and I don't want to labour the point, but always remember that when death occurs to the physical body there is a matter of time which passes, usually within the region of about three days or so, where energies are taken up from the etheric into the higher astral and spiritual bodies in a kind of an interplay or transference of energies....... taken up from the lower to the higher. These energies persist in my world and don't just dissipate."

Amanda: "That's brought up something that I have wondered about for a while. In foreign countries where it's hot, dead bodies are disposed of very quickly, either on the same day or the day after. Does that have any impact upon the spiritual bodies of the deceased?"

White Feather: "It can have a temporary impact and I do not recommend it. I understand why, but I do not recommend it. You will find that the more evolved cultures recognise that there should be a passage of three or four days or more between the death of the physical body and the destruction of it by fire or by whatever means takes place."

David: "I'll just follow up that because that thought had occurred to me as well.....how much does what happens to the physical body after death and immediately afterwards affect the etheric body?"

White Feather: "It depends upon the individual. If there is knowledge and understanding, very little. If there is ignorance then it can have an effect, albeit a temporary one. You will find that the individual who has vacated the physical body may wish to remain with it, may wish to remain close to it and also close to its place of abode. It can cause some distress to the individual concerned because they still believe, and you may find this difficult to comprehend......but they still believe that, that is who they are even though they are looking at themselves! They are looking at their body but they still believe that, that is who they are, that is where they should be. Rather like those who stand at the graveside and weep as they bury the coffin in the ground believing that, that is the person themselves whom they are burying. The same thing applies. So there can be temporary difficulties that obtain but these individuals are helped. No one is left alone or neglected. All are helped and realisation dawns to the ignorant mind that it has to move on and leave these conditions behind."

Obviously gaining a great deal from the sitting, David continued to relate further questions to the guide, some taken from the list which he had prepared beforehand, unseen by the spirit helper and others that were originating spontaneously in response to the answers which White Feather was imparting:

David: "I've got two questions which funnily enough, are similar but about different aspects of our lives. The first one is about freewill, which seems easy enough to understand, but I find it really difficult to work out where it begins and where it ends. For instance, how much of what I am is determined by my body's genes for instance and how much of the experience of my life arises from a pre-arranged need of the spirit?"

White Feather: "It is hard to draw boundaries. One cannot, when discussing these things, many of which are of a subjective nature, set them in stone. It is in reality a combination of many aspects. Your lifetimes whilst upon this earth, the blending and mixture of the directive of the soul, that facet which has chosen to incarnate into your physical form which brings with it all of the attributes that it has gathered together in past lives and which it tries to imbibe in this lifetime and of course the physical combination through the genetics of your parentage that lays down the material blueprint with all of its idiosyncrasies.With its hereditary effects, with its predisposition towards certain illnesses and conditions that may appear later in life, with its genetic coding that determines its gender, your height, your build, your mannerisms, the colour of your hair, the texture of your skin and so on and so forth. You have also to contend with the climate, the culture into which you are born with its cultural differences, with its religious viewpoints, with its educational system, with its social and moral implications and all of this goes into the mix. So where do you draw the line? It is a somewhat grey area and it is difficult to write hard and fast rules when you are speaking of this."

David: "With genetics we've been surprised to realise that rather more of how we are as people is due to our genetic representation than we expected. Would that be true perhaps as well of the soul? That rather more of our actions that we might be thinking are actually freewill actions are due to the soul's movement of what it needs to do in this life?"

White Feather: "Again.......... and I am not evading the question........ but it depends upon the individual. You can have those individuals whose lives are deeply rooted in the material sense in the physical body and the culture into which they are born because they are young souls or because they are ignorant souls, or that facet of the soul that is expressing through them displays ignorance. And so they are driven, they are lead very much by instinctive mind, by the material mind, by the ego and by all the trappings of matter.

But on the other hand you could have a more evolved soul who, even though they may be encased within a body, shall we say that is impaired in some way, perhaps severely so, and yet they are not of the body. They live in the mind, they live in the spirit, they are beyond the body and its trappings. So you see the contrast here, it depends on the individual, not the personality, which is not the individual. The personality is that into which that facet of the individuality comes. It is the individual and its spiritual development that matters in accordance with its expression upon your earth. You have to look at the two extremes and decide for yourself which is which. There are extremes, but there are many which fall between the two, if you like, and imbibe aspects and qualities of both, the higher and the lower. The difficulties arise of course where you adhere too much to the lower and it takes over to an extent and prevents the higher from expressing itself as it should do."

David: "Following on that basis, one thing that has always struck me about various different religious groups who follow their path, is that the spirituality isn't necessarily any more with any one group and yet in any community you seem to be able to sense some people who have a generosity of spirit, who you feel perhaps want it more and I wonder if that's because they are slightly more evolved?"

White Feather: "I would think so, and perhaps as you already recognise, spirituality has little to do with religion. They are not necessarily partners that walk hand in hand. Indeed religion can very often work to the detriment of spirituality. Some of the most spiritual souls that I have ever encountered have not one iota of religious opinion within them. They have no interest in religion. I recognise that perhaps for some it plays its part. For others it is a stepping stone, for yet others it is a crutch. But where one is truly liberated one moves beyond the realms of religion unto the greater realms of spiritual freedom. One recognises that the greatest temple is not built with bricks and mortar, but is life itself in all its various forms."

Amanda: "I was just wondering, on that point about spiritual evolvement, is overcoming one's physical difficulties directly proportional to their spiritual evolvement if by going through certain difficulties they then become enlightened? I do wonder as time goes by, if someone's physical body then deteriorates again will they still evolve spiritually at the same rate if you like, through the experiences that they had before?"

White Feather: "Spiritual evolvement comes through many forms, through many sources, and there are many determining factors which spark the commencement of spiritual growth. What you refer to as physical hardship, which is very often accompanied by pain, either physically, mentally, emotionally or perhaps all three, is the crucible that brings about the desire for spiritual growth, because one has been touched deep within. One begins to question, to seek more and therefore through this one begins to quicken. One's spiritual journey has begun and spiritual growth and enlightenement very often follow this. It is not the only path of course, but you recognise, as is your own experience that through that which is undertaken by the physical body, very often this brings about this innate desire to serve. Because you have had pain and suffering, you have a sympathy and compassion towards others and that in itself, leads to an awakening and quickening of the spirit within which brings about as a matter of consequence a deeper desire to understand and to unfold that which is inherent within.
Always remember that these things are catalysts for what lies within. You have to have something that sparks and brings it to life. Suffering and pain are but one aspect, there are others; deprivation, heartache, loneliness, even the simple desire to serve in the core of your being are all catalysts that start the individual acolyte on its spiritual quest for evolvement."

Amanda: "So if one's physical body does start to deteriorate, then there's still plenty to do spiritually and in the mind?"

White Feather: "Of course. And you will very often find that the more the physical body deteriorates, although this is not always the case.........but very often you will find that because of this deterioration in the physical form, the higher faculties of the spirit come into play. How often have you encountered one who is blind, who sees more than you do? One who is deaf and yet hears that which you do not? Because the faculties which were otherwise not functioning to that higher degree have come into play. The same can be applied you know, with age. Some of you in your world fear getting old. 'I don't want to be old' you say. 'I don't want to be like that gentleman over there or that lady over ther who is in a wheelchair, who never goes out, just sits and does nothing'. Yet you will find that age brings its own compensation and rewards. You cannot possibly know what these are until they come your way, until you reach the latter years. It is like a fine wine that matures. You will find that things will come to you which you did not have in your youth or even the age at which you are now. Life has a way, nature has a way of compensating the individual of age. You will find that in your older years in the physical sense, there will be many rewards that will come to you that you have not even dreamt about. Look forward to them."

These last remarks brought laughter from both Amanda and David, who had been offered an unexpected alternative view to growing old from the spirit visitor who never fails to surprise. The evening continued with the guide responding further to David's remarks about the current climate in which we live:

David: "Yes.....I think I must say that our culture is rather a young culture these days!"

White Feather: "That is another question altogether. I am sad to say that in the culture that I once operated through, age was given great respect. In your culture it is frowned upon. Something has been lost there, to a degree."

David: "Can I just ask a question about the time immediately after physical death when a spirit goes to the spirit world.......we're often told about returning to a sort of pleasant 'reception area', do all souls go to this area first and then later on rotate towards whichever is the correct level for them?"

White Feather: "Not necessarily. There are those who do not because of their actions, because of what they are, because of what they have become, who gravitate to other areas, other aspects, other levels of my world. But you will find that for most people, most souls, that when death occurs they find themselves in what I have referred to in the past as the Summerland in which they may remain for a great length of time or perhaps for a short while before moving on to that which more befits the level of devlopment and spirituality which they have reached. There are exceptions. There are many facets to life. Those for instance, who have been responsible for evil acts upon your earth, for the destruction of life. You will find that they are precluded from many things when they pass into my world. You will find that for *all* there is a period of reflection upon what has transpired through their physical lifetime. One is never alone in this time but once that has transpired you will find that very quickly one finds oneself in one's surroundings. Where one has inflicted difficult circumstances, pain and suffering upon others, that is very swift to pass and such an individual finds themselves bereft of many

of the things which they would have hoped for and indeed which they strived to achieve upon the earth through the wrong methods.
The law is very just in its operation. It is not a question of punishment. It is not a question of a vengeful deity inflicting its will or its wrath upon them. It is a matter of the law outworking itself in a natural sequence of events which cannot be transgressed or prevented by the will of any individual. It is automatic in its operation."

David: "So, if there were things in your early life, when you were immature, that even in this physical life you were very sad about and maybe even ashamed about......the fact that you've eventually come to some understanding about those events..... would that actually hold you back when you pass over?"

White Feather: "If you have come to an understanding and realisation and if has been some growth in that lifetime than that is taken into account. It is not a question of wiping the slate clean, it is not a question of anyone forgiving you. It is a question of you coming into an awareness of your limitations, of your past mistakes in this lifetime or previous lives and recognising that you have grown from it and that you have moved on. That you have progressed. The scales are balanced to perfection, always remember that. Whatever you may desire or think that you are or that you want does not alter by one iota that which you *truly* are, that which you have made yourself by your actions. But always remember that there are numerous opportunities. Nothing is set in stone. If you look at the index of an evolved soul, you will see that within that soul there are errors, mistakes, there is darkness, there is light. There is ignorance and there is truth. There are acts that one might refer to as of the lower self as well as acts from the higher self, of an altruistic nature. There are selfish acts, there are acts of altruism, good and bad......so on and so forth. You will find that all is there, of every description. But always there is a second chance. You can always strive to put right that which you consider to be wrong and that has an affect upon your progress. All things are indelibly stamped upon your soul for all to see, for all time. But we do not judge. No one causes you to hang your head in shame because if they do that, it is quickly pointed out to them that perhaps they should look at their own index, their own past lives. All have to learn to move on and to recognise that all are held in the radiant light and love of the Great Spirit. Even the lowest of low, even the most despotic of minds is still loved by the Great Spirit and all can redeem themselves in their own actions of service and love towards their fellow man and all other life around them. This is the process that forever unfolds. So don't be fearful, any of you, with mistakes that you have made. You wouldn't be human if you did not err. It is good to make mistakes but it is better to learn from them and to move on."

Acknowledging the guide's question 'Am I doing justice to what you are asking?' with an affirmative 'yes' the inquiring sitter's next question concerned 'progress' in the spirit world in relation to what is actually occuring upon the earth plane, a topic which brought an insightful response from the sage:

David: "There seems to be a difference in the thinking of each generation. The way people thought thirty years ago, seventy years ago.....does this difference continue in the spirit world when they pass over? Presumably there will be a lot of different ideas around at the same time then?"

White Feather: "It does differ, yes. There is growth, there is movement. As your earth progresses in its thinking......if that is the right term to use......I am not sure whether it is always progression by the way......but I know what you mean. Generally there is an upward trend and one is able to say that this generation can think more deeply or delve into more complex issues and discover more than previous generations and that does transfer itself to my world. You must realise that my world is not static, still. There is growth, there is movement. There are changes in people, new ideas, just as there is upon your world because it is a natural progression. Because minds and souls elevate from the earth to the spirit, they carry on with that thought process and it continues to affect the lives of those in my world. The only time that there is not such an impact, not such a difference, is when you reach the higher levels because that evolution has already taken place and that ability to think more deeply and to be more in harmony and attunement with the pureness of the Great Spirit is already there.
'Sin' tends to be at the lower levels where change is more impactful, more evident. Do you understand? The higher one goes the more refined one becomes so naturally at the higher levels, the higher dimensions that change has already taken place. It is already there so anything that happens upon the earth or the lower planes of my world does apply in the same way at the higher frequencies."

David: "That's interesting because even here on the physical world you get the sense that certain, more enlightened people in each community have a lot of empathy for some of the people in different communities."

White Feather: "That is so. Let me draw you an analogy; If you take an object, let us say a pendulum and swing it, you will see that there is movement from side to side. But at the point at which you hold it, there is less movement than at its tip. If you look at the hands of a clock, at the outermost there is great movement as the fingers move around the face. But at the centre, at the fulcrum, there is less movement. It is the same with the levels in my world. The movement at the higher is *less* evident than upon the lower. That is a good analogy I think for you to keep in mind when referring to this question."

David: "Perhaps this is the last question now......could it be said that all existence is the result of the expansion of God and the great driving force behind this is that it's almost as if God is trying to find out what is possible with creation?"

White Feather: "That is a complex question. It almost implies that if God is expanding, then into what is he expanding? That he is trying to find his existence within nature and that in some way God is imperfect? You must recognise that the Great Spirit expands, in the true sense, into nothing. Because that is already there. The Great Spirit is perfect, complete and whole. The Great Spirit is a totality of all things, past, present and future. All time, all space and all things are one in the Great Spirit. However, the spirit expresses itself through that which is not complete, which is not whole, which is not total. And that through which it comes is in a state of expansion, a state of growth, a state of awareness, so that it knows itself and becomes aware of its divine source. It is a question of the divine, infinite, infallible and perfect operating through the imperfect, through the fallible, through the material and finding itself within this. Do you understand?"

David: "Yesssssss......."

White Feather: "But to imply that the Great Spirit is expanding.......no. The Great Spirit *is*. How can you expand into that which is already there? You see what I am saying? That would imply that there is that which is *not* the Great Spirit."

David: "Would it be fair to use the expression 'consciousness' then.....an expression of consciousness, rather than God?"

White Feather: "Again, I cannot change what I have said to you in that the Great Spirit, which is perfection, operates through imperfection. Therefore you do not ever have the totality of that perfection expressing itself at this level of matter and even in my world there is not perfection. I know of no one and no thing that is a perfect expression of the Great Spirit. So always there is this movement, there is this expansion, to use your terminology. But it is not a question of the Great Spirit expanding, it is a question of that facet of the spirit expressing itself through imperfection which itself is striving to find what it is, what it is a part of and to express itself perfectly. That is an eternal process."

David: "The thing that made me think of that is that I'm fascinated about the fact that in the natural world it's as though there is this tremendous force that's trying to create as much diversity as possible without causing absolute chaos and it's as though nature never wastes energy in producing something twice and just as in the natural world, perhaps it's the same with us?"

White Feather: "That is an intrinsic part of life itself. I have spoken of this on numerous occasions before but it is a good point because you will find that inherent within every form at every level there is an innate desire to express further. To expand and to grow. To become better, to become more knowledgeable. Whether it is within the humble insect who is striving to build a nest in the soil, who is striving to build an ant-hill or whether it is man who is reaching out to the stars, or whether it is a hermit who sits in meditation trying to find enlightenment, you will find the same principles, the same processes at work. Wherever you look in nature there is this striving for expansion. Sometimes it seems to be falling into chaos, but even within chaos there is order and there is this intrinsic desire for growth and expansion and betterness that is part of life itself, because that is what the Great Spirit is. You are all parts of the Great Spirit and you will find that wherever there is life, this same trait is apparent. I could speak at length about this, but I fear that we do not have sufficient time, but it is a good point and I am pleased that you brought it up."

David: "Just as a sort or rider to that......is it true to say that our thinking is just as much affected by this force as the physical existence?"

White Feather: "Absolutely, because it is multi-dimensional. I am not speaking really of the physical evolution and change, I am speaking of the mental and emotional processes and the very essence of life itself which is beyond mind, beyond emotions, beyond material forms. It is intrinsic to the nature of the life force itself and it is within everything, in degree. And you will find that the higher you go, if you look at the evolved souls in my world, they are still striving for betterment. They still want perfection. They still want to enable the higher aspect of the divine to function through their thinking, their actions and their very being. That is apparent at so many levels of life itself."

Amanda: "So do the higher, advanced souls in your world accept that they are fallible, that they are not perfect?"

White Feather: "Oh absolutely! Without exception. You will find that humility is a wonderous trait that an evolved soul has. The ability to look at itself and see, not only its divine potential, but also its failings and its imperfections, is always apparent. There are no greater souls and no harsher critics than those evolved minds in my world who recognise what they once were, what they have become and what they have yet to be."

David: "As you were saying that, I was thinking that there comes a point when a soul becomes so evolved, so enlightened that it almost merges with that life that is the original God and becomes inaccessible to those people in our life?"

White Feather: "There is an element of that because when one reaches the highest levels of my world one cannot touch directly, your world. There is no point of contact. The gulf in vibration and frequency is so vast that the one cannot impact directly upon the other, there is no means to do so, which is why one has to come back through various intermediaries in a kind of waterfall effect, to touch your world. You must recognise that as I think you do."

Reaching the conclusion of a very enlightening meeting with the spirit mentor, Amanda gave White Feather the opportunity to express any thoughts he held concerning the evening itself and also the fact that this was the last such session especially arranged for the purpose of this book. The guide did not disappoint:

Amanda: "Before we come to the end of the tape, this session is actually going to be the last chapter in the book and I just wondered if you have anything that you would like to add or say as an epilogue to the teachings and the sessions that we've had to this point?"

White Feather: "Only that I am very grateful to all who have been partakers in this work. I speak to you my son [David] who sit before me and to the many others who have sat in that seat. To you Sunflower, and the many who gather at my side. You have all played a wonderous part in these proceedings and these sentiments, these thoughts, these questions, these words, will travel far and wide beyond the confines of these walls to touch many souls. Some less knowledgeable than you, some who are in need of help and guidance, weary, downtrodden individuals who are filled with pain and despair and hurt, and others who are more fortunate in that they are enlightened but who are seekers upon the pathway of life. These words will reach out to them all like beacons of light in the darkness and illuminate their pathway. As you have been helped, so your words and mine also will help others and that is a wonderous thing in itself. But it is only part of the great procession of life that sees each individual linked to the next. You are all partakers in the wonderous evolution, this wonderous shift that man is taking part in. From ignorance to truth, from darkness to light, from captivity to freedom. It is an ongoing process, it is an ongoing work in which you each play your part and I want to thank you from the deepest recesses of my heart for allowing that to take place."

Amanda: "May I also say then, on behalf of everyone who has sat here, everyone who is here now and will be in the future, that the humility that you impart to every soul that you touch is something that we wholeheartedly respect and something that is a great joy to us all. I'd like you to know that we and many other people vey much thank you and have a great deal of love and respect for you and for your friends in spirit. I hope that these commuications will continue for many, many years to come. Thank you and God bless you."

White Feather: "That is noted Sunflower. I thank you for those words. Let me reiterate as I always do, that I am but the messenger. It is the message which has the greatest import. I am only pleased that I have been able to give it wings and bring it like a bird, to settle here in this place. Now it is the time for me again to spread *my* wings and to fly into my realm where there are many who await me. But I thank you for this time, for the great respect you have given me, for the many other times that we have joined in one union together and for all that is yet to come. I thank you all. And to the Great Spirit who seeks always to express itself in all that we do I give my utmost thanks and gratitude."

On that emotional note, and having spoken for almost an hour, the teacher from the next world took his leave. Yet in truth, he is always with us. For his presence permeates much of our daily thinking and his words linger long after he has returned to his true home. It is our hope that his revelations will have touched you also and that they may have helped to bring a little joy, comfort, and knowledge into your life. If they have, there will be none more pleased than the spirit teacher who has graced our presence on so many occassions and of whose teachings and wisdom we never tire.

Epilogue 12

That it has been our privilege to spend time with our dear friend White Feather over many years cannot be disputed, but the recording, collation and transcription of material for this book can only be described as a labour of love. Arranging sittings, sifting painstakingly through hours of recordings, compiling and editing over two hundred pages of information, re-editing and re-reading, spellchecking.......the list is endless. Yet our efforts are nothing when compared to the efforts and sacrifices that many in the spirit world make regularly on our behalf. It cannot be an easy decision to commit to returning to the heavy vibrations of this earthly plane having enjoyed the sweetness of the elysian realms. Being a spirit guide is perhaps not as romantic a notion as we would think it to be. Yet White Feather and others of his ilk adhere unswervingly to their game plan, seeking always to deliver service to mankind and asking nothing in return except perhaps our brief attention and consideration. We owe them all a great debt of gratitude. For just as a world without sunshine would perish, so a world without hope and some form of enlightenment would be an intolerable place in which to dwell.

Spirit teachers not only offer us a way forward out of the mists of ignorance towards more illumined spheres of existence, they also provide us with the means to acheive greatness. What is greatness? It is the realisation of who and what we are, the recognition of the divine that lies at the very heart of our being and a deeper knowledge of our eternal existence.

Long may the work of those loving and wise spirit souls continue and long may there always be available the earthly channels through which they can operate. Mediumship is a vital component in bringing understanding to a largely ignorant population, yet each can play their part. For in the words of the wise teacher 'look and you will see, listen and you will hear, seek and you will find, ask and it shall be given'. All doorways are open to the earnest seeker and in a universe where the miraculous is only that which is not yet understood, all

things are possible. For us now all that remains is to wish you all the best upon your journey of self discovery and realisation and to offer a few words of encouragement from one whose truth has illuminated many a dark corner of this world................

What if

What if tomorrow you put aside all fear and anxiety
What if tomorrow you decided to respect your fellow man
What if tomorrow you resolved to be still and to listen in the silence
What if tomorrow you closed your eyes for a moment and began
to see clearly
What if tomorrow you removed all pride and selfishness
What if tomorrow you transcended your ego
What if tomorrow you thought and spoke only in truth
What if tomorrow you said a kind word or performed a good deed
What if tomorrow you helped someone in need for the love of service
What if tomorrow you were thoughtful and caring
What if tomorrow you overcame worry and self doubt
What if tomorrow you allowed the light of the spirit to shine through the
windows of your soul
What if tomorrow you were yourself
What if tomorrow you spread your wings and took flight
What if tomorrow, you understood
What if tomorrow you loved

What if……..

Section 2
A brief guide to Trance Development

Developing Mediumship

There are without doubt many misconceptions about what constitutes a 'trance state' and many differing opinions concerning the most appropriate methods to employ when endeavouring to develop trance mediumship. Having been aware of being mediumistic since my late teens (prior to this I was aware of being 'different' to others, but unaware of having mediumistic qualities) I have encountered many opposing views, some of which have been quite hostile, and much ignorance about what is considered to be a genuine trance condition.

Essentially, all mediumship constitutes an altered state and all altered states can be viewed as trance states. Having worked for a period in my life as a qualified hypnotherapist I am only too aware that even during 'normal' everyday states, people drift quite unconscioully from one altered state to another without ever being aware of doing so. This fact alone quite often amazes people.

Mediumship, and in particular 'trance mediumship' is an extension of these naturally occuring states and differs only in as much that the medium usually enters into the altered condition by a wilful act of attunement and a 'third party' in the form of a spirit based control, or guide is also involved. The actual altered state of consciousness remains similar to many of the afformentioned normally occuring mind states which each of us enters during any given twenty four hours.

One thing that a trance state is not, is a sleep state. Even in the deepest of trances where the medium appears to be asleep, with eyes tightly closed, breathing heavy and limbs immobile, there is still a discernable difference between the two states. To the onlooker, they would appear to be identical, but there are many internal differences which are undetectable by outside sources.

Altered states of consciousness can vary quite considerably from what are sometimes referred to as 'upbeat' states to the opposite end of the spectrum and what are called 'downbeat' or deeper states. Brain wave patterns have been shown to vary markedly during these different 'levels' and activity is less apparent during deeper states such as meditation than during higher states such as excitement. The commonly referred to Beta, Alpha, Theta and Delta states correspond to a lessening of activity from something in the region of 14-30Hz per second in the Beta state of normal waking consciousness to 1-3Hz in the Delta range as the mind, operating through the brain decreases its mental activity. *(see fig 1.)* It is when this 'mind chatter' subsides that other aspects, both internal and external can become apparent. The student of mediumistic development should understand that the 'mind' is not one dimensional. It has many levels of expression, some of which we are consciously aware such as those involving everyday thinking and activity, but many which are unconscious until accessed through an altered state such as sleep, meditation, hypnosis, mediumship or simply a naturally occuring shift of the kind which sometimes happens during brief moments of insight or 'bliss'.

Fig 1. **Changing brainwave patterns**

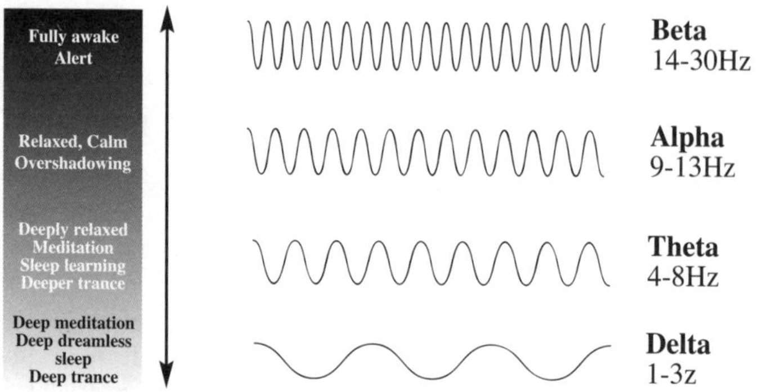

When referring to the development of a state sympathetic to the emergence of trance mediumship the student should strive towards reaching a level where the mind is passive and yet alert. Stilled and yet open to movement. This can only be achieved through self discipline and regular practice, preferably within the safety and comfort of a well run development group or 'circle'. It is essential that such a group be run by an established and well developed medium who, acting as the leader can not only observe what is taking place during the meditation but also actively assist both the aspiring mediums and their spirit 'controls' to work together. Their encouragement to both the sitters and the spirit based teams is important in building confidence and also ensuring that both common sense and discipline prevail at all times. On many occasions I have witnessed inexperienced sitters deluding themselves with unnecessary posturing, bodily movements such as rocking backwards and forwards, facial contortions and even speaking in 'pigeon English' because they have assumed either consciously or unconsciously that this is how guides link with their medium. Other myths include the belief that the spirit body of the medium has to 'step out' of the physical in order to allow the spirit body of the communicator to 'step in'. I have also heard it said that the sitter must 'open his/her chakras' before spirit control can commence. Quite clearly, the majority of this is all nonsense and should be firmly discouraged by all concerned. If one feels the need to 'open the chakras' at the commencement of meditation, that is acceptable and some disciplines, particularly eastern philosophies actually assert that knowledge of the chakras is of great importance, but in my view it is not essential for mediumistic development and will certainly not prevent spirit controlled trance from taking place if it is meant to. I feel certain that the great pioneers of the past who demonstrated trance and physical mediumship did not need to know about opening or closing their chakras.

All that happens when a medium is entranced by someone from the spirit dimension is that a *mental* link is established that allows a thought flow to occur from one mind to another. There is no displacement of bodies (although this *can* happen if required, particularly in physical mediumship) just a linking of one mind to another, one spirit to another. The fact that this takes place at all is due to several factors, the most important of which is the ability of the medium to attune with the spirit helpers and the law of attraction which draws the two parties together. No one can force communication to occur or 'call up' any spirit person in the vain hope that they will manifest to order. The only reason that the spirit world communicate with a medium is because they choose to. Nothing and no one can in any way force the issue.

Even where there is consent on both sides, a degree of spiritual development is required on behalf of the medium to facilitate a 'point of contact' with the spirit world. If there is insufficient 'spirituality' or spiritual development then it becomes more difficult, particularly for more evolved spirit teachers to link with the medium. There have of course been many documented cases of so called 'ignorant' or 'earthy' type individuals who have demonstrated the most sublime mediumship. But a closer analysis of these people will reveal that however 'base' their physical make-up, however lowly their social status, however lacking in intellect or appearance, they still possessed a more evolved 'spiritual' aspect to their constitution which allowed the spirit guides to draw close.

History shows that many of the so called 'saints' and spiritual giants of the past frequently emerged from very humble backgrounds. Never judge a book by its cover. Although there are no hard and fast rules governing spiritual training and unfoldment and everyone who has ever developed their mediumship to any degree will invariably claim that *their* system is the best, there are I believe, certain parameters which should be adhered to in order to allow the spiritual potential of those who aspire to the noble art of mediumship to blossom.

It should be stated that there are no short cuts to spiritual attainment. There is no 'quick fix' or ready made formula that will in any way bypass the requirements of discipline, high aspiration and the innermost desire to serve humanity. Spiritual teachers have no time for egos and will inevitably seek to impart this to any personality that sees itself as more important than its fellow man. I have seen many an inflated ego cut down to size by a great, yet humble spirit teacher, whose aim was not to hurt, but to heal, not to chastise, but to teach and lessons of this type learned early on are usually worth their weight in gold and are seldom forgotten.

Generally, the best way to progress with any form of mediumistic unfoldment and most certainly with the development of trance is to find a sincere, dedicated group of people who share similar aims and aspirations and with whom one can feel empathy.

The group should essentially meet at a regular interval and meditation should commence and complete at a set time. Each sitter should have their own 'place' or seat within the circle and the members of the group should occupy these places at each sitting. Ideally, upwards of five people should form the basis of the circle, with seven or nine members of opposing gender being the ideal combination. If sitters can alternate around the circle in a male - female - male configuration, this is even better as it compliments the balance of energies within the group dynamics.

Peaceful surroundings are preferable and should encompass comfortable seating, correct temperature according to conditions, suitable lighting (preferably subdued) and soothing, appropriate low level background music (optional). It goes without saying that complete harmony between all students is essential and any conflict, jealousy, resentment or egotism should be quickly dealt with by the group leader.

The proceedings should commence with a silent or spoken 'prayer' either by the group as a whole or by a nominated individual on a rotation basis. In this way, everyone gets to 'open' in prayer sooner or later. The speaking of a prayer or as I prefer to call it an 'invocation' should never be read from a book. Nor should it be religious in any way. Religion has little to do with true spirituality and the idea behind the invocation is not to promote a religious attitude but simply to unite the group as one and to invoke the help of the divine intelligence which we refer to as 'God' through those in the spirit world who act as ambassadors and facilitators of spiritual unfoldment.

Following the invocation, a period of meditation preferably lasting for one hour should commence. Each sitter should enter into their own silence and seek to attune with their group of spiritual helpers. During this period the spirit people will draw closer to each individual and attempt to employ and utilise whatever psychic abilities they have. Throughout this time the leader of the group will most certainly be both watching the proceedings, taking time to focus on each student whilst also communicating with the guides of each group to both encourage and assist them in linking with their chosen medium.

Indeed, a good group leader will often direct energy to a particular sitter and their helpers by means of thought and also by reaching out a hand and allowing power to flow into their auric field. During my own development the circle leader would often tip-toe carefully up to me, taking great care never to make physical contact which could have resulted in a form of psychic shock to my system, in order to place his hand close to my chin and direct power to the guides who were building an 'ectoplasmic voice box' through which they could later speak. Even though deeply entranced, I was aware of a great light emanating from his upturned palm and was able to feel a gentle warmth around my throat. Often during this time the urge to speak would grow ever stronger within and as my own development progressed this became the signal for White Feather to commence his talk.

Each student should be encouraged to 'work' during their meditation and it should be emphasised here that there is a degree of difference between many meditative states and the type of meditation required for mediumistic development. For example, when sitting in contemplative meditation or when meditating for the purpose of relaxation a slightly different approach is required whereby one can attempt to subdue the thought processes and literally go 'beyond mind' where any thought is minimalised, whilst at the same time the body becomes very still and almost 'transparent'. It is at these deeper levels that 'out of the body' experiences can occur. For the purpose of trance mediumship however, a different type of approach is needed. One where, as previously mentioned, the mind is sufficiently calm to be considered passive and yet remains alert to the subtle thought influences of the spirit guides. This condition can be likened to that of a jelly which although still, vibrates when touched. In a similar way the medium's mind responds to the thought flow of the spirit person attempting to communicate and thoughts ascend from the unconscious levels up into awareness where they are witnessed by the conscious mind. Often these thoughts, which invariably follow a spiritual theme are thought to be the sitters own mind and are rejected as such because of a fear of self delusion. Indeed, in the early days there may well be some aspect of unconscious self delusion taking place, but this is to be expected as there will inevitably be a degree of colouration by the both the conscious and unconscious aspects of the mind. However, as development proceeds, there will be a greater emergence of the spirit influence at the expense of the medium's own thought processes - a gracious sacrifice of the self and a yielding to the deeper thoughts of another, which is the essence of mediumship. There will always remain some colouration, but where development is balanced and ego is subdued or surpassed, this can be kept to a minimum.

A good marker of whether a spirit controlled trance state is genuine, particularly where development appears to be advanced and speech is regularly evident, is to note both the eloquence of the language employed, the contents of the subject matter being given and the flow of the communication. If the words used are barely above those normally spoken by the medium in their normal waking state or if there is a degree of hesitancy then it is likely that the communication is suffering through interference from the medium's own mind. As the seance progresses, those sitters not drawn to philosophy or to working at deeper levels of trance should occupy their time in other ways, whilst remaining still and silent and aligned to the rest of the group. Seeking clairvoyance for other members of the group is one option, as is sending out healing thoughts to those in need. Some sitters are used as 'power packs' for the rest of the group and these wonderful souls who often fail to develop to any great degree as active mediums, despite their best efforts, are some of the most valuable individuals around. For their energies are used by the spirit guides to assist in the development of others in the group and every circle will have at least one of these people present. They are of course compensated in other ways and are often more advanced spiritually than many of their compatriates who appear to have overtaken them on the path to spiritual progress.

It should be noted that sitters who are receiving clairvoyant messages during the hour's meditation should be discouraged from 'giving off' their findings until after the quiet time has been completed and the circle leader invites each person to reveal what they have undertaken during the evening. This keeps any disruption to a minimum and avoids any disturbances which may affect other sitters who might have entered a deeper state or who are under the control of a spirit helper.

A warning here; an entranced medium should never be touched by another in the group unless invited to do so by the spirit guide. To physically touch someone who is in this state can be at the very least dangerous to their health and at the worst, fatal. Even a pin dropped, can sound like a loud thunder clap to a person in this state of trance control, so one can imagine what a physical touch might do.

At the end of the meditation, the circle leader will call the rest of the group to time. This can be done by a softly spoken command or simple request that the sitters 'come back' to full awareness. A more eloquent way however, is by thought alone and in a well attuned group the thought sent forth from the group head will be picked up by each sitter as they return to their normal waking states. This may sound implausible, but I have witnessed this myself on many occasions. Over time, even this request will probably become redundant as sitters will awaken and simultaneously open their eyes at the allotted time, much to their surprise.

It will be noted that those who have entered deeper states will take a little longer to return to normality and care should be taken to allow this to happen. If they fail to open their eyes, as sometimes occurs, the circle leader should note whether the sitter remains under spirit control and if so inform the helper that it is time to relinquish this or if this does not appear to be the case, should make a pass of the hand above the medium's head, taking care not to touch them in any way. This will have the effect of gently distrurbing the auric field without imposing any harm and is similar to one person shaking another out of their slumber. Whisperings of 'time' can be uttered and after a few moments the entranced student should return to normality. If all else fails, a few loud coughs usually do the trick!

Once the entire group has regained full consciousness, the leader should ask each sitter to deliver any clairvoyance which they may have received along with any other comments concerning their experiences during the meditative hour. They in turn can be given whatever constructive comments the circle head deems appropriate along with any further guidence if needed. Whilst discipline is essential to maintain harmony and focus it is also required to prevent any unnecessary egotism or posturing which sometimes can arise within development groups of this kind. But care should be taken to retain a positive outlook within the circle as negative thoughts about mediumship are likely to produce negative results. Right thinking enhances and assists unfoldment and a good circle leader will demonstrate fairness, discipline, wisdom, insight and confidence to the sitters. Favouritism should be avoided and all students, whatever their level of progression should be treated with equal respect. Where resentment and disharmony arise, mediumistic development can be severly hampered.

When the evening is drawing to its close and everyone has completed their work a closing prayer should be said, again by alternate group members and the proceedings brought to an end. Sitters should refrain from talking about their circle experiences to others outside of the group, even family members and endeavour to 'keep their own council' whenever possible. This is not to create an atmosphere of secrecy but simply to retain the group energies and futher strengthen the group dynamic over a period of time.

The mechanics of spirit control

How exactly does a spirit helper or guide gain sufficient control of a medium to facilitate a trance state? The process is a gradual one which requires time, discipline and patience to develop. Both the guide and the medium have to learn to adapt to each other and the spirit control has to discover and implement to best ways to utilise whatever mediumistic qualities exist so that they can be honed and employed in the best way possible.

Initially, having linked with a medium, the guide will begin the process of making a more intimate connection through the unconscious or subconscious aspect of the sitter's mind with a 'thoughtflow' that can eventually emerge into the conscious mind as either inspiration, clairvoyance or controlled speech (trance). To understand more fully how this occurs, one has to consider the nature of the mind. The simple model in *(Fig 2.)* explains this more fully.

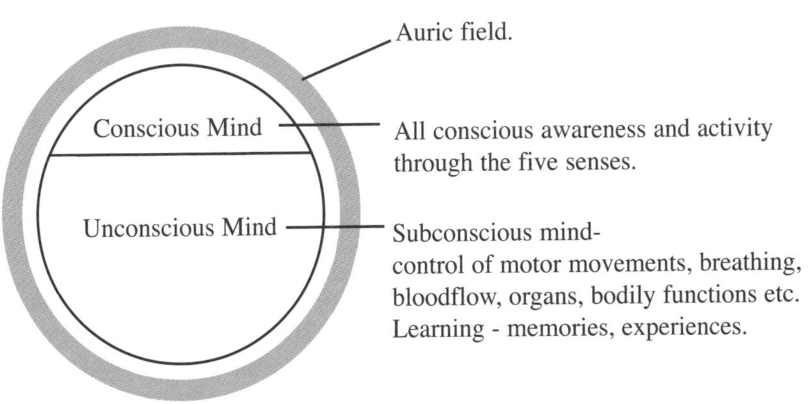

Fig.2

The reason that a spirit helper will link through the unconscious mind or as I prefer to call it 'the back door' is to avoid contamination from the conscious aspect. Also, within the realm of the unconscious mind lies the main control mechanisms of the body which the brain employs to regulate everyday functions such as breathing, blood flow, blood pressure, heart rate, temperature, motor movements and functioning of all internal organs. The unconscious mind also houses memory, language and all of our life experiences amongst its many treasures. It is amongst other things, a vast storehouse with links to every aspect of our being. It makes sense therefore, for a spirit guide to obtain some measure of control over this centre in order to then exert influence over the smaller, but in many ways more significant conscious mind.

The controlling entity will then, draw close to the medium through their auric field, blending their energies with those of the sitter before establishing a mind link with the unsconscious mind and its various control centres. The medium will sometimes experience this linking through feelings of expansion, with the head area feeling as though it has ballooned to several times its size. This is the actual auric field which itself expands in meditation but does so greatly when a spirit guide links through it. *(seeFig 3)*

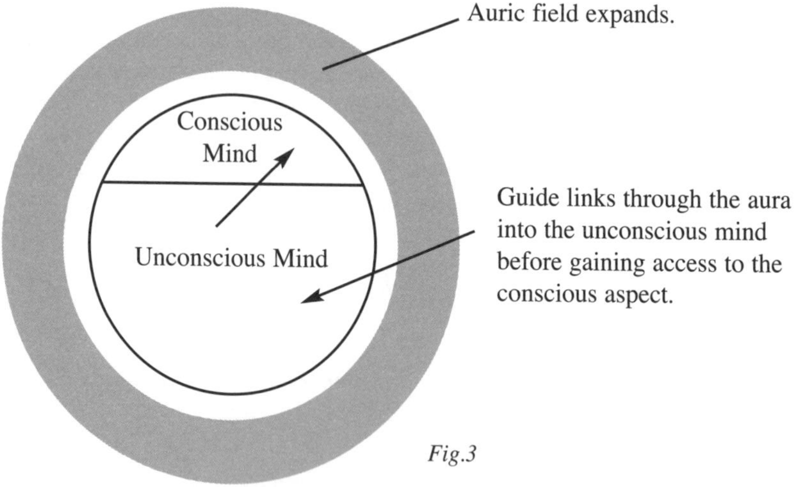
Auric field expands.
Conscious Mind
Unconscious Mind
Guide links through the aura into the unconscious mind before gaining access to the conscious aspect.

Fig.3

Having learned through a process of trial and error how to best work with their medium a guide (and their group) will begin working in earnest to implement whatever flow of spirit intelligence is to be directed through the instrument. In the case of trance development this will invariably be aimed at spiritual philosophy, with the thought flow from the guide being one of words and perhaps pictures. The medium will experience this firstly as 'inspiration', often mistaking it for their own thoughts and then as it gathers momentum over a period of weeks or months as a more definite and concrete message, distinctive from their own thoughts. To aid this process spirit guides will often blend their thought directive with one which occupies the sitter's own mind before altering it to their own. For example; a sitter may be contemplating a quiet country scene and thinking about the way in which nature organises the pageant of the seasons. The spirit helper, sensing this, will join their thought flow with this before enhancing it with deeper meanings and more profound imagery. Later, providing attunement is maintained, they may change the thoughtflow into something quite different, having established sufficient rapport with their student.

Over a period of time, when both sitter and guide are more at ease with each other, the one will sense the other's presence and control will be obtained more swiftly and easily. From taking perhaps an hour or so for trance control to take place, this will now be assumed in a matter of minutes, such is the ease with which an experienced guide will entrance his medium.

One concern which is often raised regarding what can be actually classified as 'trance control' as opposed to 'inspirational speech' is the level at which the one takes over from the other. When does 'inspiration' become 'spirit control'? There seems to be much confusion over this issue and many misconceptions have arisen as to what actually constitutes 'spirit control' and what is mere 'overshadowing'. The lines are somewhat blurred and as with many aspects of the mind, which are often subjective in nature, it can be difficult to draw definitive boundaries. The illustration below *(Fig 4.)* goes some way to addressing this problem, but even this should not be thought of as absolute.

Fig 4. **The River of Trance**

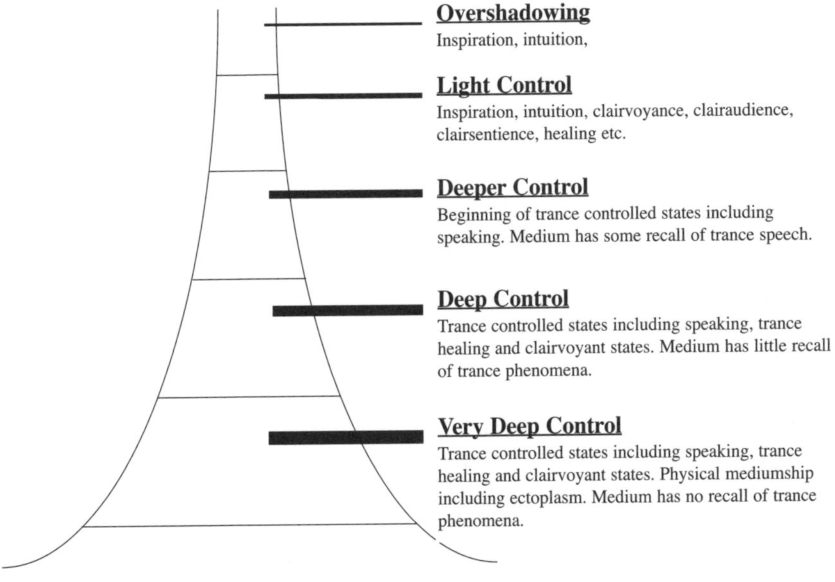

Overshadowing
Inspiration, intuition,
Light Control
Inspiration, intuition, clairvoyance, clairaudience, clairsentience, healing etc.
Deeper Control
Beginning of trance controlled states including speaking. Medium has some recall of trance speech.
Deep Control
Trance controlled states including speaking, trance healing and clairvoyant states. Medium has little recall of trance phenomena.
Very Deep Control
Trance controlled states including speaking, trance healing and clairvoyant states. Physical mediumship including ectoplasm. Medium has no recall of trance phenomena.

In practice a true trance medium will fluctuate between a deep and very deep control state, with the later being conducive to a more reliable communication, although even at this level there is likely to remain some colouration from the subconscious mind. It is doubtful whether a pure spirit communication is achieveable, for even in the most highly developed states of mediumship the mind of the medium can never be totally excluded. One hopes, that where mediums are correctly developed and spirit control can be employed to its fullest degree the amount of contamination can be kept to minimal levels.

Demonstrating in public

The question of when mediums should be permitted to publicly demonstrate their gifts, particularly in regard to trance, is debatable. The golden rule should always be one of proceeding slowly but surely rather than the current trend of 'get them on to the platform as quickly as possible'. In my own case, I sat in a development group run by a very able circle leader and trance medium, Arthur Phelps, for several years and I will always be indebted to him for his patience and wise council. He knew before I, when the time was right for me to move from the protection of the circle to the more vunerable arena of public demonstrations.

As a guide, when a developing medium - I refrain from using the word 'fledgling', is able to demonstrate proficiently on a regular basis to the satisfaction of the group leader that they are in true communication with the spirit world, whether that be through trance, or any of the numerous other forms of mediumship, then they should be trusted to work publicly. Spiritual organisations such as the SNU and the Greater World do offer training and qualifications to help maintain standards and there is nothing wrong with this provided that it does not become a concern of the ego to become 'a qualified medium'. I know of many 'unqualified mediums', myself included, who are equal in their abilities to many so called 'International Mediums' and Spiritualist Ministers. The pages of the spiritualist press are filled with such publicity seekers. It is better is it not, to let your public and your spirit helpers be your judges, rather than those who have placed themselves upon the pedestals of fame. A medium is only as good as his or her last demonstration and as previously discussed, humility is the greatest virtue that any medium can acquire.

It is hoped then, that this brief guide will be of some value to the aspiring medium. The principles discussed herein are only to be used as a guide and are open to interpretation and hopefully, improvement. For mediumship is in many ways a science and as such is open to development upon all levels. One should never consider oneself to be 'fully developed' because then there is a danger of the mind becoming closed to new ideas and ways of thinking. All mediums should be prepared to experiment and to push back the boundaries of both research and knowledge for as White Feather himself might utter, 'many pathways lead to one place'. I hope that what we have outlined in this brief chapter may find accord with you and your pathway and that it may help deliver you to the place of your choosing. If that place is in serving the Great Spirit and humanity through the able demonstration of your gifts, then it has been well worthwhile. I wish you the very best in your endeavours.

Robert Goodwin
November 2004

Visit the White Feather web site:

http://web.ukonline.co.uk/mandrob